LEGENDARY LOCALS

OF

DOVER

OHIO

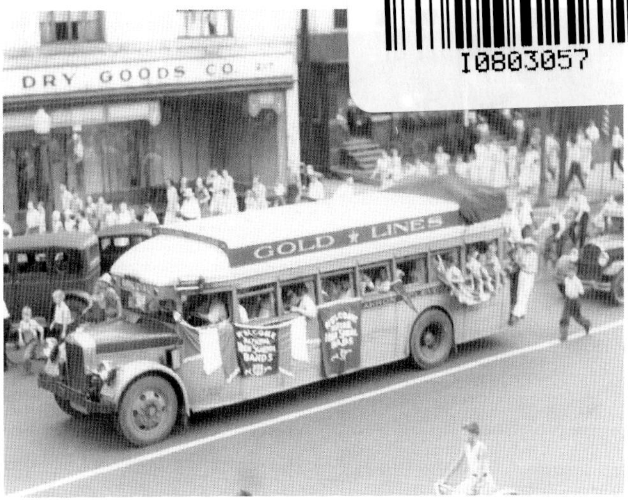

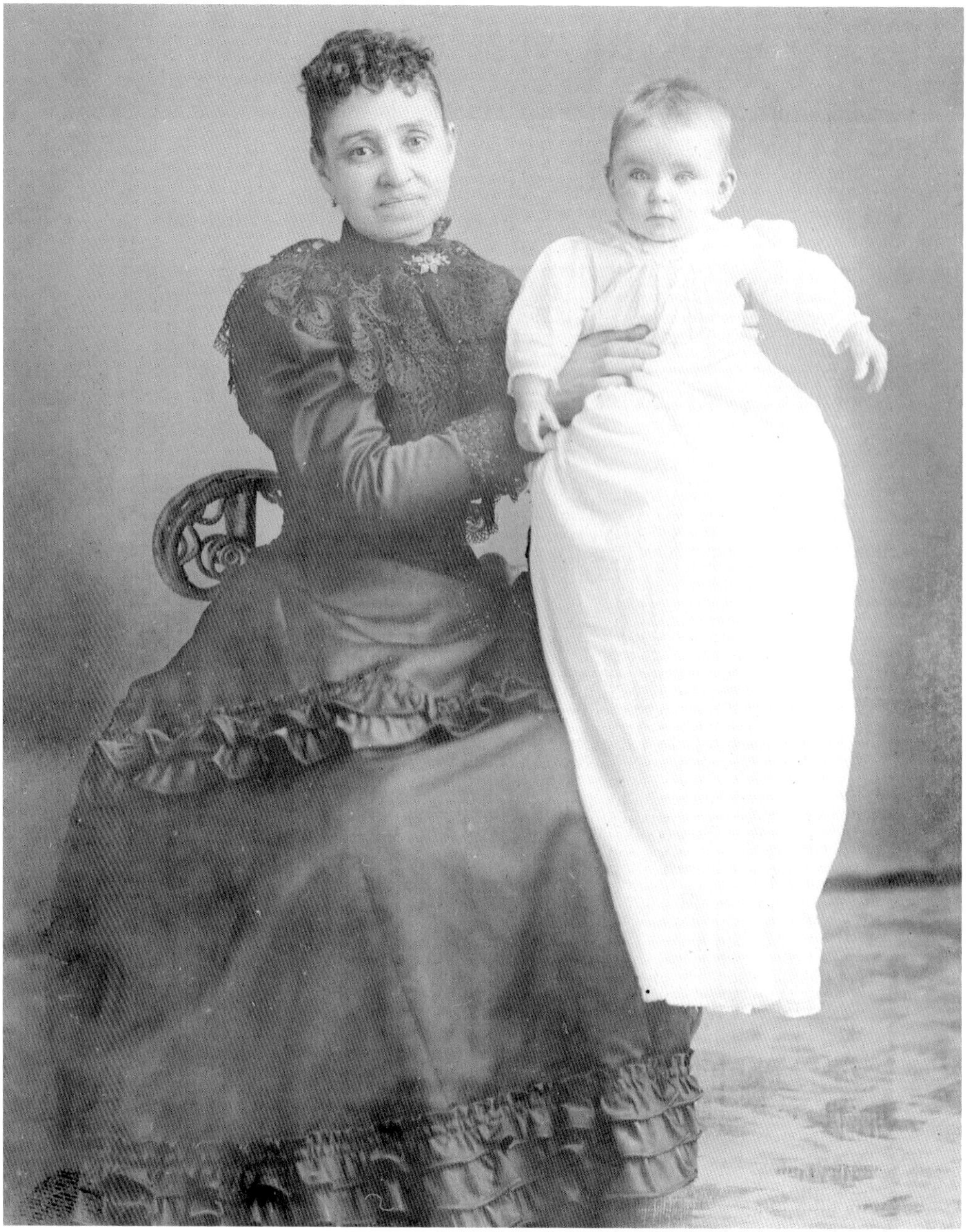

Jane Reeves and Samuel Reeves Jr.

Jane Reeves is pictured holding her grandson Samuel Reeves Jr. After the untimely death of Sam's father, Jeremiah and Jane Reeves had a home constructed next to their own on East Iron Avenue for Sam, his mother, and two sisters. (Courtesy of Dover Historical Society.)

Page 1: 1933 National Championship Band

L.H. Alexander led Dover's 73-member marching band. After being named champions at a national band competition, the marching band performed at the 1933 World's Fair in Chicago. (Courtesy of Dover Historical Society.)

LEGENDARY LOCALS

OF

DOVER

OHIO

MATTHEW S. LAUTZENHEISER

LEGENDARY LOCALS

ISBN 978-1-4671-0099-1

Legendary Locals is an imprint of Arcadia Publishing
Charleston, South Carolina

Printed in the United States of America

Library of Congress Control Number: 2013935597

For all general information, please contact Arcadia Publishing:
Telephone 843-853-2070
Fax 843-853-0044
E-mail sales@arcadiapublishing.com
For customer service and orders:
Toll-Free 1-888-313-2665

Visit us on the Internet at www.arcadiapublishing.com

Dedication
For Douglas and Benjamin

On the Front Cover: Clockwise from top left:
Dover basketball champs 1932–1933 (Courtesy of Dover Historical Society; see page 76), Guy Smith, Dover's second-longest serving mayor (Courtesy of Dover Historical Society; see page 56), Samuel Toomey, owner of the Toomey Carriage Manufactory, inventor, and community leader (Courtesy of Dover Historical Society; see page 11), Kathy Pietro, prominent local realtor and real estate investor (Courtesy of Kathy Pietro; see page 63), Reeves Military Band, local marching band funded by the Reeves family (Courtesy of Dover Historical Society; see page 111), Ray Mears, University of Tennessee head basketball coach (Courtesy of Denny Rubright; see page 78), Harry Crater, donated the land used to construct Crater Stadium (Courtesy of Dover Historical Society; see page 40), Christian Deardorff, Dover's founder and most prominent early pioneer (Courtesy of Dover Historical Society; see page 14), George Elford, founder and coach of the Dover Basketeers (Courtesy of Dover Historical Society; see page 75).

On the Back Cover: From left to right:
World War I War Chest Drive, group of community leaders who raised funds for the war effort (Courtesy of Dover Historical Society; see page 34–35), Alvin Rausch, local merchant whose store became a fixture in Dover's downtown (Courtesy of Dover Historical Society; see page 38).

CONTENTS

ACKNOWLEDGMENTS

Like any book, this one is not perfect. The list of people included in this book is by no means exhaustive. I know there are a few I have missed, and there are others who are working today to become legendary locals of tomorrow. For anyone I left out, I sincerely apologize. In a perfect book, the number of pages would be doubled. Alas, there are deadlines and page counts to meet. My hope is that, perhaps, another historian will pick up where I left off.

As with any project of this magnitude, success would be impossible without the help and feedback of many great individuals. More so than any other book I have worked on to date, I have needed to rely on others for their help. This includes many of the legendary locals you will read about in the pages that follow. Many of these people and their family members invited me into their homes or offices to share a piece of their life's work. Many of the photographs are from their private collections with the remainder coming from Dover Historical Society's archives. I feel really privileged to have gotten to know these great people. They have helped me to connect to my community in new and different ways. I hope that you, too, reader, will connect with the stories in this book. They teach that success and giving back go hand in hand. Without the help and support of their family, friends, and the community, the legendary locals in this book would not have accomplished as much as they did.

I would like to thank several people who have worked with me throughout the process. My two editors, Tiffany Frary and Amy Perryman, have been patient and supportive. They and the rest of the staff at Arcadia Publishing run a great organization. The work they are doing to support local history and local history publications is commendable. Arcadia's books allow small museums, like the J.E. Reeves Home, to share their collections with the world.

I would also like to thank my dedicated researcher, Larry Lautzenheiser. I am sure he never dreamed that he would spend his first year of retirement digging for obituaries, searching cemetery records, and hunting down old photographs. Perhaps, the only thing he does better than research is be a father to his children.

Finally, I would like to thank the three most important people in my life, my wife, Kelly, and two boys, Douglas and Benjamin. You are my legendary locals. Thanks for supporting me and being the best family I could ever ask for.

INTRODUCTION

Nestled on the banks of the Tuscarawas River, the town of Dover, Ohio, is pure Americana. The story of Dover is the story of small-town USA. Founded by Christian Deardorff and Jesse Slingluff, Dover benefits greatly from its rich natural resources, fertile land, and hardworking, blue-collar mentality. When Christian Deardorff filed a plat map of Dover at Zanesville in 1807, he was realizing his dream. Throughout the rest of his life, he would work to make this dream come true. Many of the aspects of that original plat map are visible today. This includes the town square and many of the current roads. Every town that has enjoyed success needs a Christian Deardorff, someone who has the vision to make a dream reality.

Although Christian Deardorff started the community, he would not have succeeded alone. Many others came after him and continued to work to better the community. Whether it was through business, transportation, recreation, innovation, or manufacturing, Deardorff's vision has been picked up and advanced by hundreds of individuals here in the community. Many of these great individuals are in the pages that follow. Whether it was Jeremiah Reeves, who turned Dover into an industrial center at the end of the 19th century; Christian Deis and Samuel Fertig, who operated the county's largest wholesale grocery; or Charlie Deeds, whose numerous projects and community service have shaped Dover in the past 40 years, all of these men shared Deardorff's vision and drive.

Dover is truly fortunate to have such a wealth of great individuals in such a small town. Equally as important as the economic impact of these legendary locals is their impact as role models in the community. One could argue that, without someone to lead and show the way, perhaps, many of the current leaders would not have developed the skills and know-how to lead.

In 1993, Charles Barkley famously claimed, "I am not a role model" in a Nike advertising campaign. In the advertisement, he encouraged young people to look to their families and community leaders. Just because a person can dunk a basketball, does not mean he is a role model. Unfortunately, it appears that Sir Charles's message has been lost. In a 2008 study, most young people still point to sports heroes and even pop stars as their primary role models. In this reality-television, famous-for-being-famous culture, it is time to return to the basics and look to those who truly deserve to be role models. Luckily, there have been many great individuals in Dover to be emulated.

Several traits are associated with great role models. These are things like courage, work ethic, creativity, adaptability, and a desire to give back.

Courage

Courage comes in many forms, but it is easy to recognize once looking for it. It took courage to move to the wilderness in 1807. At the time that Christian Deardorff arrived here, there was not much other than trees. He built and lived in a bachelor's cabin on the banks of the Sugar Creek, spending 10 years alone. This is not a romantic or easy life; it is a very difficult one. Surely, there were many nights when Christian Deardorff felt homesick and wished he had remained in York, Pennsylvania. In the end, his courage and drive persevered, and he built his dream.

Courage is leading one's fellow men into battle. In 1861, when the Civil War broke out, Rufus Ricksecker joined the Dover Light Guards. Less than a year later, he enlisted as a member of Ohio's 126th Ohio Volunteer Infantry (OVI). He served his country bravely, and by June 1864, he was promoted to first lieutenant. Twice during his service, Ricksecker nearly died from disease. Despite his hardship, he showed leadership and dedication to his men. Never was this more apparent than during the Battle of Opequan in Virginia's Shenandoah Valley. As commander of his company, Ricksecker was mortally wounded on the battlefield. Although his men tried to carry him back to camp, he ordered them not to. He realized his wounds were fatal and did not want the men to risk their safety.

Work Ethic

Jeremiah Reeves was born the grandson of a tenant farmer in rural England. At the age of 10, he went to work at the Victoria Ironworks in Wales. Throughout his time in the mills, Reeves saw the opportunity to learn and prepare for the chance he hoped to someday get. This first opportunity to pull himself out of the role of laborer came when he partnered with his brothers to form the Reeves Brothers Boiler Works in Niles, Ohio. Though a strong work ethic, the brothers made their first business a success.

In 1883 came Jeremiah's real test. That year, he heard of a struggling steel rolling mill in Dover. The mill had just gone bankrupt for the second time in 15 years. Where some saw financial ruin, Reeves saw his future. After being turned down by nearly every bank in town, Reeves convinced local banker C.F. Baker of the Exchange National Bank to loan him $14,000 to buy the mill. He bought the mill and worked incredible hours. It was rumored he left his home before 6:00 a.m. some mornings and did not return home until after midnight. His hard work paid off, as the mill employed 1,200 men by the time the family sold the Reeves Ironworks.

Creativity

A chance encounter with a hobo forever changed Ernest "Mooney" Warther's life. His father passed away when he was just a young boy, and Mooney was forced to work herding cows for a penny a day. While on the job, he encountered a vagrant who taught Mooney to carve a pair of working pliers using a single piece of wood. Who would have known that this would be the first of hundreds of carvings that Warther would make in his lifetime.

Mooney Warther would go on to carve his "History of Steam" series of scale trains as well as a second series, titled "Great Events in American Railroad History." All of his carvings were done by hand, and all of the calculations done solely in Mooney's head. His talent and creativity would take him on a six-month tour of the United States and to New York's Grand Central Station, where his work would be displayed. His creativity and talent also led to the founding of the Warther Museum, which continues to enrich and benefit the community today.

Adaptability

During his high school career, James Black was a record-setting running back for the Dover Tornadoes. His talent took him to the University of Akron, where he played under Coach Dennison. Black excelled at Akron and achieved All-American status twice. After his college career had finished, Black bounced around professional football. He was twice signed by the Cleveland Browns and, for a time, played with the Ottawa Rough Riders. Unfortunately, by his mid-twenties, James Black's football career was over. Many in his situation are left with nothing to fall back on; however, that was not the case with Black.

After his playing days were over, Black moved to Hollywood where he decided to try his hand at acting. Through his hard work and adaptability, Black has caught lightening in a bottle twice. Many people strive to succeed in either sports or acting, James has seen success at both. He has appeared in numerous television shows and in movies alongside stars like George Clooney and Jennifer Lopez.

A Desire to Give Back

The truest mark of a role model is the desire to give back. These men and women understand that they did not accomplish all they have alone. Many of the individuals in this book feel a deep appreciation for their communities and have dedicated themselves to giving back. They understand that this is perhaps their greatest responsibility.

Both John Toland and Charlie Deeds exemplify this ideal. These men have donated countless hours to their communities. John Toland served generously with the Young Men's Christian Association (YMCA) and Salvation Army. He also donated time and energy to the Dennison Canteen during World War II.

Charlie Deeds has served the community in too many ways to count. One would need an entire chapter here just to detail the boards, fundraisers, and volunteer hours he and his wife, Virginia, have given to the community. Both are shining examples of community service and excellent role models for the leaders of tomorrow.

In the end, that is what it means to be a role model. Those chronicled in this book provide a road map to not only success but also a life well lived—a life that breeds personal advancement and also community improvement. To find role models, one does not need to look to professional sports or Hollywood; they can be found a lot closer to home. They are neighbors and community leaders; they are volunteering with the Salvation Army, the Kiwanis, or the local Exchange Club, and members of the community should follow their examples.

CHAPTER ONE

Building the Foundation

For every city to change and grow, it must have catalysts. These forces can come in the form of natural resources, transportation networks, or innovative individuals. The latter makes the difference in many communities. How many times are there examples of two small towns in a region that develop in vastly different ways. One town develops into an industrial center, while the other remains a one-stoplight town. The difference between these two towns is the presence of innovative leaders. These men and women of vision transform their communities.

Like many other small towns throughout the United States, Dover benefited greatly from its founding families. In the early years, there were men like Christian Deardorff who saw the potential of the Ohio and Erie Canal and lobbied for it to pass through town. That decision alone saw Dover's population grow 10 times in just 20 years. Deardorff also pushed for the county's only tollbooth to be located at Dover. In doing this, he impacted Dover's downtown businesses. As the boats would wait to pay their tolls, their captains, crew, and passengers would wander into downtown for accommodations, dinner, drinks, or shopping.

After the canal era came to a close, Dover was fortunate to have men like Jeremiah Reeves. Reeves saw the potential in the area's resources, both natural and manpower. Through hard work, he transformed a twice-bankrupt steel rolling mill into a thriving ironworks that employed 1,200. Later, he would found the Reeves Manufacturing Company, which supported the area with 1,500 jobs during the war years. Once he was established in the steel trade, Reeves branched out, eventually opening a bank, hotel, real estate company, and construction company.

While not all the men in Chapter One accounted for the prosperity that Deardorff and Reeves gave the community, all are significant. They impacted Dover whether through business, politics, or charity. More importantly, they provided role models for future generations and laid the groundwork for the community's success.

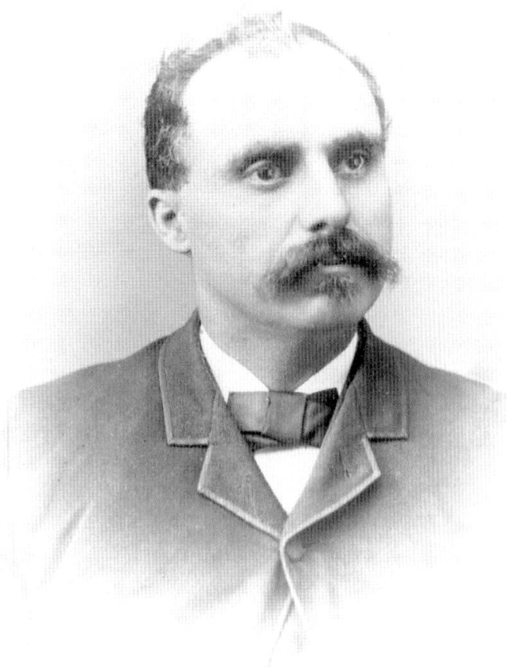

Jeremiah E. Reeves
Born on June 23, 1845, in England, Reeves went to work in the Victoria Ironworks at age 10. In 1867, he immigrated to the United States, where he continued his work in the steel industry, and in 1872, he and his brothers established the Reeves Brothers Boiler Works in Niles, Ohio. This venture was successful, and in 1883, Jeremiah took advantage of this success to purchase a struggling steel rolling mill in Dover.

Reeves Ironworks Office Staff
In 1899, the Reeves Ironworks was sold, and in 1900, a new business venture was founded under the direction of Jeremiah and his son Samuel. This venture, the Reeves Manufacturing Company, would grow to be the industrial backbone of Dover for nearly 100 years.

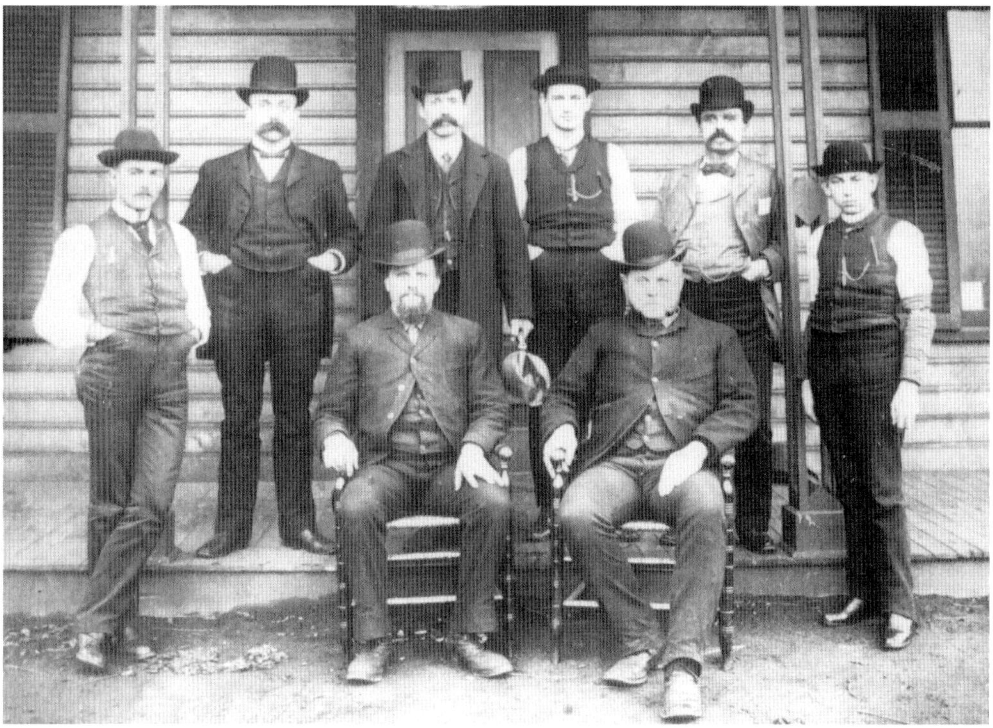

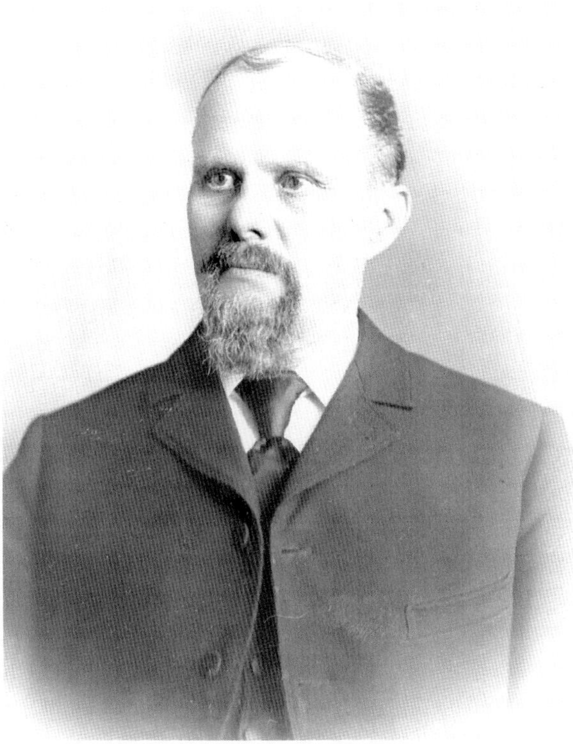

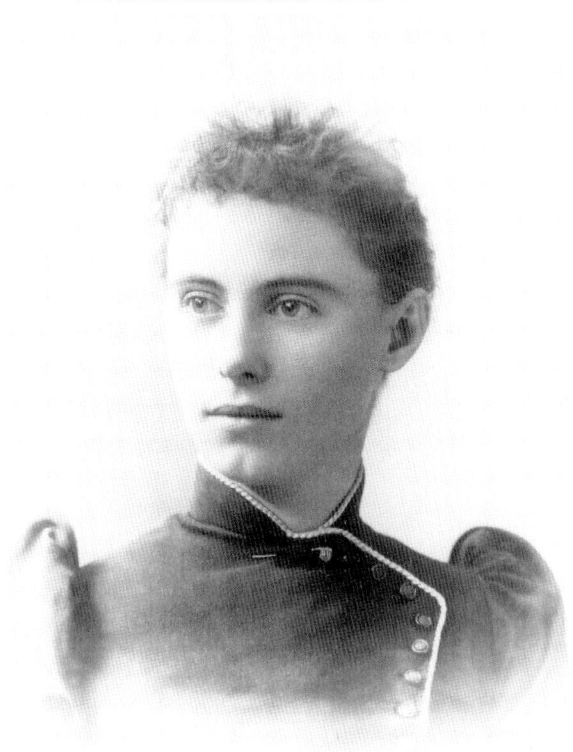

Jabez and Mary Ann Reeves
Jabez Reeves, like his brother Jeremiah, went to work in the steel mills at a very young age. He would eventually learn the trade of a puddler. Puddling is a critical component of steel making in which molten iron is removed from the smelting furnace. Jabez was the first of his brothers to immigrate to the United States in 1865. He settled in Niles, Ohio, just outside of Youngstown, where he married Mary Ann Jenkins in 1868. In 1882, it was the advice of Jabez Reeves that led to the purchase of the Dover Rolling Mill by the Reeves brothers. Beginning in 1883 and stretching through 1884, Jabez oversaw the remodeling of the mill. He later served as the superintendent of the mill, earning the title the "blue-collar" Reeves.

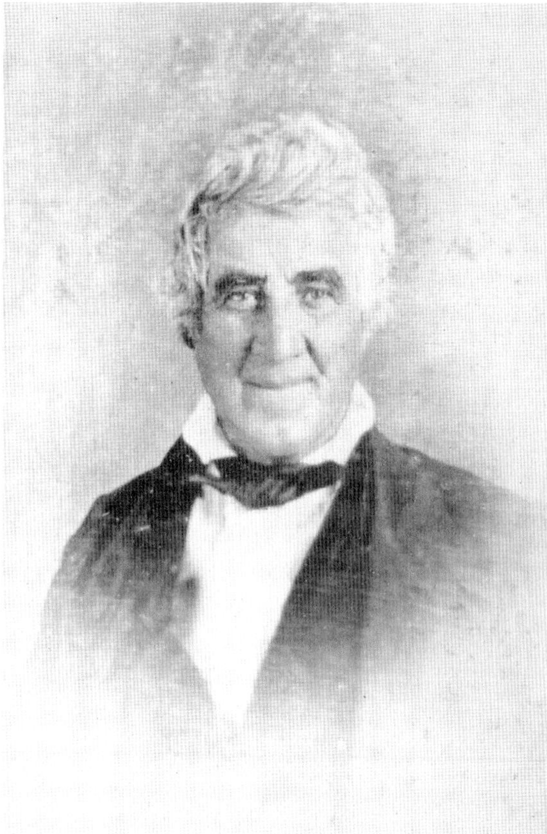

Christian Deardorff

Although he was born in York County, Pennsylvania, in 1781, perhaps no man in Dover's History has done more to shape the community than Christian Deardorff. In 1802, at the age of 21, Deardorff and his brother-in-law Jesse Slingluff set out for the Ohio frontier. That first trip proved fruitful, and in 1806, the two men agreed to purchase 2,175 acres from Col. James Morrison of Lexington, Kentucky. Morrison had acquired the land in exchange for his military service during the Revolutionary War.

After the sale was final, Deardorff moved to the area, filing a plat map at Zanesville in 1807. Deardorff's original plat map showed great vision. It included many of the current downtown Dover streets, 256 lots, and a grand public square.

Deardorff constructed a bachelor's cabin on the banks of the Sugar Creek. He utilized this water source to construct the area's first gristmill. Deardorff would eventually become a man of many firsts. He was responsible for the area's first bank, post office, first bridge to cross the Tuscarawas River, and the first store, which he kept in his home.

Personally, Deardorff must have been lonely in those early years. Settlers were few, and he lived alone in his bachelor's cabin for 11 years. That changed, in 1817, when Deardorff married Margaret Butt, daughter of another area pioneer. Married life suited Deardorff as he served the area as a judge of the court of common pleas and, later, as a state representative in 1825–1826.

Despite everything that Deardorff accomplished, perhaps nothing was more important than the role he played in securing that the Ohio and Erie Canal would pass through Dover. This greatly benefited Dover and its growth, taking the community from a population of 46 in 1820 to 598 in 1840. Much of this growth, as well as the cropping up of downtown businesses, was a direct result of the tollhouse that was built just off downtown. This, too, the only tollhouse in Tuscarawas County, was secured by Deardorff.

Jesse Slingluff

Jesse Slingluff was born on January 1, 1775, the eighth child of John Slingluff. John Slingluff was born in England of Swiss parents. Originally, the family's name was Schlingwolf, which meant "devouring wolf," but the name was changed after the family immigrated to the colonies.

In 1805, Jesse Slingluff, Christian Deardorff, and Charles Boehm pooled their resources to purchase 2,175 acres on the Ohio frontier from Col. James Morrison of Kentucky. The men had been intrigued by the possibility after traveling west together in 1802. In 1807, Deardorff moved to Dover and began to lay the foundation for the men's dream of a frontier town. Slingluff remained in Baltimore where he continued in business with Charles Boehm. Boehm would later sell his interest in Dover to Slingluff, who saw real potential in the town. To manage his interests in Dover, Slingluff sent his sons George and Joseph. Both men would be lifelong residents of Tuscarawas County.

In 1812, Jesse Slingluff left Baltimore to pursue farming about 20 miles outside of the city. He would spend the rest of his days on that farm. Despite the lack of good transportation, Slingluff made yearly trips to Dover. On one such trip, when he saw the work being completed on the Calico Ditch, Slingluff predicted Dover's great industrial future.

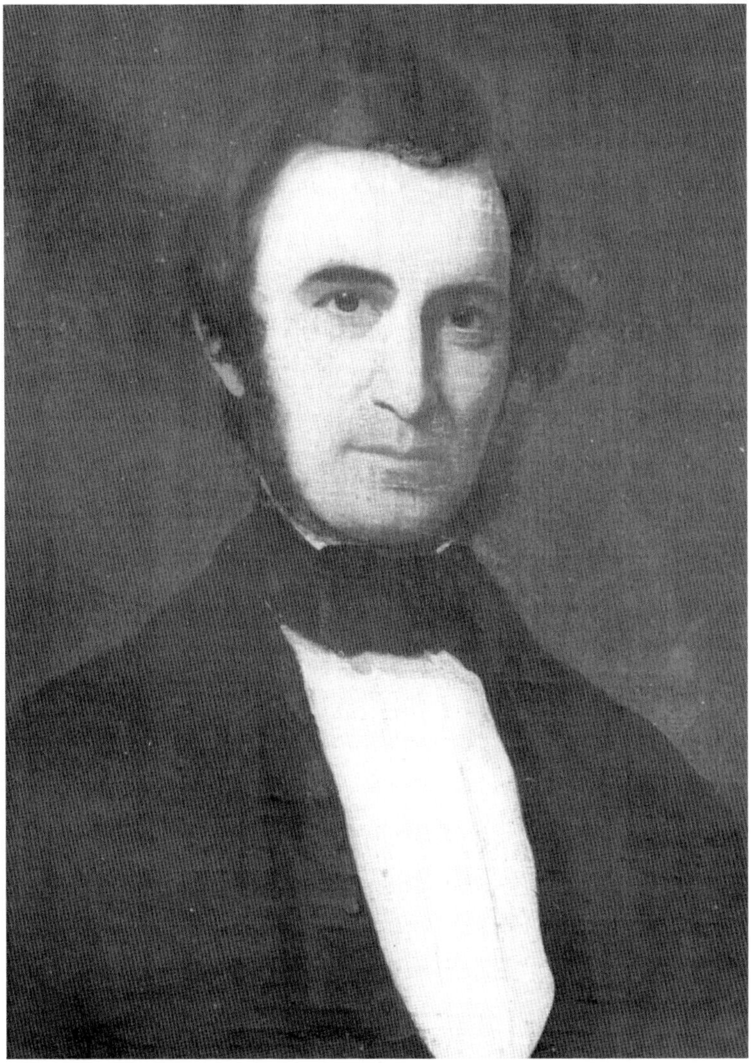

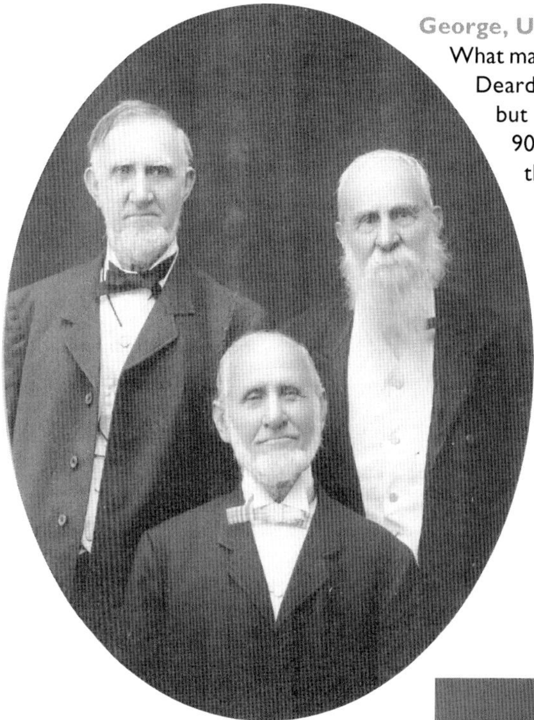

George, Upton, and Isaac Deardorff

What makes the three sons of Dover's founder, Christian Deardorff, so interesting is not as much what they did but what they saw. All three men would live to be 90 or older, all three were successful, and all made their community a better place to live.

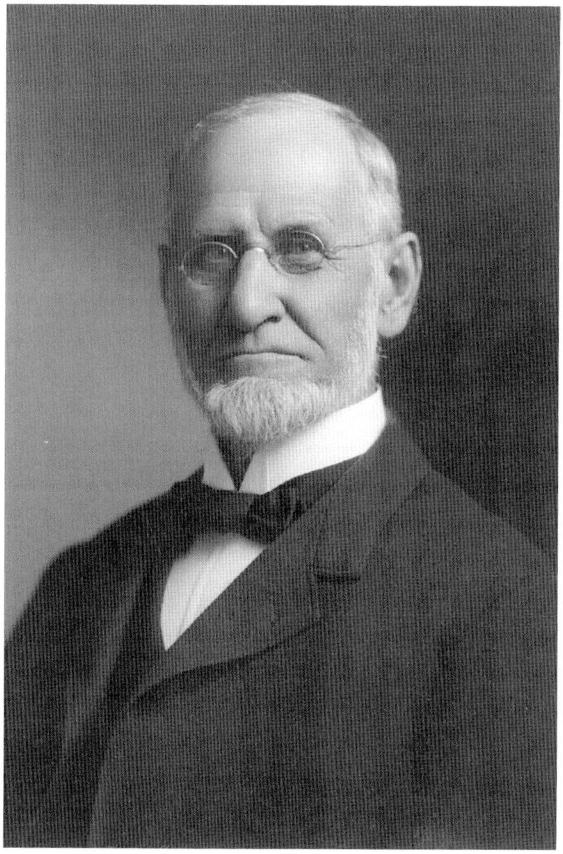

Upton Deardorff

Born in 1827, Upton Deardorff spent much of his life as a farmer. He maintained an original portion of the land first purchased by his father, Christian, in 1806; there, Upton raised sheep. Deardorff was a big supporter and eventual founder of the Tuscarawas County Agricultural Society. In 1869, he switched gears and decided to go into business. He bought into the new salt industry that took hold just after the Civil War. He was one of the founders of the Dover Salt Works that incorporated in 1869. Away from work, Deardorff was known for being a lifelong Mason. He was a member of the organization for 69 years.

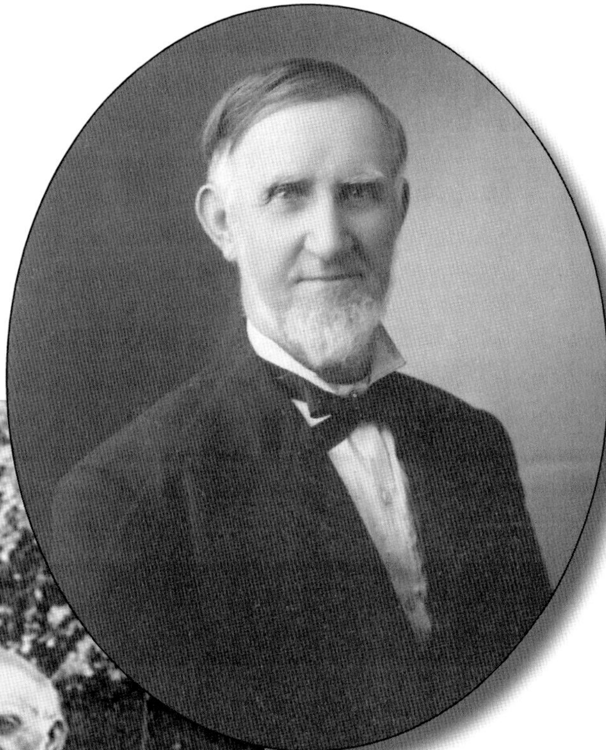

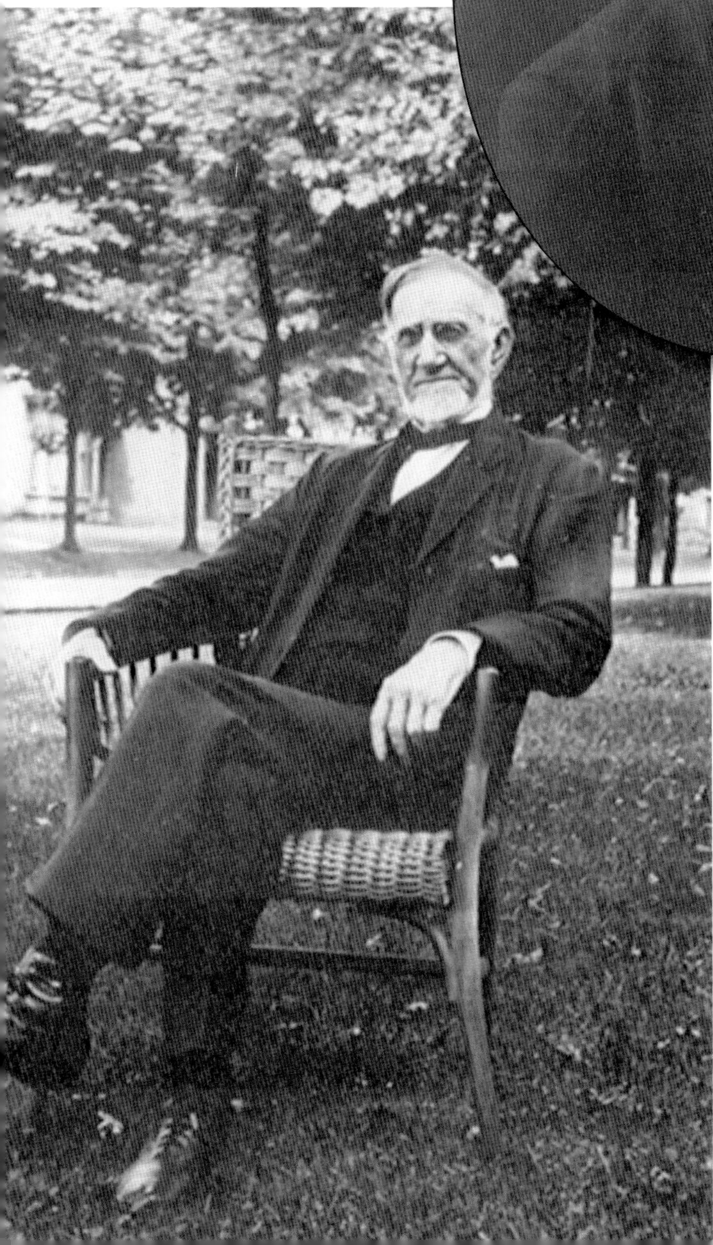

George Deardorff
George Deardorff was born in Dover on January 29, 1823. As a boy, George was sent away from Dover to learn the mercantile trade. He went to Berlin in Holmes County to clerk in the store of Joel Hall and Company. He stayed there for about 18 months before returning to Dover and continuing to clerk at Butt, Burnett, and Co. In 1846, he joined his brothers Jesse and Upton in business, but he left in 1849 and established a dry goods business. In 1852, he sold out and returned to farming. Although farming suited George, after 12 years of hard labor, he decided to pursue another business interest. In 1871, he opened a hardware store. The G.B. Deardorff and Son store would remain a fixture in downtown Dover for many years.

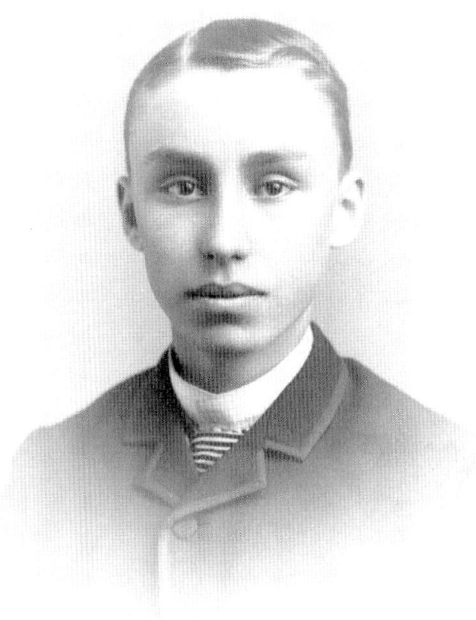

Samuel Reeves Sr.

Samuel J. Reeves Sr. was born on September 14, 1870, in Connellsville, Pennsylvania. In his twenties, Samuel proved gifted in matters of business. This, combined with his energy and drive, earned him the label of a "coming Carnegie." With his father as mentor, Samuel took a greater role in the family's business as the years passed. By the time he reached his 28th birthday, his father, Jeremiah, was able to step back and enter a state of semiretirement.

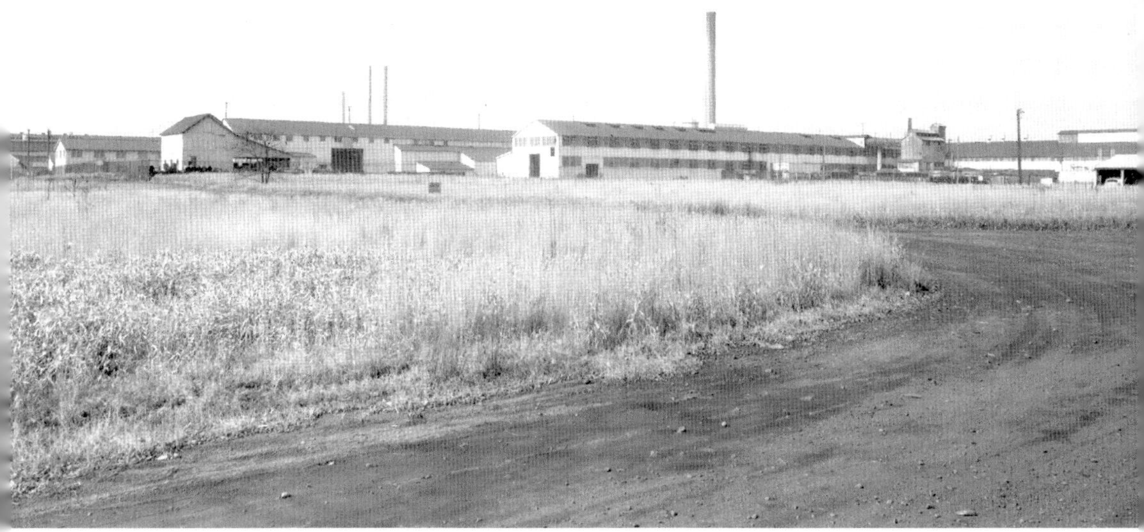

Reeves Manufacturing Company

Unfortunately, Samuel Reeves's story does not have a happy ending. In 1901, at the age of 31, he died of typhoid fever. Among his many accomplishments, Samuel Reeves began construction of the Toledo, Fostoria & Findlay Railroad and oversaw the sale of the Reeves Iron Company in 1899. It was also his vision that helped in founding the Reeves Manufacturing Company.

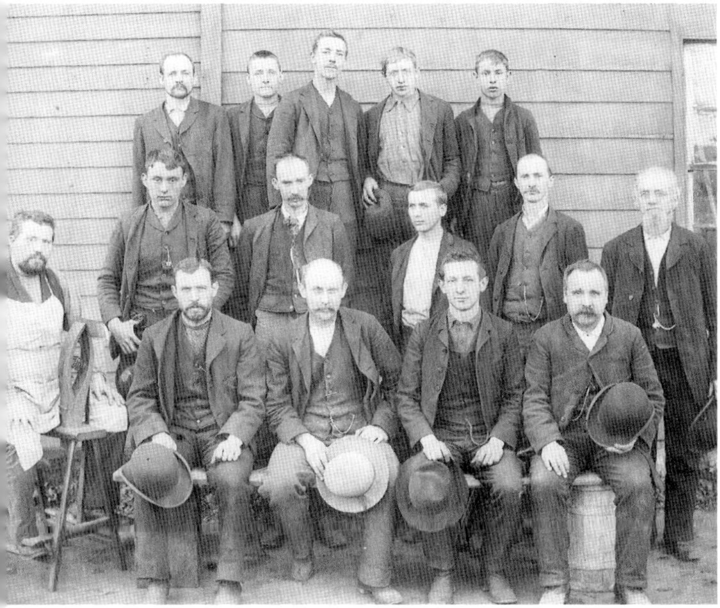

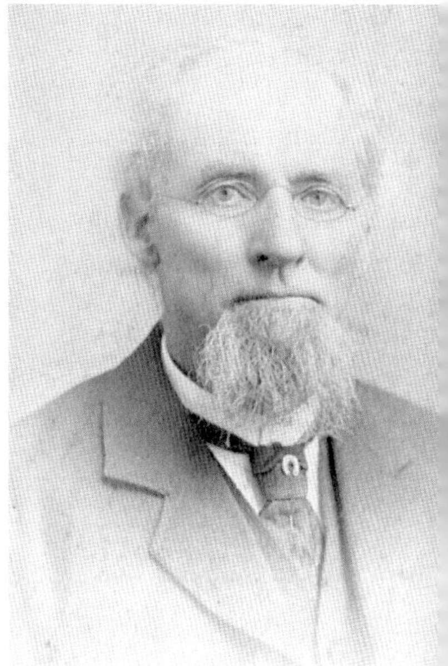

Samuel Toomey

Born on March 1, 1830, Samuel Toomey was the 11th of 23 children. Like many who are born into such large families, Toomey was forced to begin working at a young age and relied on his wits and work ethic to make a success of his life. As a teenager, Toomey worked for a local blacksmith near his York, Pennsylvania, home. In 1847, when he was just 17, Samuel Toomey set off to find his way in the world. He left Pennsylvania and headed for Ohio. He had only the possessions that he could carry on his back and $14 that he borrowed for the trip. He arrived in Tuscarawas County at Sugar Creek Falls and began working immediately for a local blacksmith. Fate smiled on Toomey when the shop's owner left for California and the Gold Rush of 1849. At the age of 19, he took over operation of his own blacksmith's shop. Unfortunately, this was not to be Toomey's big opportunity. In 1850, the blacksmith shop caught fire and burned to the ground.

Seeking a fresh opportunity, Toomey moved to Wilmot, Ohio, where he opened a carriage manufactory. While a great deal about his business in Wilmot is not known, it is known that, in 1868, Toomey returned to Tuscarawas County and opened a carriage manufactory at Dover. The first carriages that Toomey produced at his Dover business were traditional high-wheeled buggies. Toomey's carriages were well made, and he quickly earned a reputation for quality. In later years, Toomey built an oval track on his property in Dover and would personally test all carriages and sulkies before he would allow them to be sold under the Toomey name.

While his business began with high-wheeled buggies, Toomey's true fame came because of his racing sulkies. His design and patenting of the truss axle revolutionized the construction of sulkies and changed the landscape of one of America's favorite sports. At the time of his death in 1910, Toomey held nine patents.

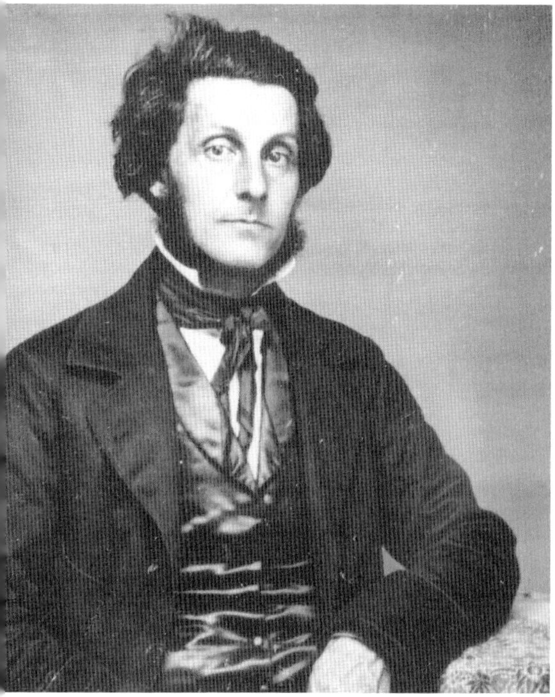

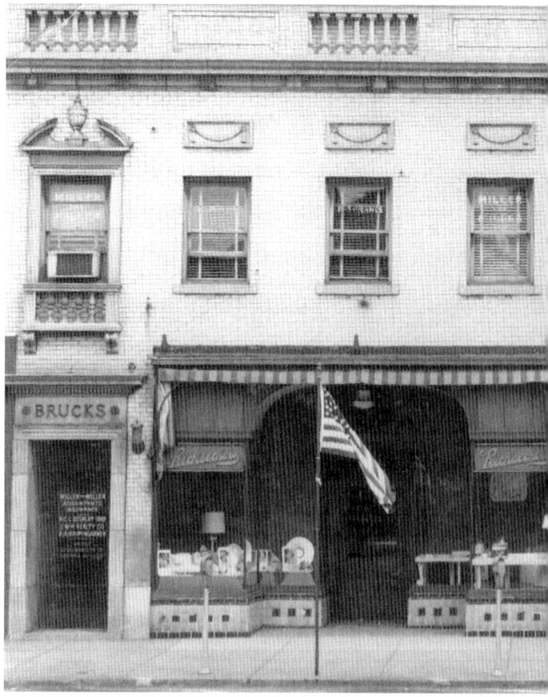

Israel Ricksecker

Israel Ricksecker came to Dover from Bethlehem, Pennsylvania, and opened a jewelry shop in Dover's downtown. At the time of its opening, it was the only shop of its type in all of Tuscarawas County. While Ricksecker's innovation as the area's first real jeweler is significant, his real contribution came as one of the founders of the local Moravian church, which was organized in 1842. Away from his charitable and business interests, Israel Ricksecker was a talented musician who imparted this talent and its importance on all of his children. It is said that he was responsible for bringing one of the first pianos to the area. (Courtesy of Deborah Rinderknecht.)

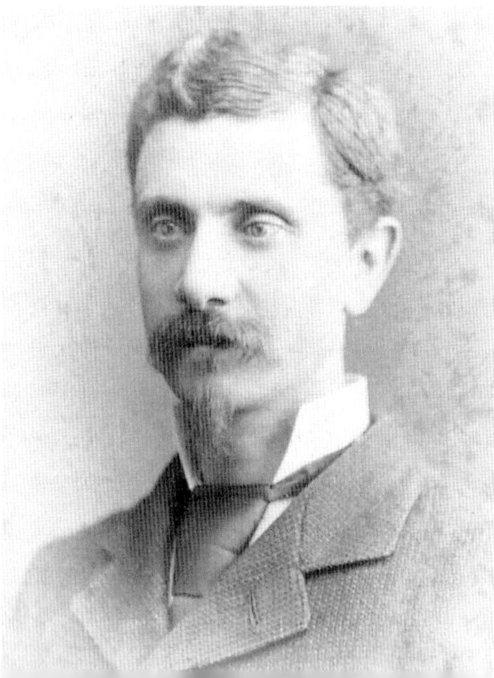

Julius Ricksecker

Julius Ricksecker was born in Dover in 1848. As a boy, he attended Dover schools, where his father served as director for several terms. In 1870, Julius became a partner alongside his father in the family business. This changed in 1872 when he became sole proprietor after his father's death. Ricksecker retired in 1901. (Courtesy of Deborah Rinderknecht.)

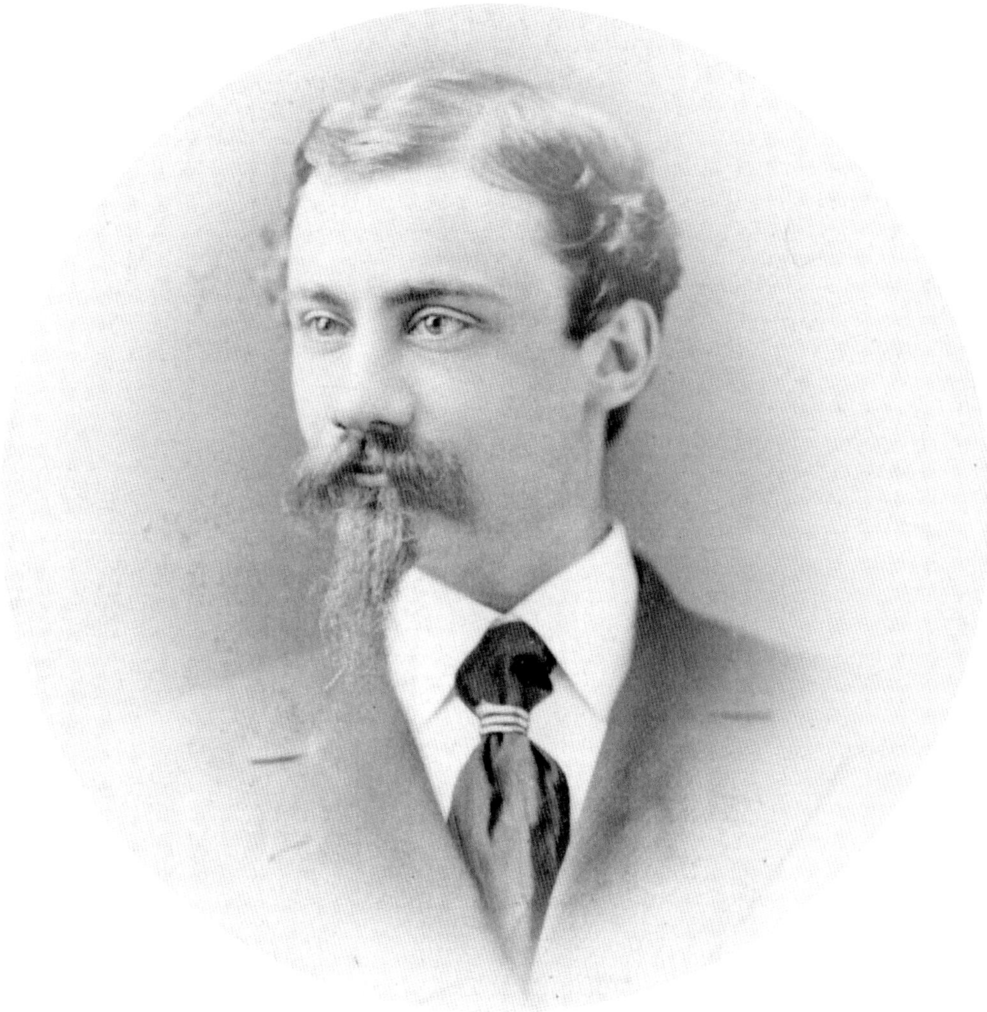

Theodore Ricksecker
Although he was to achieve his greatest success elsewhere, Theodore Ricksecker was influenced by his upbringing in Dover and his family's strong ties here. When he was just 15, he began publishing his own monthly newspaper titled the *Dover Monthly News*. A year later, in 1862, he decided to set out on his own and seek his fortune in New York City. This would prove one of the best decisions of his life.

Upon arriving in New York City in 1862, Ricksecker went to work with Shieffelin Bros. and Co., a wholesale druggist. While working at Shieffelin Bros., Ricksecker paid close attention and learned the business. Six years later, in 1868, he decided to try out some of his own ideas. He partnered with Timothy L. Waters, and the two men opened Waters and Ricksecker Druggists. He continued with Waters until 1875, when he bought out his partner's share and took sole control of the business. In the intervening years between 1875 and 1896, when the business was officially incorporated, he relocated several times while continuing to grow and redefine his vision.

At some point, the company began the manufacture of high-quality perfumes and toiletries. Ricksecker would design the bottle himself and have them manufactured in Europe. In 1893, his attention to detail and high-quality product paid off as he was bestowed the highest award for perfumes at the World's Fair. His company would eventually open stores in London, Paris, Amsterdam, and New York. (Courtesy of Deborah Rinderknecht.)

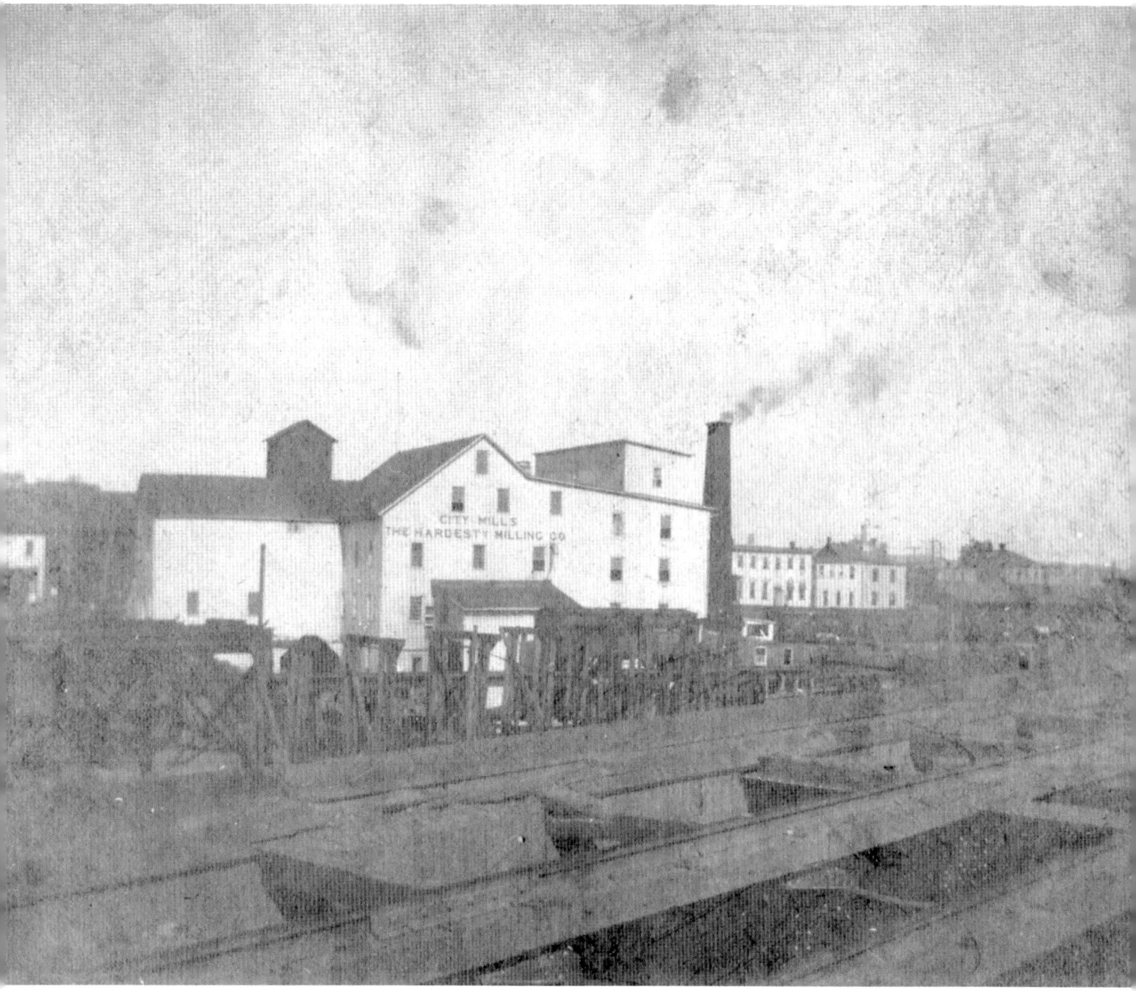

Hardesty Brothers Mill

Born in 1845 and 1848, respectively, Alonzo and William Hardesty had millwork in their blood. Their grandfather founded the first flouring mill in Carroll County.

The Hardesty family's involvement in Dover City Mill began in 1866 when Thomas Hardesty purchased the Dover City Mill from Simpson Harmount. Nathaniel Hayden and Elijah Welty founded Dover City Mill in 1842. After Thomas's death, the mill fell to Alonzo and William. In 1872, the brothers purchased the original Deardorff Mill, completely overhauling it. Only four years later, the brothers constructed a modern brick steam mill. Their innovative approach and entrepreneurial spirit resulted in the Hardesty Brothers Mill's potential to produce 400 barrels of flour every 24 hours by 1879. That same year, the mills were valued at $90,000.

Tragically, the life of Alonzo Hardesty ended prematurely. In 1891, Hardesty was injured after falling down an elevator at the mill. Although he appeared to be recovering from the fall, he succumbed to heart failure. He was only 45 at the time of his death.

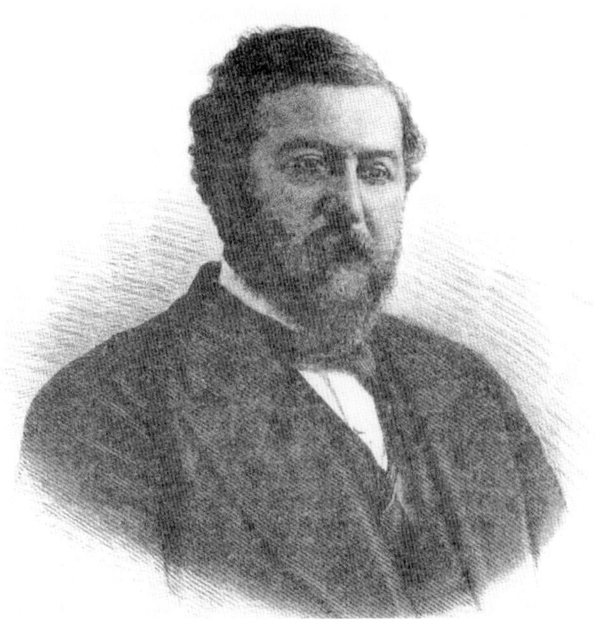

Dr. E.C. Lewis

E.C. Lewis was born in Holmes County on December 26, 1840. He studied at the Columbus Medical College. Afterwards, he moved to Pennsylvania, where he attended the Philadelphia Medical College. At the time, the Philadelphia Medical College was the most respected institution for doctors in the United States. Finishing his education at Jefferson in 1862, Lewis immediately went to work in the war effort. He accepted a position as a surgeon in Louisville, Kentucky. Following the Civil War, Lewis returned to Tuscarawas County and continued to practice medicine. He also served in the Ohio General Assembly and the Ohio Senate.

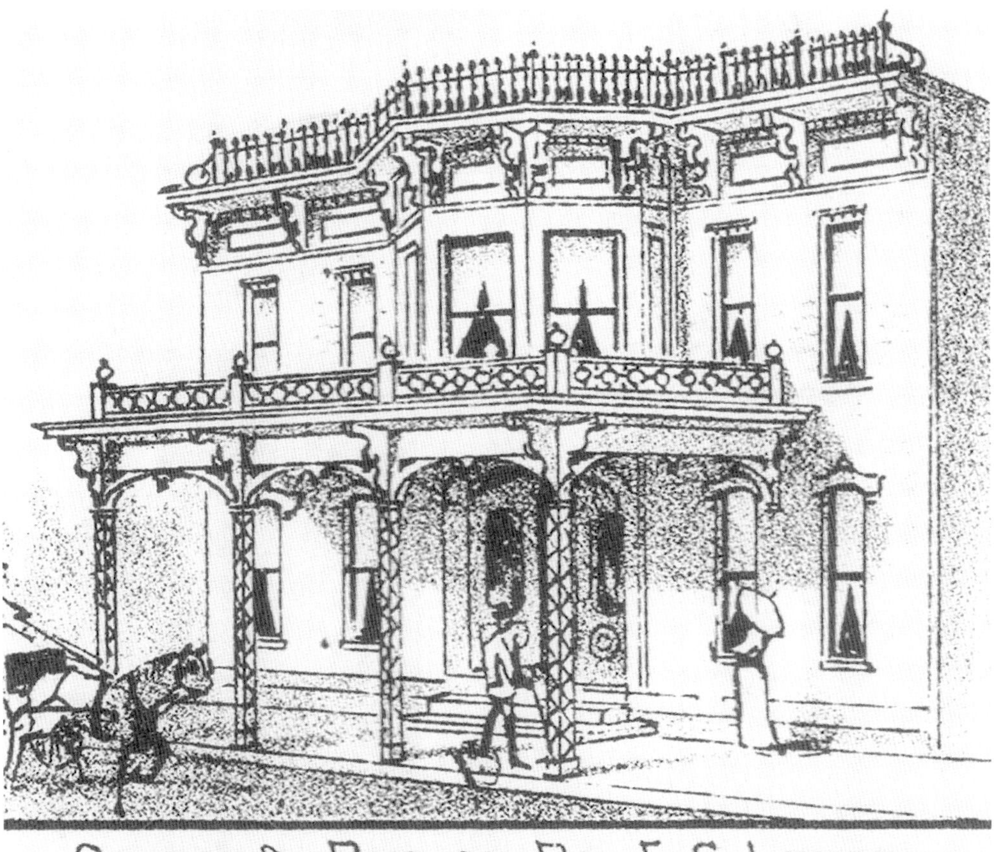

OFFICE & RES. OF DR. E.C. LEWIS,

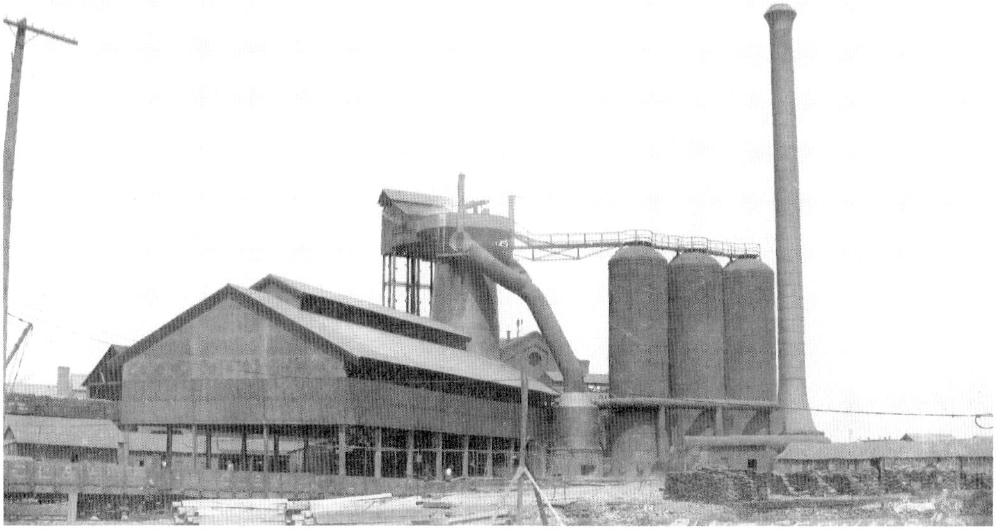

Edmund Burnett

Edmund Burnett was born in Wyndam County, Connecticut, on December 11, 1814. In 1834, his family moved west to Ohio, and at the age of 22, Edmund landed in Dover. As a young man, Edmund Burnett taught school for six months before accepting a job as a salesman for a mercantile company partially owned by Dover's founder, Christian Deardorff. Later, Deardorff left the firm, and Edmund Burnett became a partner along with C. Ritter and John Sterling.

Burnett sold his interest in the firm in 1842 and, later, formed his own mercantile business. He also developed additional business interests, including holding stock in the Dover Planing Mill and being named president in the Dover Furnace Company (pictured above and below) and the Dover Rolling Mill.

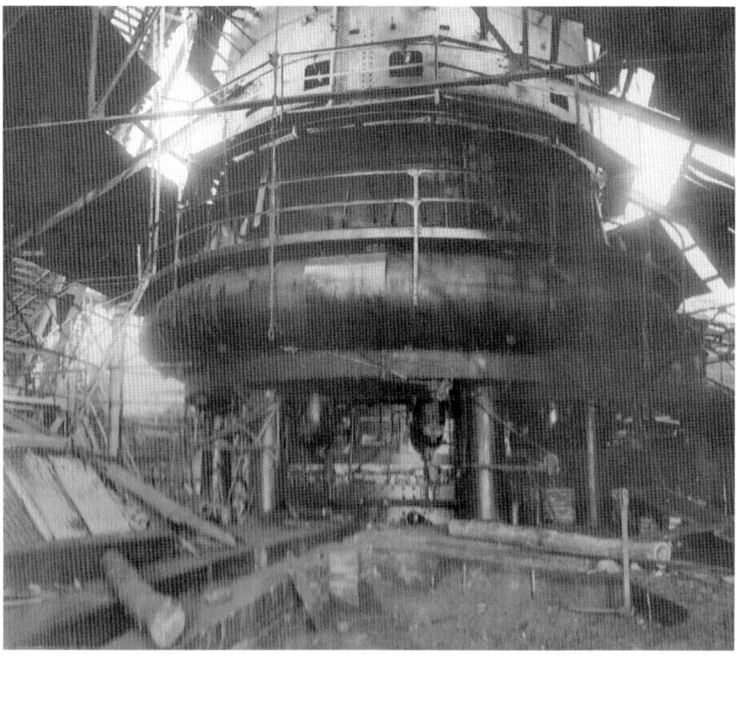

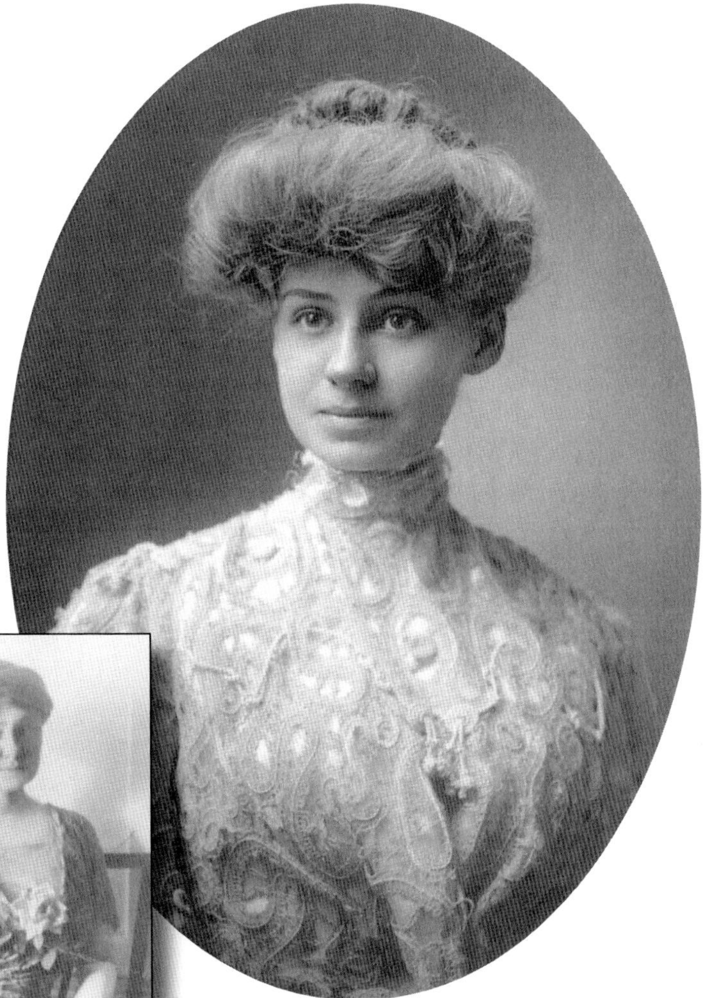

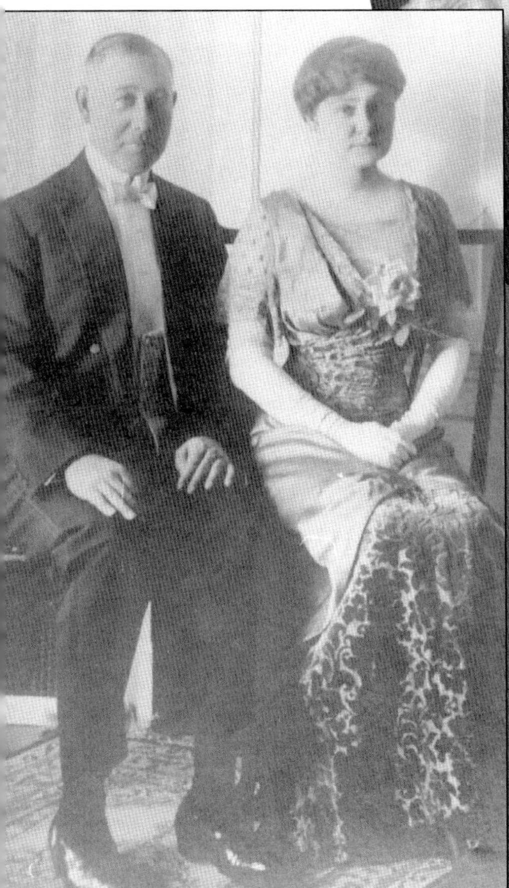

Agnes Reeves Greer and Herbert Greer
Born in 1880, Agnes Reeves married Herbert Greer in 1908. Their marriage united two strong industrialist families and created a partnership that dramatically increased the wealth and success of the couple's business ventures. Agnes took a special interest in the media. She owned multiple radio stations and newspapers. Among these is Dover's own WJER, which she founded in 1949. Despite her responsibilities at home and in the boardroom, Agnes still found time to engage her creative side. At the time of her death, Agnes Reeves Greer held 18 patents on inventions that she had created.

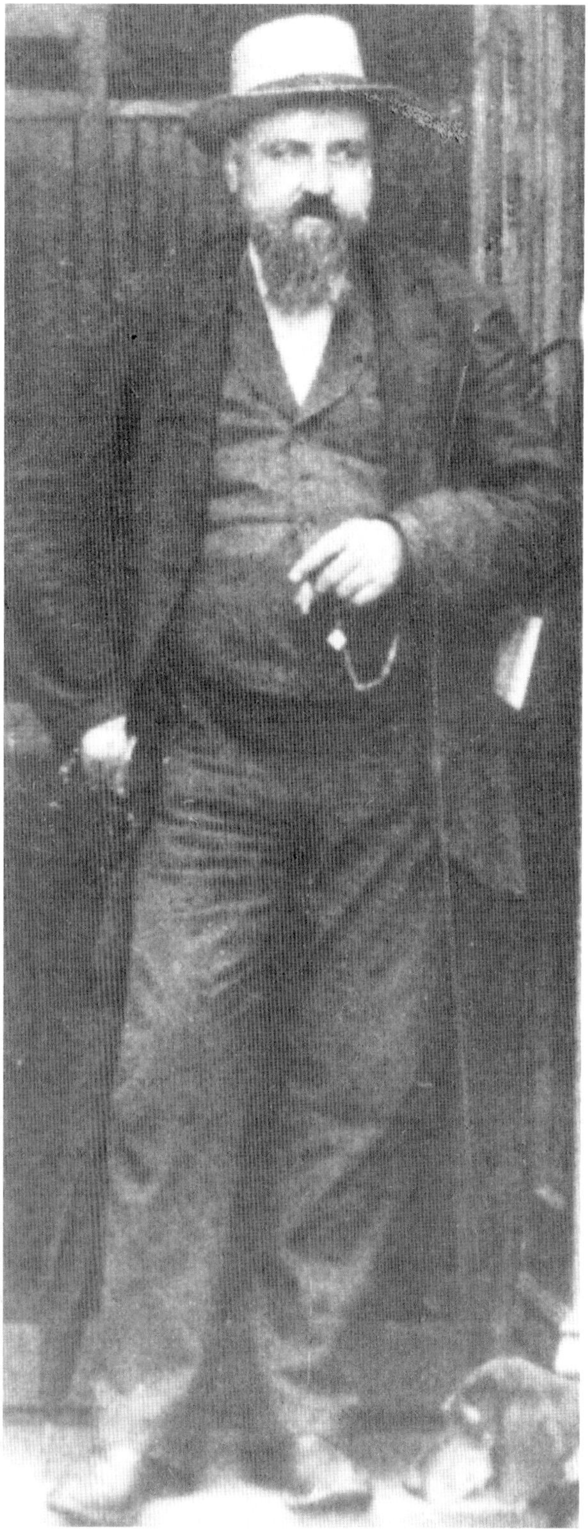

Frederick Bernhard

Born in Germany in 1845, Frederick Bernhard came to the United States at the age of 21. In 1872, at the age of only 27, Bernhard founded the Bernhard Brothers Brewery. The company manufactured lager beer. In the 1870s and 1880s, breweries were one of the first industries to utilize industrial ice-making equipment. This allowed them to make beer in the summer, to preserve their product, and to form a lucrative side business selling ice. In 1890, Bernhard extensively renovated his brewery, building a new brew house, a cold storage department, and a 20-ton ice-making machine. This allowed the brewery to produce 90 tons of ice per year. Bernhard continued to operate his brewery through 1899, when he sold out to the Dover Brewing Company. Although he retired, Bernhard's son Christian remained on at the Dover Brewing Company as the brewmaster.

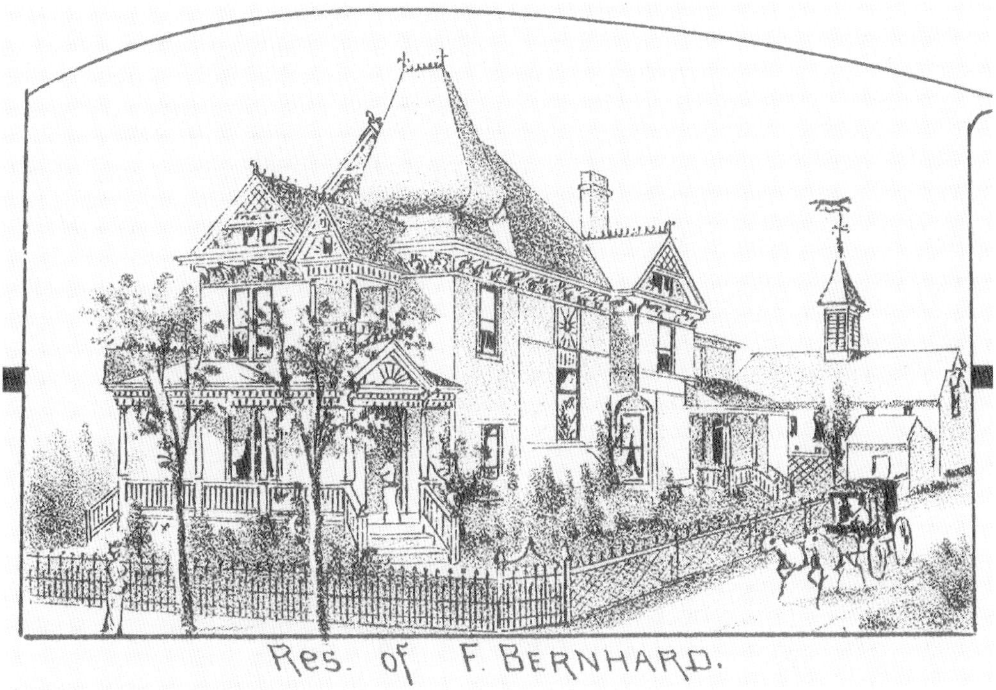

Frederick Bernhard Home

The home of Frederick Bernhard was located in the 200 block of Front Street in Dover. It was only a block from Bernhard's Brewery.

Bernhard Brewing Company

The smokestack in the center of the photograph belongs to the Bernhard Brewing Company.

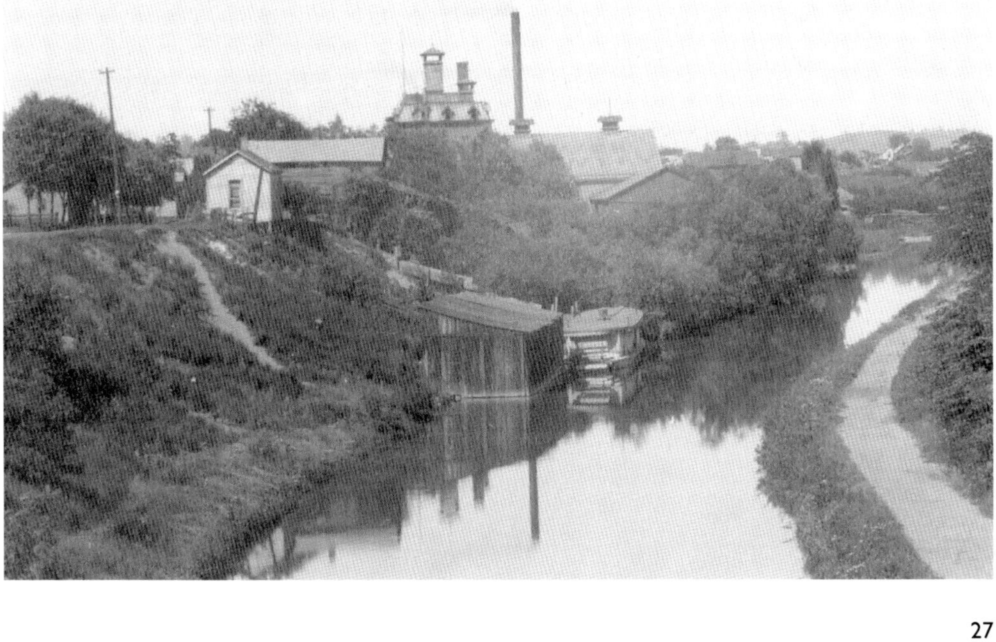

Christian Deis

One of 10 children, Christian Deis was born on October 23, 1843. At the age of 18, Deis, caught up in the circumstances of his age, enlisted in the Union army as a private. He would be promoted several times during his initial stint from 1861 to 1864. As a member of the 80th Ohio Volunteer Infantry, Deis saw action in the battles of Iuka, Corinth, Jackson, and Mission Ridge. He also took part in the siege of Vicksburg.

After finishing his initial service, Christian Deis reenlisted and served under fellow Ohioan William Tecumseh Sherman. With Sherman, he was part of the siege of Atlanta and Sherman's March to the Sea. He mustered out in August 1865, having earned the rank of captain.

Returning to Dover, Deis married Rosanna Harbold, a daughter of one of Dover's pioneer families. For the next five years, the couple busied themselves in farming, but in 1870, Christian partnered with his brother Phillip in establishing a hardware business.

Eventually, Christian sought to strike out on his own. He founded a wholesale grocery in 1878 and took on a partner, Samuel Fertig, in 1881. This move established the Deis-Fertig Wholesale Grocery. This business went on to become the largest wholesale grocer in the county.

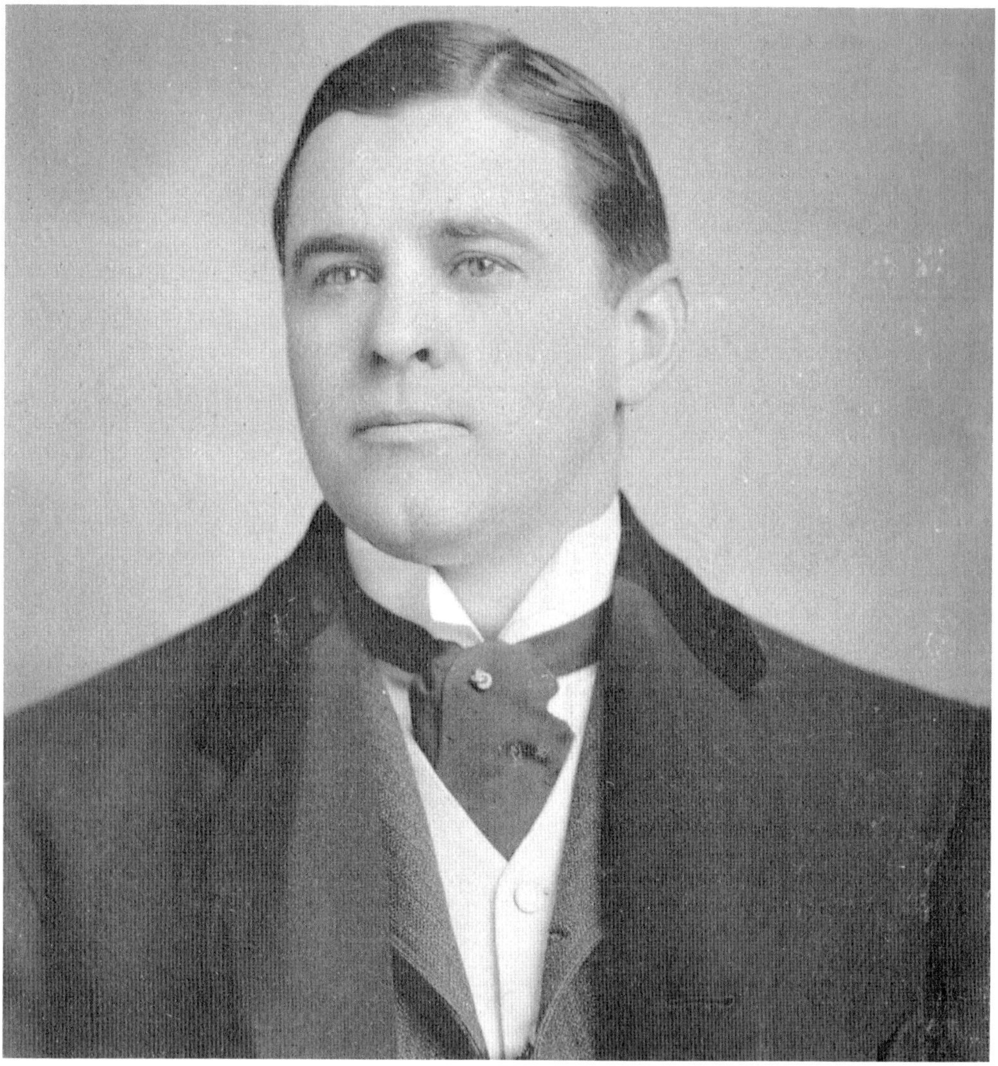

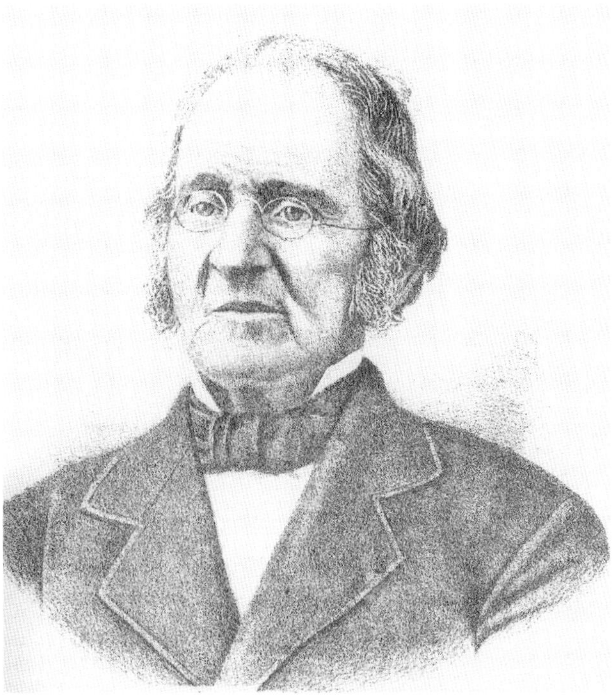

Samuel Fertig

Samuel Fertig was born in Lancaster, Pennsylvania, in 1812. He moved to Ohio at the age of five. In 1834, Fertig accepted a job working on a canal boat. Using his connections as a boatman and capitalizing on Dover's canal boom, he broke into the grocery business in 1837. In 1881, he partnered with Christian Deis to form the Dies-Fertig Grocery.

Deis-Fertig Wholesale Grocery

Below is a fire department demonstration in front of the Deis-Fertig Wholesale Grocery.

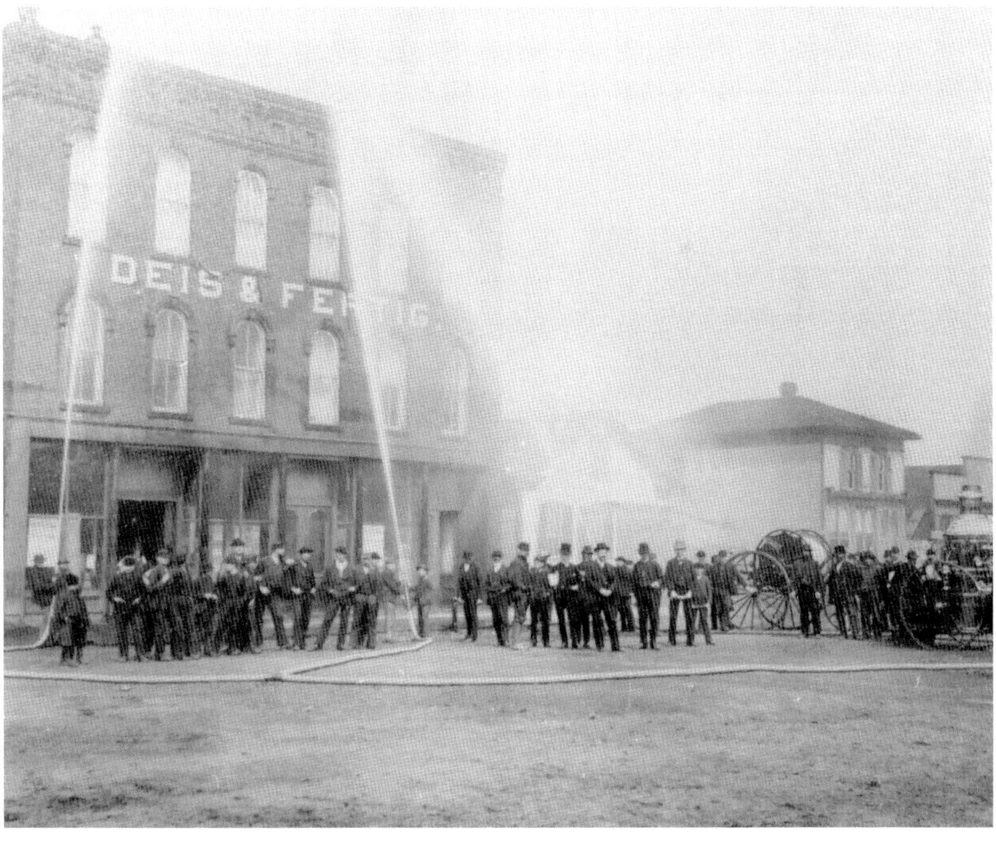

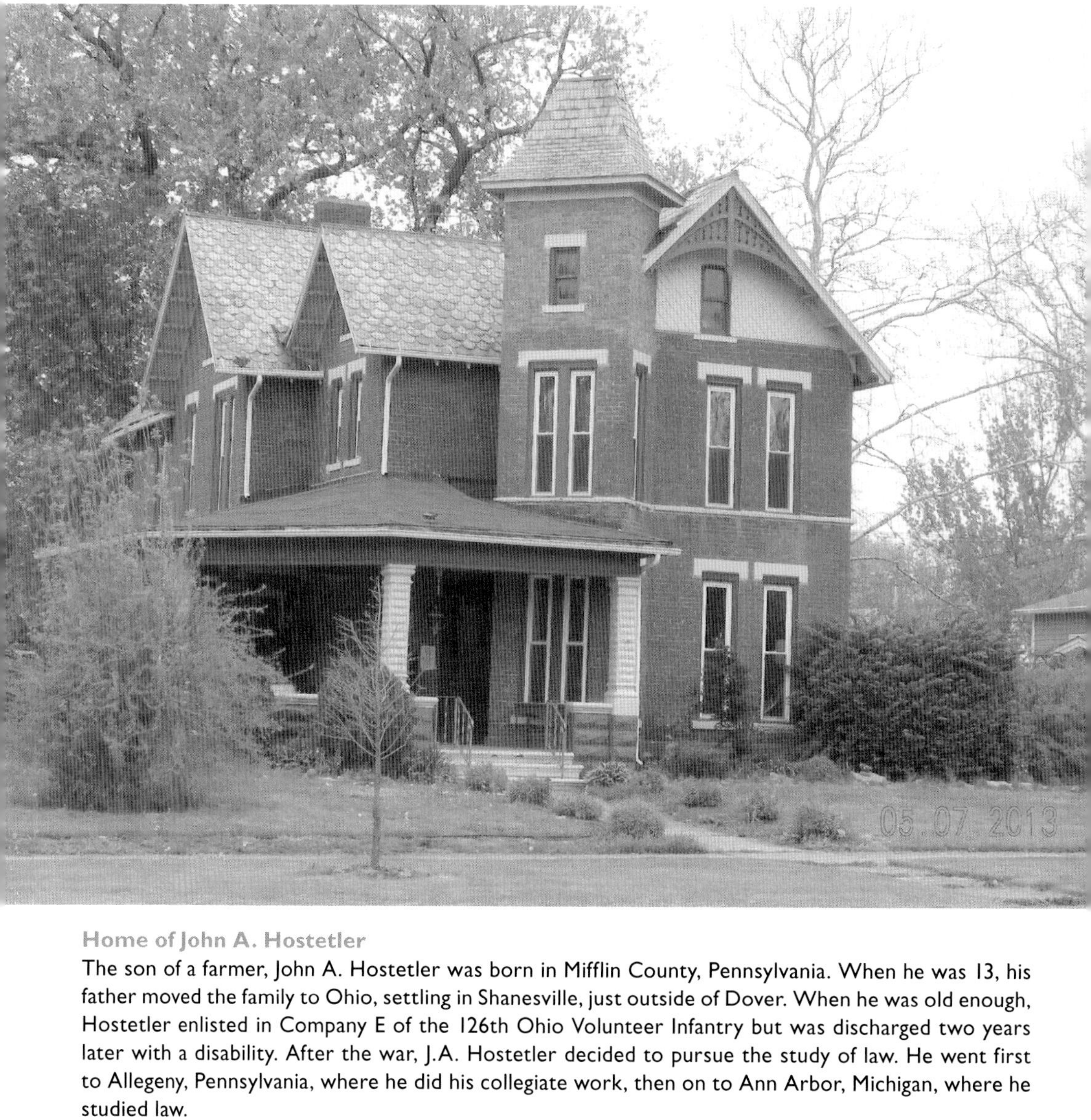

Home of John A. Hostetler

The son of a farmer, John A. Hostetler was born in Mifflin County, Pennsylvania. When he was 13, his father moved the family to Ohio, settling in Shanesville, just outside of Dover. When he was old enough, Hostetler enlisted in Company E of the 126th Ohio Volunteer Infantry but was discharged two years later with a disability. After the war, J.A. Hostetler decided to pursue the study of law. He went first to Allegeny, Pennsylvania, where he did his collegiate work, then on to Ann Arbor, Michigan, where he studied law.

The University of Michigan at the time was a very progressive law school. It was founded in 1859 and had already secured its place among American law schools. In 1870, it graduated only the second African American in the United States to attain a law degree, and in 1871, it graduate the first female to complete law school in the United States.

Hostetler would have attended the law school at the same time as Sarah Kilgore, the first woman to graduate from the school. J.A. Hostetler graduated from the University of Michigan Law School in 1872, passed the Ohio Bar Exam, and began practicing in Dover in 1873. Hostetler must have been popular among the citizens of the town; in 1882, he was elected mayor. (Courtesy of Larry Lautzenheiser.)

John J. Jurgens

John "Jerome" Jurgens was born in Baltimore, Maryland, in 1847. He was the first generation of his family born in the United States as both of his parents were born in Germany. Jurgens graduated from Calvert Hall College in 1862, with a degree in music, and spent several years teaching music before coming to Ohio. In 1866, Dover's St. Joseph's Parish hired Jurgens. At the time, it was looking for someone to take over administration of the newly constructed St. Joseph's School on West Sixth Street. The new frame school had two rooms and could accommodate up to 80 students. Jurgens spent 18 years as the principal of the school, retiring in 1884. In addition to his duties in the school, Jerome Jurgens also served the parish as its organist. St. Joseph's Church is pictured here.

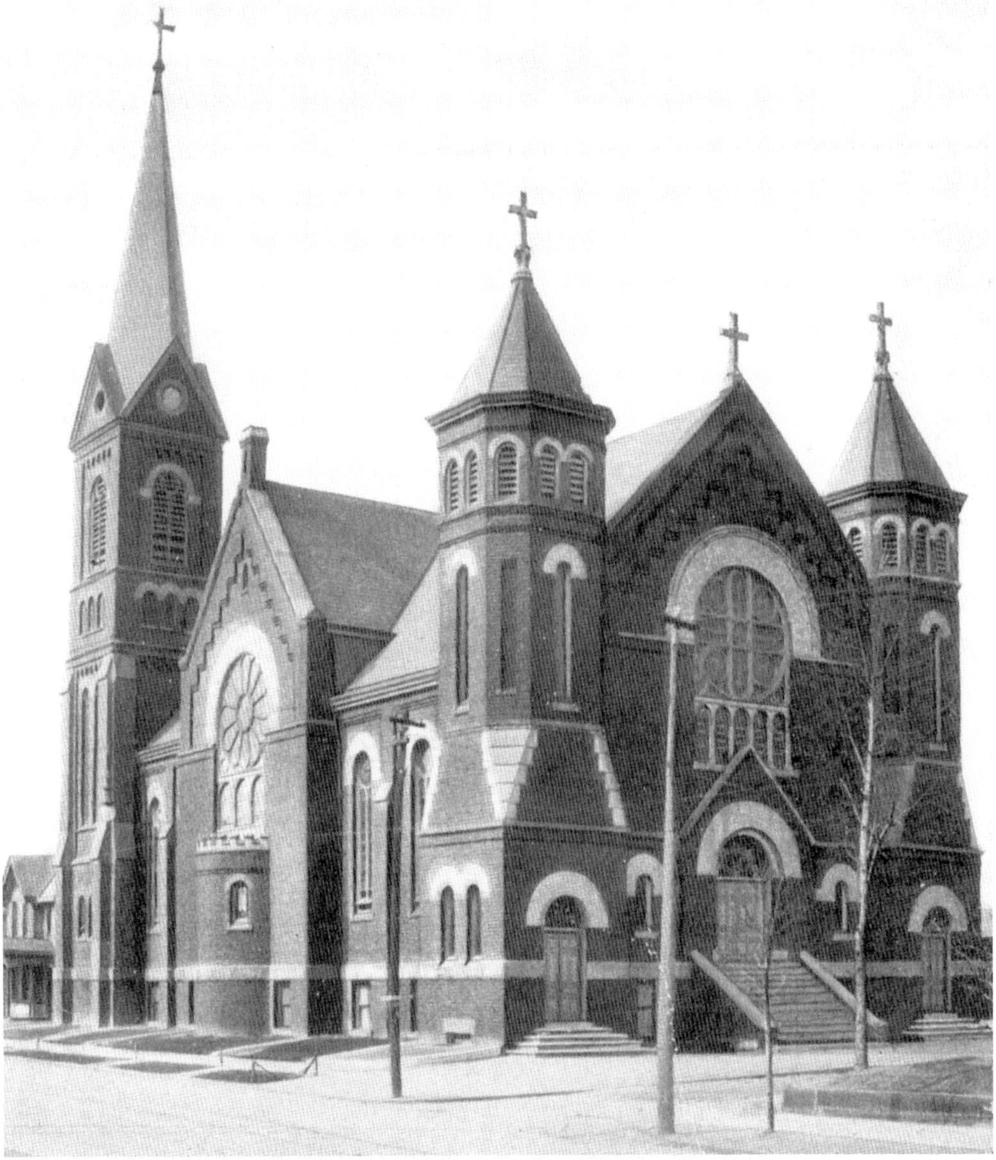

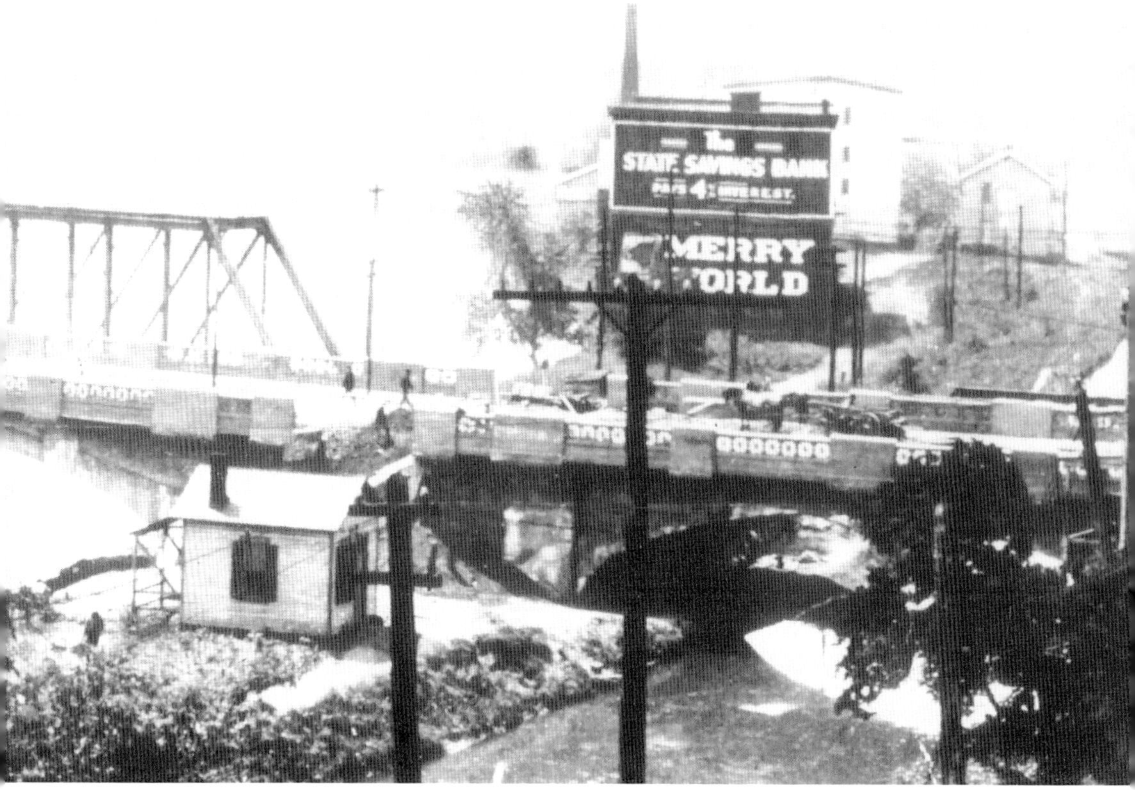

Simpson Harmount

Simpson Harmount was born on April 3, 1828, in Franklin County, Pennsylvania. When he was seven, his family moved to Ohio and settled in Canal Dover. As a youngster, Harmount studied under Edmund Burnett. Burnett would remember the bright young man and hired him to work as a salesman at the age of 16. Later, Harmount would work for the Deardorff brothers in a similar capacity until he accepted a position with the board of public works. In 1849, the board of public works named Harmount the toll collector for the Ohio and Erie Canal at Dover. He remained as the toll collector for four years until he was named Tuscarawas County treasurer. Undertaking a career in politics, Harmount was elected to the state legislature in 1868 and to the Ohio Board of Agriculture in 1872. Despite his political success, Harmount's greatest honor was being chosen to deliver Tuscarawas County's centennial address in 1876. Pictured is the tollhouse on the Ohio and Erie Canal.

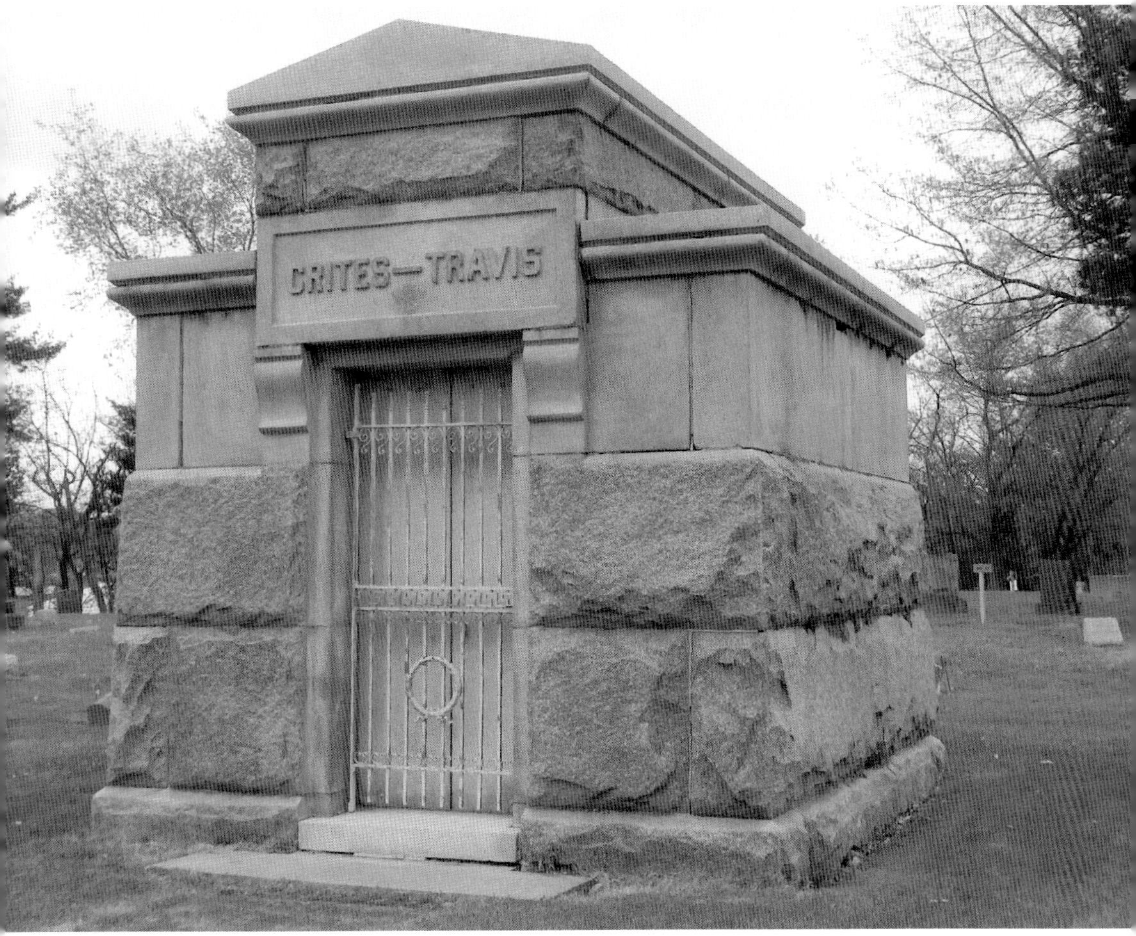

George Crites

George Crites was born on March 9, 1842, the son of a local carpenter. His father worked to build many of the community's prominent buildings. Coming from humble beginnings, George Crites attended the local schools. His first job after finishing school was as a teacher. Also during this time, he worked with his father doing carpentry work. In 1865, he began work with William Rickert and Sons Druggists as a clerk. He would spend the rest of his professional life working in drugstores.

In 1867, he felt that he had learned enough and partnered with another young ambitious Doverite, W.W. Scott, to form Crites and Scott Druggists. The partnership with Scott lasted until 1873, when Scott left, and George Crites was joined by E.C. Dickson. When Dickson dissolved the partnership in 1877, Crites decided to continue on alone. For many years after, his business was simply Crites Druggists. In addition to his professional interests, Crites also took an interest in politics as an active Democrat. He was elected as a state representative in 1879 and was reelected in 1883.

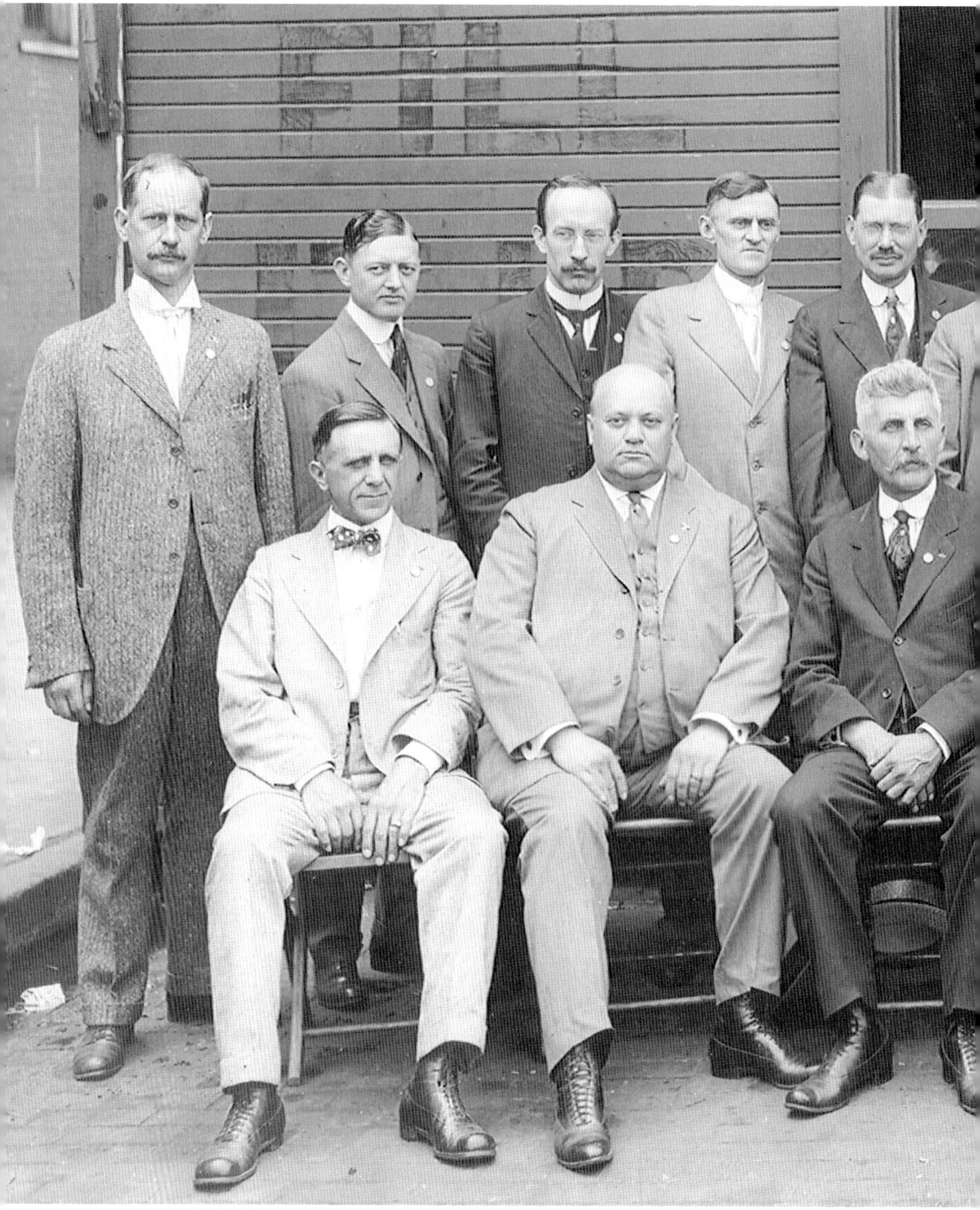

Arthur J. Krantz

Arthur Krantz was one of Dover's leading industrialists for more than 50 years. Born in Dover in the mid-1870s, Krantz maintained a long relationship with the Reeves family and their businesses. Together, Krantz and Samuel Reeves Sr. established the Reeves Manufacturing

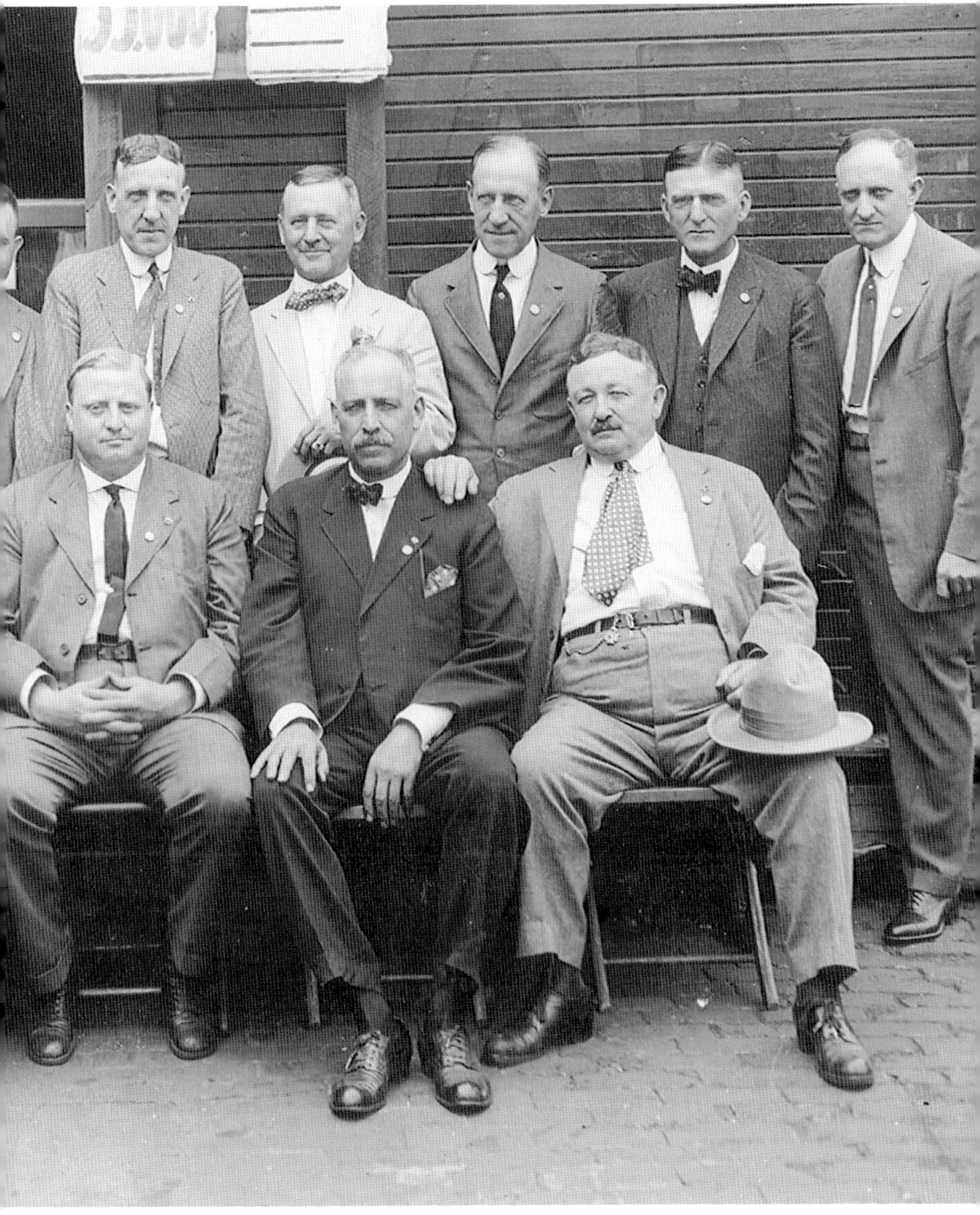

Company in 1900. Krantz (first row, fourth from left) worked first as a manager and then as the president of the Reeves Manufacturing Company. Dover's War Chest Drive raised money for the war effort during World War II. Arthur Krantz is pictured as part of the group.

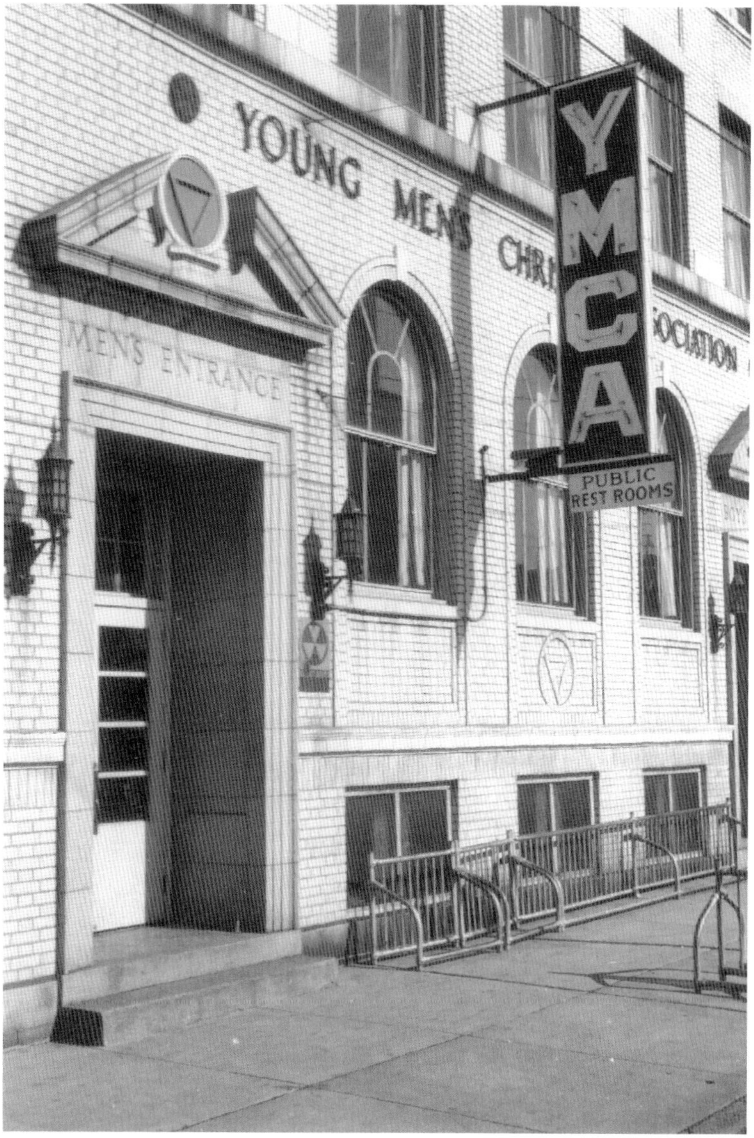

Andrew Deis

Born on December 11, 1847, Andrew Deis was a man of many interests. His primary employment came as the head of the Wagner Lumber Company. He held this position for a record 72 years from the age of 22 until his death in 1941. Originally founded as the Dover Planing Mill, the Wagner Lumber Company was incorporated as the Wible-Enck Company in 1870. In 1890, the Wagner family purchased the shares of all the investors except Andrew Dies, renaming the business the Wagner Lumber Company. In addition to his interest in the lumber business, Andrew Deis was also an investor in many other Dover businesses. These included the Dover Manufacturing Company and Invincible Vacuum.

While Andrew Deis enjoyed business and proved very successful, he did not forget the community that he called home. His generosity made the local Young Men's Christian Association (YMCA) possible. He gave $75,000 and the land for the first YMCA to be constructed on Factory Street (Tuscarawas Avenue). Deis also negotiated the deal that allowed the Dover YMCA to reorganize and become the Tuscarawas County YMCA after money problems during the Great Depression.

CHAPTER TWO

Community Builders and Businessmen

Once the foundation for a community has been laid and industry has grown, the next era of success must begin. In the case of Dover, this saw continued efforts by old names and new, those whose fathers were founders and those who were newcomers to the community. These individuals strengthened the foundation and continued to work toward the betterment of the community. Today, the benefits of these community builders and businessmen are still enjoyed by many. In fact, exceptional individuals have taken up their causes even today. Building on the success and vision of the Deardorffs and Reeveses were men and women like Sam Reeves Jr., Mrs. P.G. (Elizabeth) Justice, John Toland, and Guy Smith.

Sam Reeves continued the work begun by his grandfather Jeremiah and father, Sam Sr. He continued to promote the family's steel mill, served on the board of the Reeves Bank, and gave generously to his community. One of Sam's greatest gifts was the establishment of the Reeves Foundation and the gift of his grandfather's home to the Dover Historical Society. To date, the Reeves Foundation has granted millions to community improvement projects and worthy local nonprofit organizations. Since Sam's gift of the family home to the Dover Historical Society in 1975, the museum has welcomed thousands of visitors and actively preserves the area's rich history.

Mrs. P.G. Justice worked hard to grow the Dover Public Library from a small community room at the local high school to an independent institution. She also presided over a collection that grew from 5,000 volumes to 20,000 and watched monthly circulation grow to 10,000 volumes. Although she had already retired after 22 years of service, it was fitting that she was there when Dover dedicated its new library building in 1953.

John Toland was yet another of the caretakers of the community. Among his many contributions to the growth of the community, he worked tirelessly for the YMCA and Salvation Army. He also played an important role in the Dennison Canteen and helped to plan the route for Interstate 77. For his work in the community, he was awarded the Golden Deeds Award from the Dover Exchange Club in 1956.

Until current mayor Rick Homrighausen passed him, Guy Smith was Dover's longest-serving mayor. First taking office in 1972, Smith devoted 20 years of his life to making Dover a better place to live. Among his many accomplishments are the construction of Dover City Pool, expansion of the parks, and key improvements to the city's electric generating facility. Perhaps his greatest gift, though, was the way he transcended politics. A Republican, people do not remember him for his party affiliation; they remember him for the way he cared for the city.

While those above are great examples of community builders and businessmen, they are just a few of many. Dover has been fortunate, and continues to be fortunate, to have great people who have accepted the responsibility passed onto them from the founders. Their dedication and hard work will assure that the next generation enjoys the same strong community amenities and opportunities that they have.

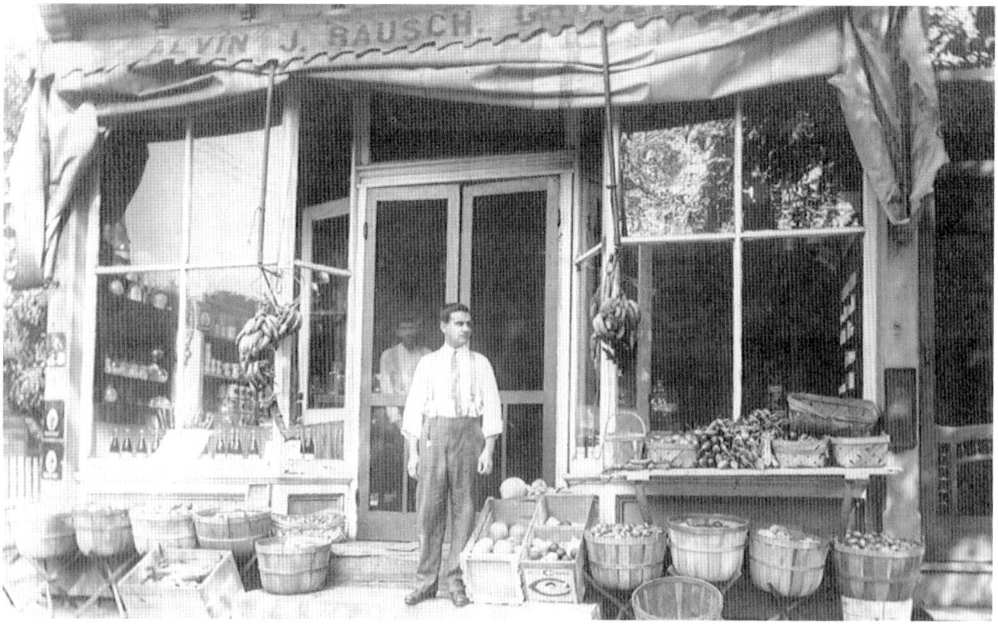

Alvin J. Rausch

After a difficult early life and the loss of both his parents, Alvin Rausch (pictured above) got his start as a delivery boy for the Davis Grocery in New Philadelphia. In 1909, Alvin met and married Mary Helmsdoerfer. Alvin's relationship and eventual marriage reaped huge benefits for the young grocer. Mary became not only a companion but also a valuable partner in establishing the Alvin J. Rausch grocery in Dover. Prior to their marriage, Mary worked at the Garver Brothers department store in Strasburg. Once the pair was united, things began to move in the right direction. They outgrew their first store in Dover and, in 1914 or 1915, began working toward building a larger store at 119 West Third Street. Although it took the family many years of hard work and dedication, the phrase "Rausch your grocer" became synonymous with quality shopping in downtown Dover. Below, Alvin J. Rausch is pictured with his brothers, George, Jacob, and Harry.

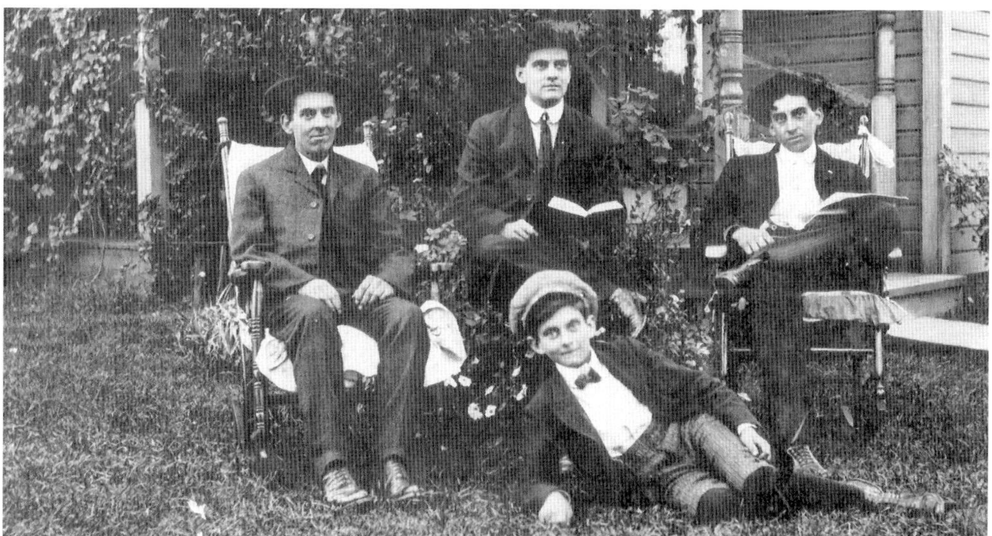

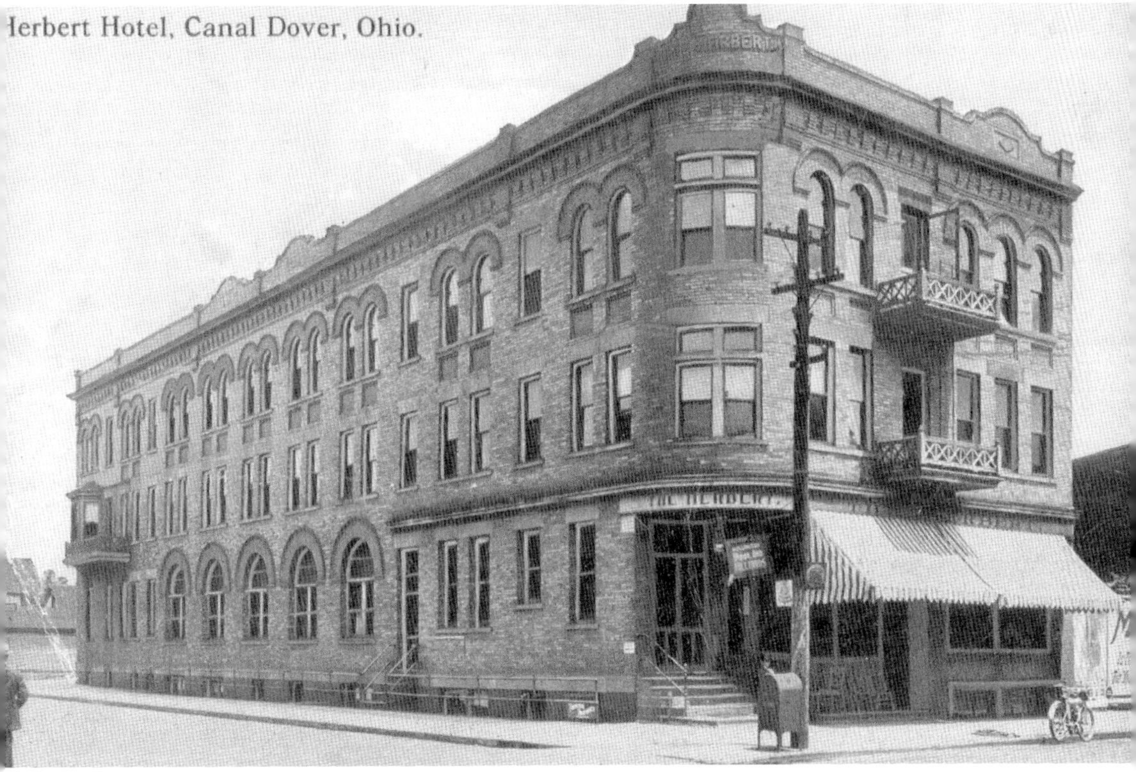

Daniel Defenbacher

Daniel Defenbacher was born to German parents on September 14, 1855. He came to Dover from Bowerston and quickly showed an aptitude for managing a hotel. In 1889, he purchased the Iron City Hotel, the same hotel that would later be known as the Riverside Inn, on Front Street in Dover. He ran the inn successfully for eight years but decided to sell the business in 1897. After selling the Iron City Hotel, Defenbacher tried his hand as an investor in the iron industry. In this pursuit, things did not go as well as they had with the hotel. Defenbacher decided to return to his roots.

In 1889, he set to work on the brand new Herbert House Hotel on the corner of Second and Factory streets (Tuscarawas Avenue). The hotel had its grand opening on July 10, 1900.

In addition to his hotel business, Daniel Defenbacher was very active in the business community. He served as the president of the Ohio Shovel and Stamping Co. and as director of the First National Bank and the Dover Building and Loan Company. Outside of business, Defenbacher was the first exalted ruler of Elks Lodge No. 975 and was elected mayor of Dover.

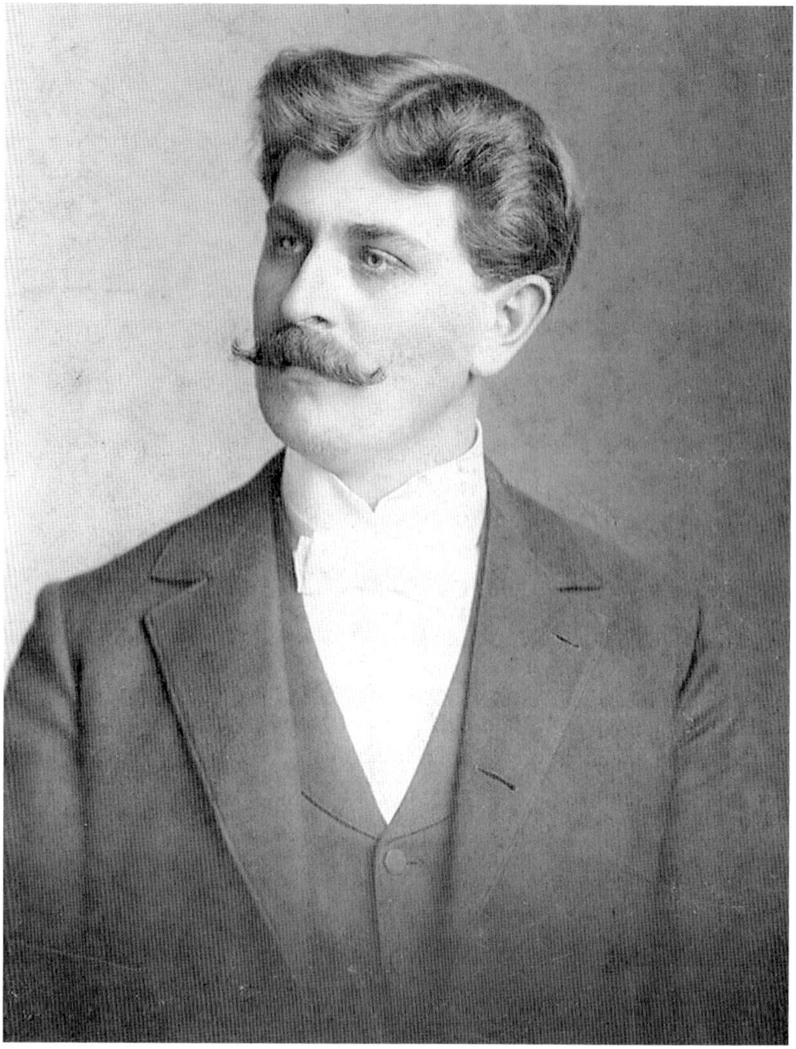

Harry Crater

One of Dover's most prominent citizens of the early 20th century, Harry Crater was born in Dover on June 9, 1873. Crater owned a great deal of land on the east side of Dover and worked as a contractor throughout his life.

The Crater family history in Dover is a rich one. Harry Crater's great-grandfather John George Crater was a member of Napoleon's expedition to Moscow. After fighting in the Battle of Waterloo, John Crater returned home to find that his parents had died and that all of his siblings had divided their assets and left him out. With no other choice, Crater sought his fortune in the United States.

In addition to their extensive land holdings, the Craters are well known for their generosity toward Dover City Schools. In 1866, they donated the land for a timber schoolhouse to be constructed at the end of Second Street in Dover. This building would be remodeled twice, in 1883 and 1896; during the latter renovations, brick replaced the timbers. Dover's Second Street school would remain a fixture until the current East School was opened in 1952.

Harry H. Crater is responsible for another gift to Dover schools in 1935. That year, Harry and his sister Leah Senhauser donated the land for what would become Crater Stadium. The Stadium was opened on September 18, 1937, and, to this day, still bears the family's name.

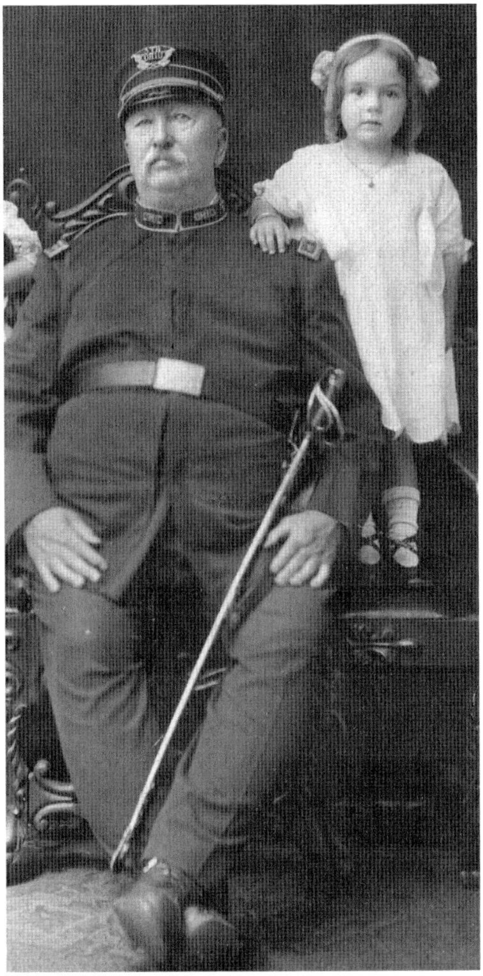

Edward Horn and the Horn Block

The grandson of German immigrants from Bavaria, Edward Horn was, for many years, a successful businessman in Dover. Edward's father, Jacob, pioneered the family's success locally by founding a tavern and a bakeshop. Jacob was known as the typical German *tavernmeister.* His jolly disposition was passed onto his youngest son, Edward, who continued in the family business while expanding his own interests. Edward Horn was the proprietor of the Central Hotel in downtown Dover and renovated the Horn Block downtown, which included his family's bakery, restaurant, and saloon. Horn was also a pioneer in Dover's cultural scene. Along with three other men, Joseph Beiter, Philip Schaefer, and Christian Deis, Edward Horn helped make Dover's Big Four Opera House a reality.

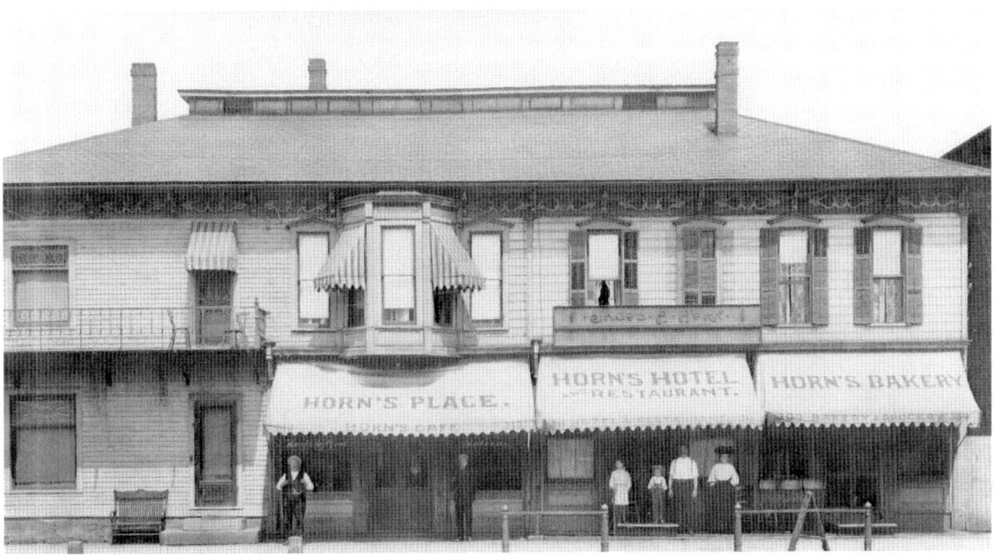

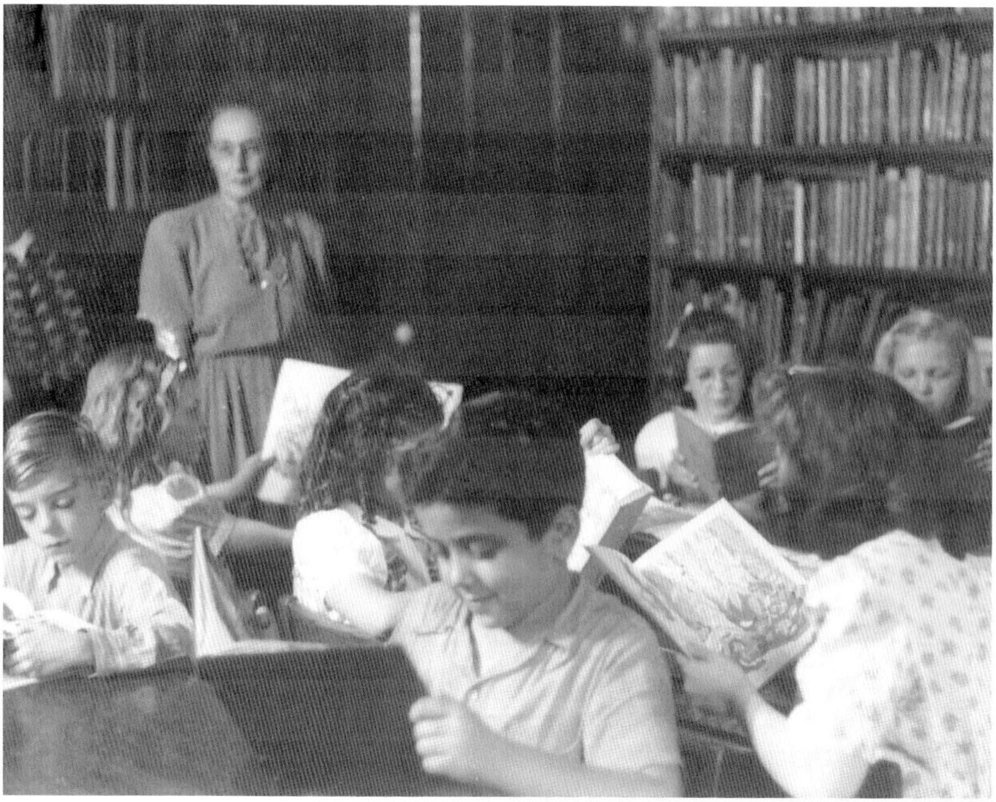

Mrs. P.G. (Elizabeth) Justice

To tell the story of Elizabeth Justice is to tell the story of Dover's Public Library System. The first known library in Dover was founded as a reading room for the employees of the American Sheet and Tin Plate Company. It was located at the corner of Front Street and Tuscarawas Avenue in Dover. After the closing of the mill, the library was moved to a room in the old Downey residence on the Oak Grove School property. Later, when the Downey residence was razed to make room for the new Roosevelt High School, the library was moved again.

Elizabeth Justice arrived in Dover in 1914. She was educated at Western Reserve University, although it is unclear as to whether she graduated. In 1923, she was asked to serve on the newly created board of trustees for the Dover Public Library, but only six months later, she was asked to step down. At first, she was concerned but quickly learned that they had asked her to resign so that she could join the library's staff. That first year, Elizabeth Justice worked under a high school senior who had been administering the library. The following year she was named the library's director.

As library director, she oversaw the opening of the library's first independent building on Walnut Street in 1934. She was also responsible for the remarkable growth of the collection. Under her watch, the library went from 5,000 volumes to 20,000 volumes, with a monthly circulation of 10,000. Although she retired in 1946, after 22 years of service, Justice was on hand in 1953 when the library constructed and dedicated a brand new building for its collection. Elizabeth Justice died October 16, 1965.

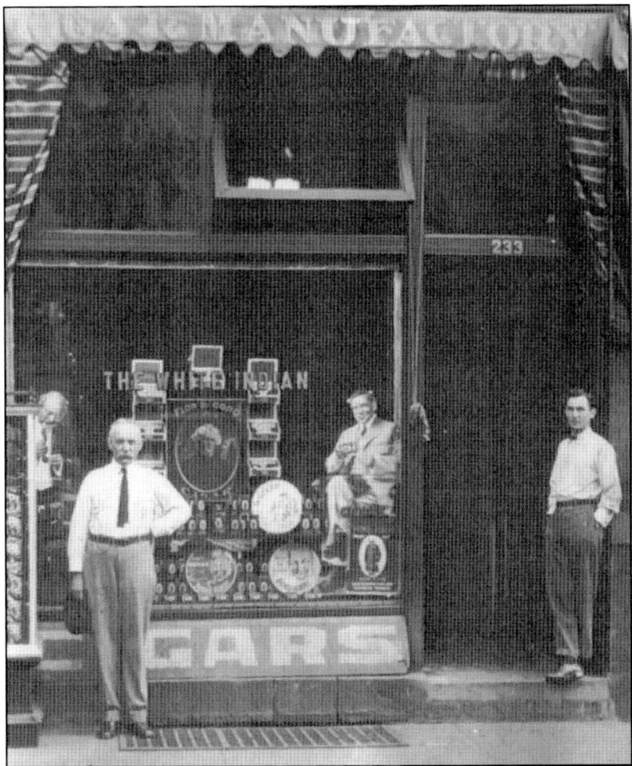

Joseph Ress

Born in Massillon on October 29, 1849, Joseph A. Ress (left) was the son of German and Swiss immigrants. In 1887, Ress opened a cigar store in downtown Dover. His store, which was called the White Indian, was both a retail establishment and a manufacturer of fine cigars. Eventually, Ress's two sons, J. Matthew and Joseph T. Ress, would join their father in the family business. (Courtesy of Don Whittingham.)

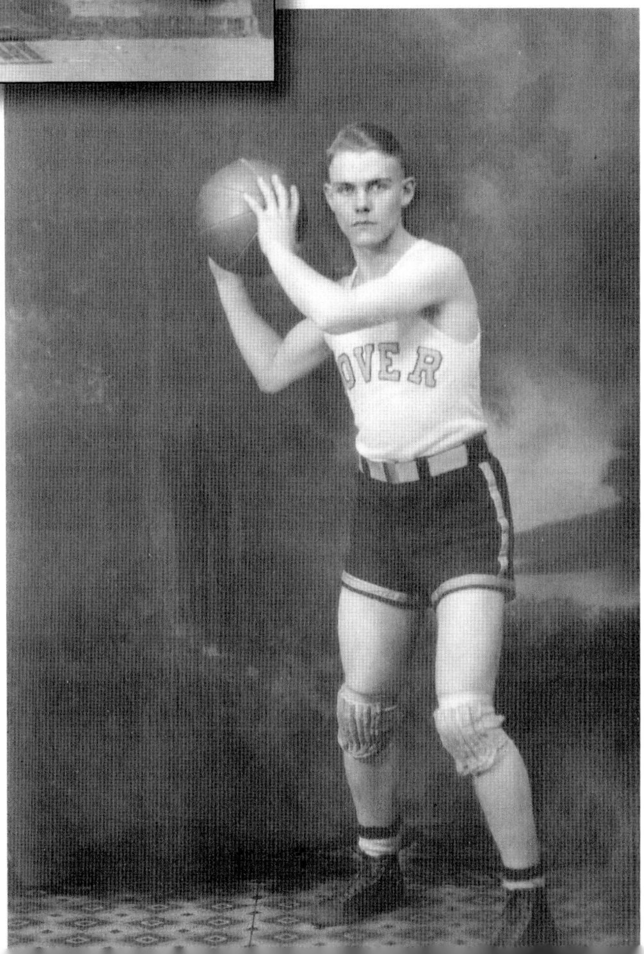

Bill Beitner

Bill Beitner was born on December 14, 1910, in Dover. As a Dover freshman in 1927, he helped his team to its first state championship in basketball. After high school, Beitner enrolled at the Ohio State University (OSU). He was a three-year starter in basketball for the Buckeyes from 1932 to 1935. During his senior season, Beitner was named team captain and an All-American. In 1939, Beitner returned to Dover, where he opened Bill Beitner Tire, Inc. He would run the business until his retirement in 1978.

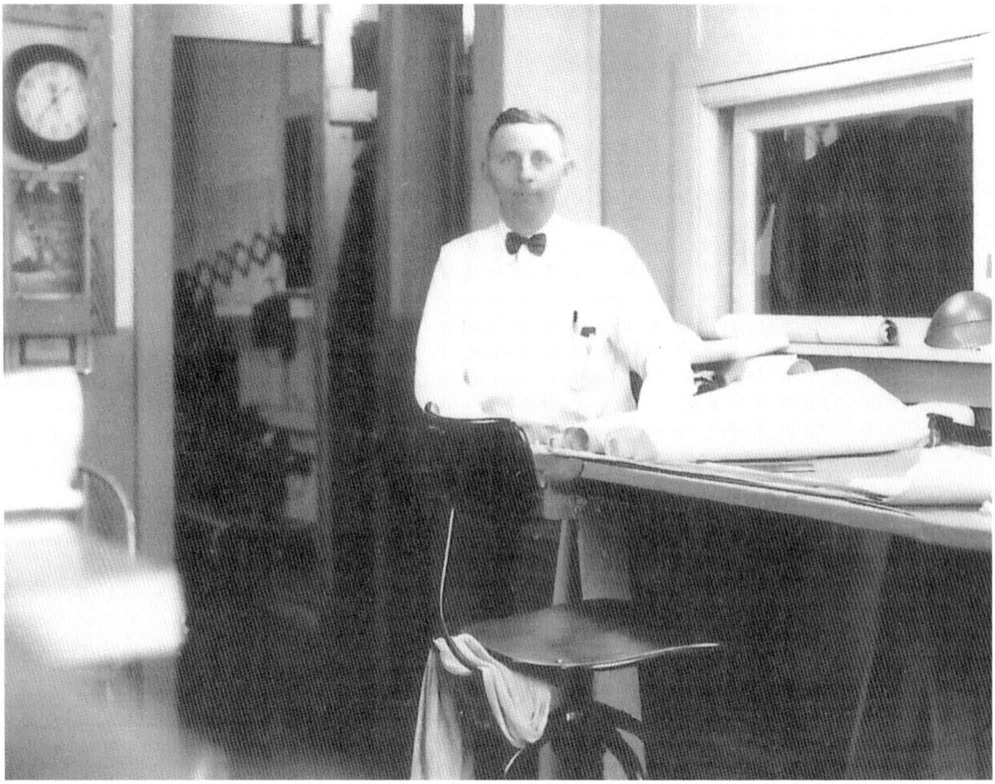

Arthur B. "A.B." Klyne

Imagine the change that Dover chief electrician A.B. Klyne witnessed in his lifetime. At the time of his birth, December 23, 1900, only three percent of American homes had electricity. At the time he took over as the city's chief electrician in 1923, things were a little better, with about 500 local homes wired for power. To its credit, the city also boasted one stoplight on the corner of Wooster Avenue and Third Street. After moving to Dover to take over as chief electrician, Klyne watched the city's department grow exponentially. He is also credited for setting up the first illuminated downtown Christmas displays on the square. After his retirement from the city in 1964, after 41 years of service, Klyne continued to stay busy plying his trade. He volunteered his time and expertise in the renovation of the J.E. Reeves Home when the Dover Historical Society acquired it in 1976. (Courtesy of Larry Lautzenheiser.)

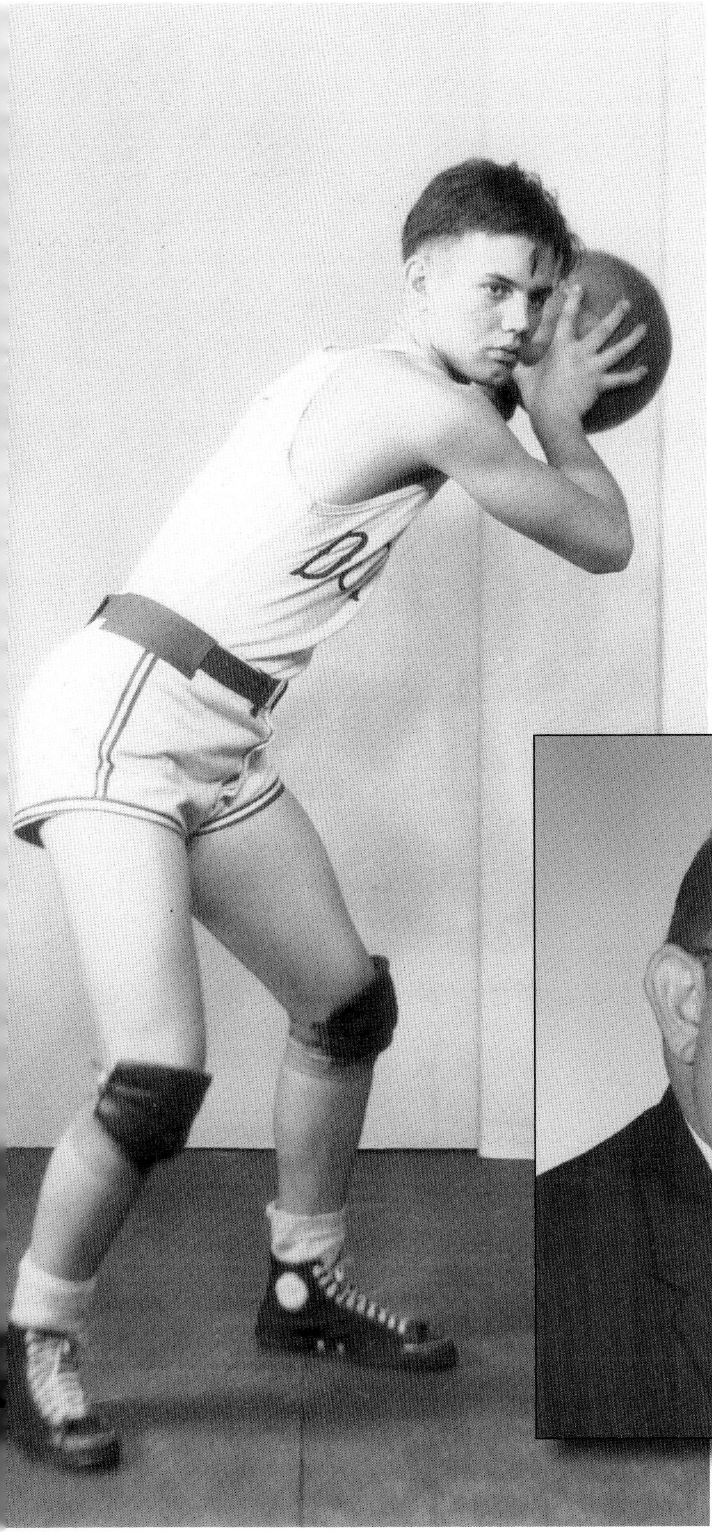

J. Richard "Dick" Klar
Dick Klar was born in Dover. Much of his life was devoted to what he loved most, sports. As a high schooler, he was the captain of Dover's 1933 state championship basketball team. Klar is shown at left as a member of Dover's 1933 team. As a businessman, Klar continued to work in the world of sports. For 29 years, he operated Klar Athletic Supply store in Dover. For many of those years, Klar also served as a high school official for both basketball and football. He would later be inducted into the Eastern District Football Officials Association Hall of Fame as its inaugural member. (Courtesy of Doug Klar.)

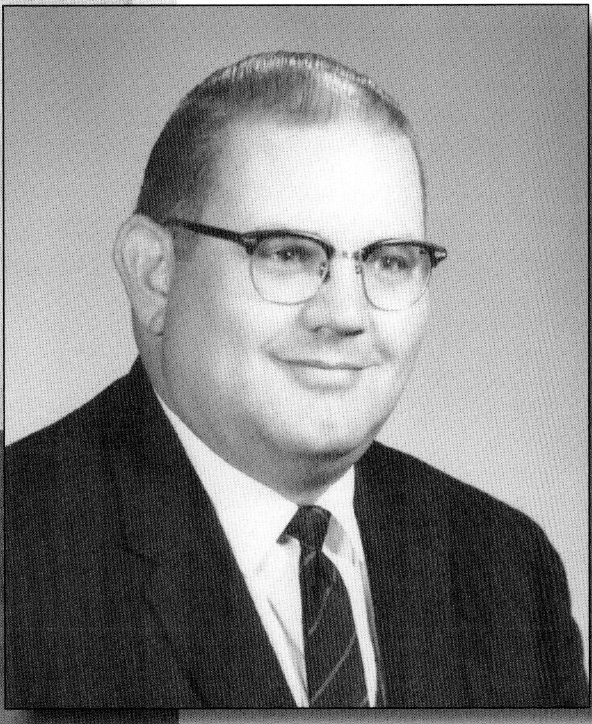

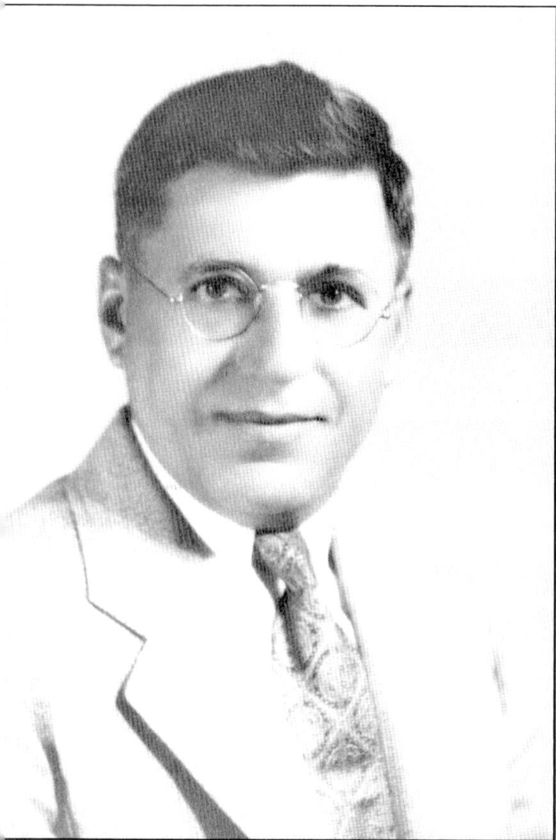

Fred Potschner

Born at the end of the 19th century, nothing in Fred Potschner's life was short term. A native of Dover, he enlisted in the service during World War I. After the war, he returned to Dover and founded the area's first Ford franchise dealership. He would operate that dealership until 1971, a remarkable 52 years. Also in 1919, Potschner married Gertrude Whitmire. The couple remained together for the next 62 years. (Courtesy of Mary Ann Ellwood.)

Potschner Ford

Fred Potschner's Ford dealership was located on the corner of Fourth Street and Wooster Avenue in Dover. Today, Lehman's Big Open Road occupies the building. (Courtesy of Mary Ann Ellwood.)

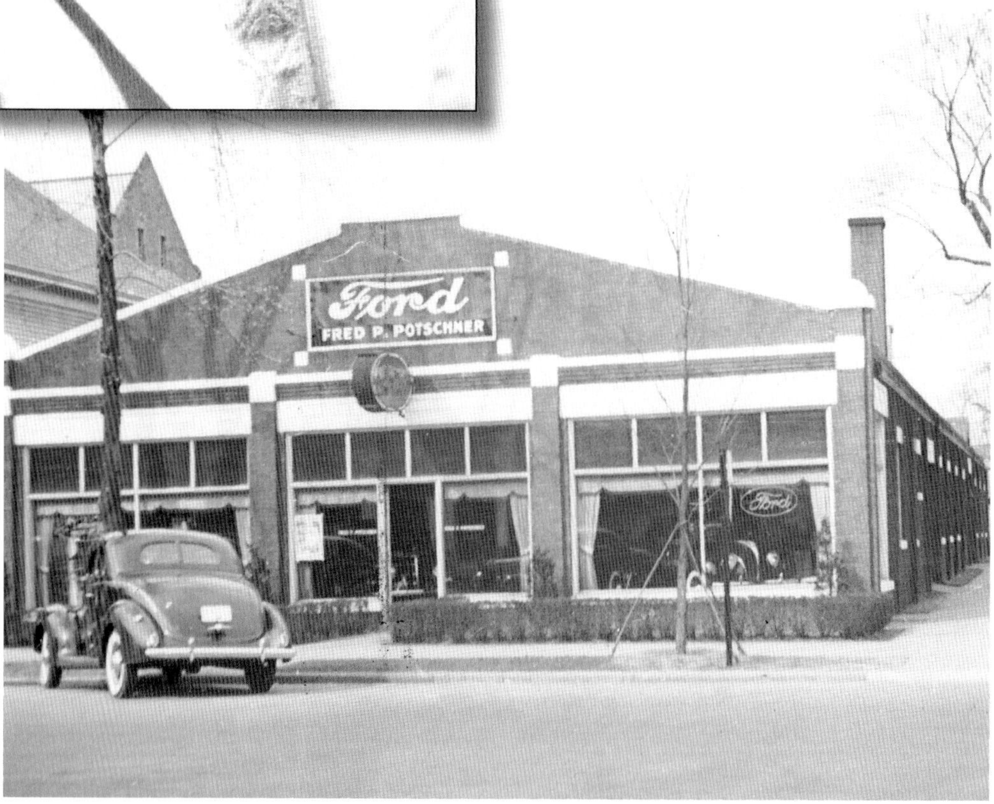

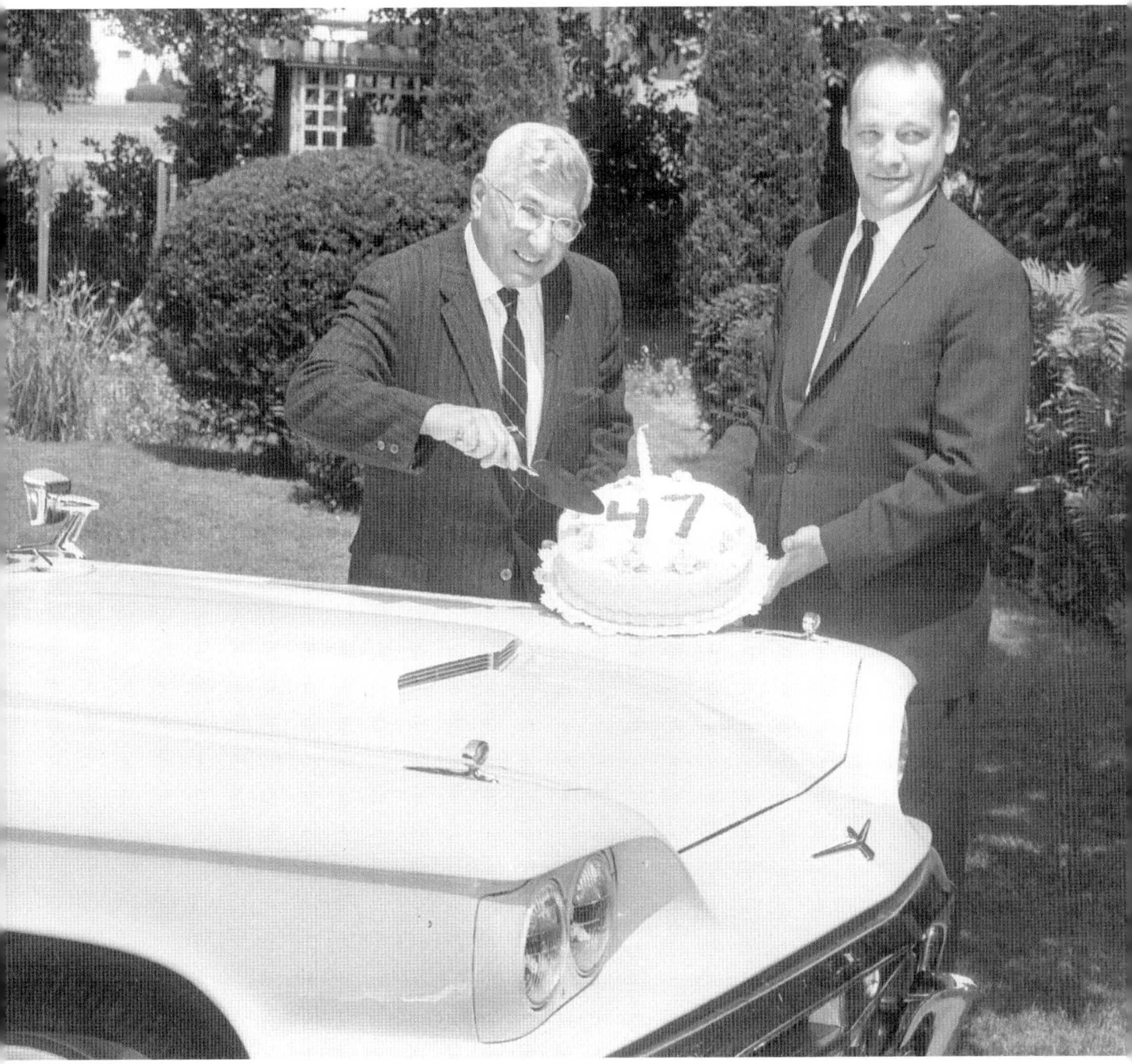

Fred Potschner and Bill Ellwood

Fred Potschner and son-in-law Bill Ellwood are pictured. After his marriage to Potschner's daughter Mary Ann, Ellwood went to work at the dealership. (Courtesy of Mary Ann Ellwood.)

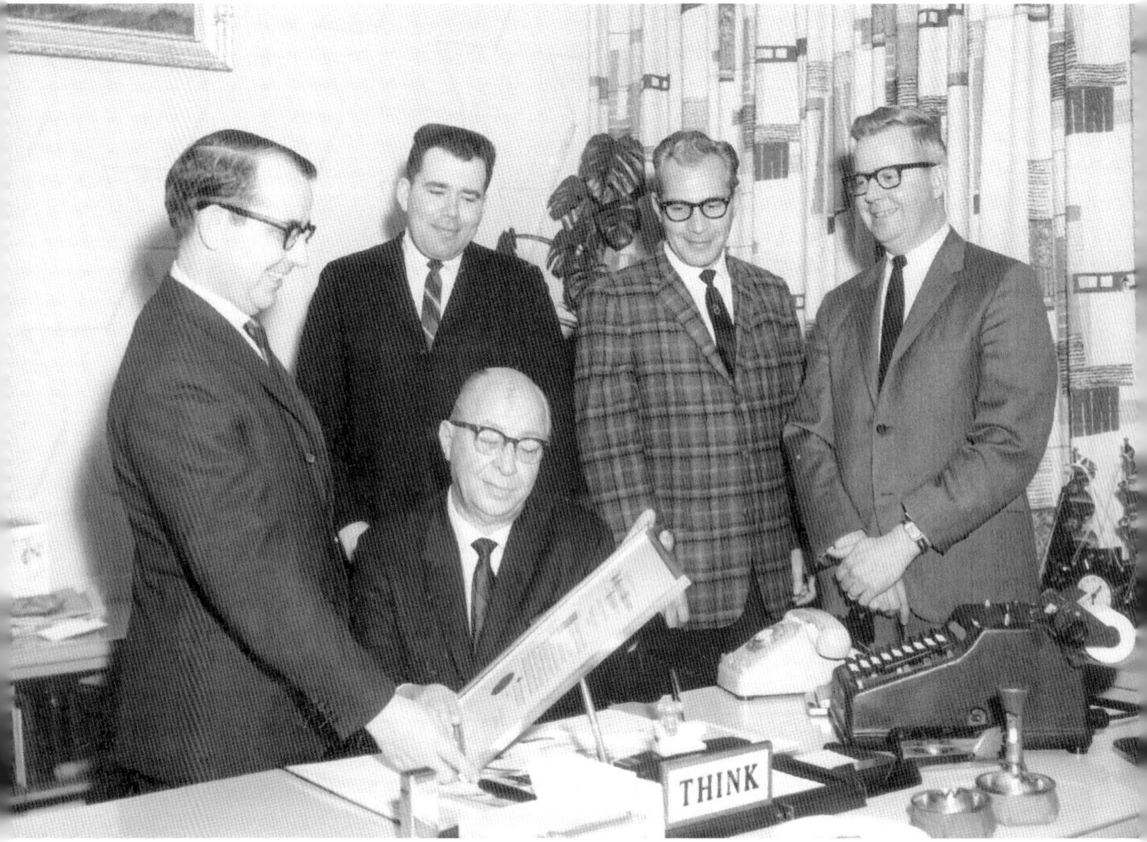

Eugene "Cheese" Hanhart

Born in 1904, Cheese Hanhart (seated) was the son of a baker. He received his unusual nickname either because he delivered cheese pies as a boy or for his family's Swiss heritage.

In 1929, Hanhart purchased the Voherr Insurance Agency, renaming it the Hanhart Insurance Agency. He would remain active as the owner for the next 53 years. Outside of his professional work in the insurance business, Hanhart was a very active member of the Democratic Party. He served on the Ohio Democratic Party Executive Committee from 1948 to 1956 and worked hand in hand with Ohio governor Frank J. Lausche on his five gubernatorial campaigns. Through his work in the Ohio Democratic Party, Hanhart met and got to know Pres. Harry S. Truman and served on the Ohio delegation that cast its ballot for John F. Kennedy at the 1960 Democratic National Convention. (Courtesy of the Hanhart Agency.)

Sam and Peg Reeves

Samuel Reeves Jr. was born on April 10, 1899, in Dover. His family, which included his mother, Belle Croxton Reeves, and sisters Margaret and Jane, was forced to deal with adversity early on. In 1901, when Sam was not quite two, his father, Samuel J. Reeves Sr., died of typhoid fever. Fearing for the family and seeking to provide guidance for the young man, Sam's paternal grandfather, Jeremiah Reeves, had a home constructed next to his own on East Iron Avenue for Sam, his mother, and sisters to live in. Jeremiah would live until 1920 providing guidance and mentoring for the young man.

Sam followed his father and grandfather into the family business. He was active in both the Reeves Manufacturing Company and the Reeves Banking and Trust Company, where he served as vice chairman. Perhaps Sam's greatest gift was the establishment of the Reeves Foundation in 1967. This philanthropic foundation has distributed millions of dollars within Dover and Tuscarawas County and continues to be an important factor in many local projects that benefit the community and its youth.

Away from business, Sam was active in the Dover First Moravian Church, the American Legion, Union Country Club, and the Masonic lodge. In 1967, Sam married Margaret Hostetler Wagner.

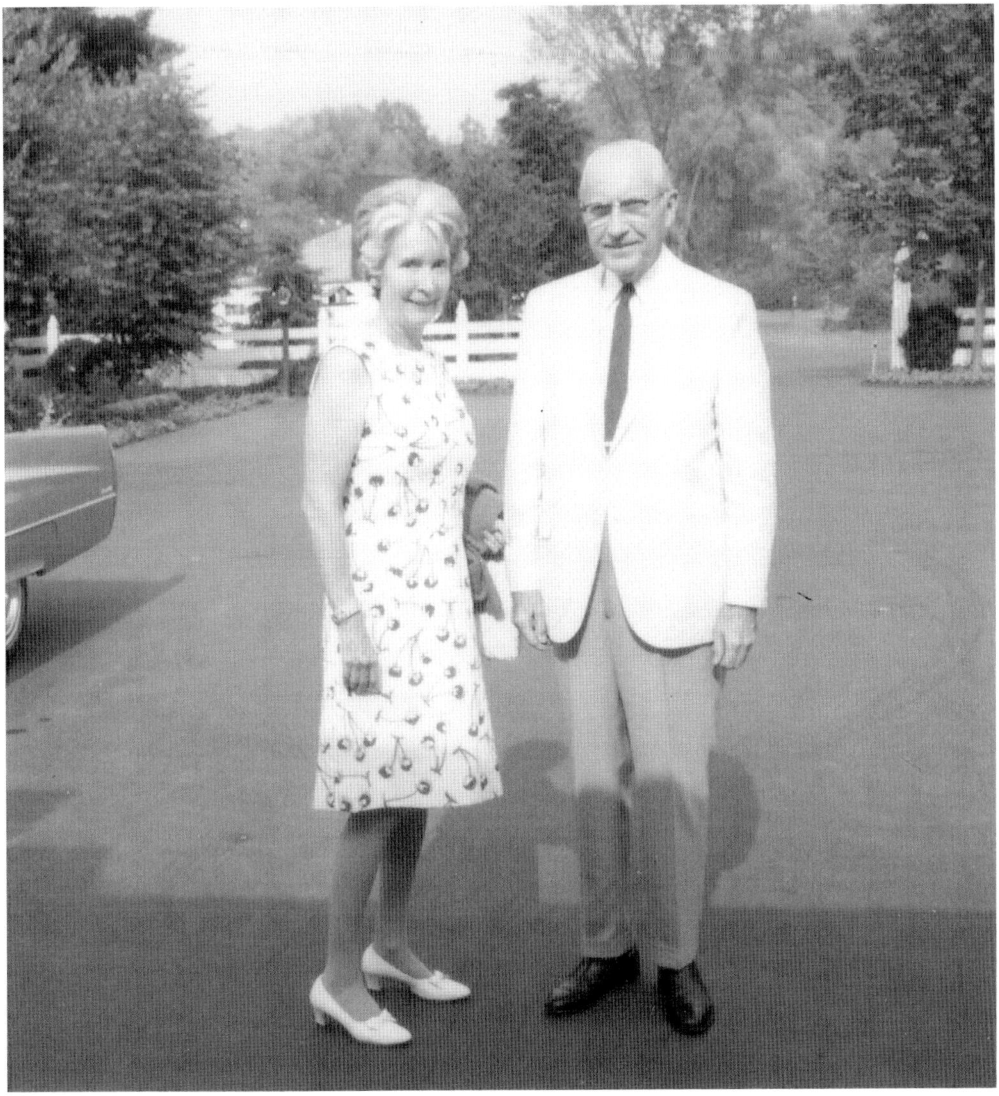

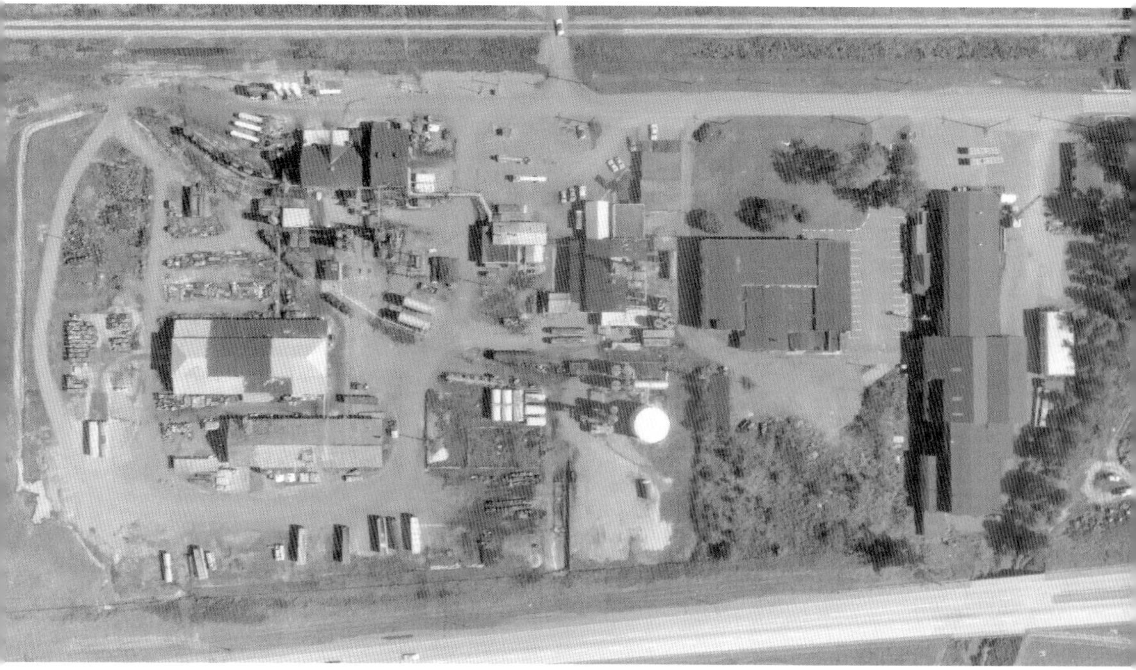

Robert S. Cohen

Robert Cohen was born on September 23, 1923, in Rochester, New York. After finishing his bachelor's of science from the University of Michigan in 1944, he entered the US Army. Cohen was chosen to work on the Manhattan Atomic Bomb Project. The Manhattan Project began in 1942 and grew to employ 130,000 people at its height and involve 30 separate sites throughout the United States, Canada, and the United Kingdom. The Manhattan Project was responsible for producing the two atomic bombs that were detonated at Hiroshima and Nagasaki, which effectively ended World War II. After the war, Cohen was involved in the Bikini Atoll nuclear tests in 1946.

After his work on the Manhattan Project, Cohen received a master of science in physics in 1947. In 1949, he founded the Dover Chemical Corporation. He would serve as the president of the company until 1976. In addition to his work at Dover Chemical, Cohen would go on to found several other successful business ventures. These include the Enterprise Chemical Corporation, the JC Technology Corporation, and the Cripple Creek Trout Farm in Rural Retreat, Virginia.

Away from his business interests, Cohen was involved in the community. He worked alongside the Wilderness Center, was active with Kent State University, and served in a number of professional chemical organizations. Above is an aerial view of Dover Chemical Corporation. (Courtesy of Dover Chemical.)

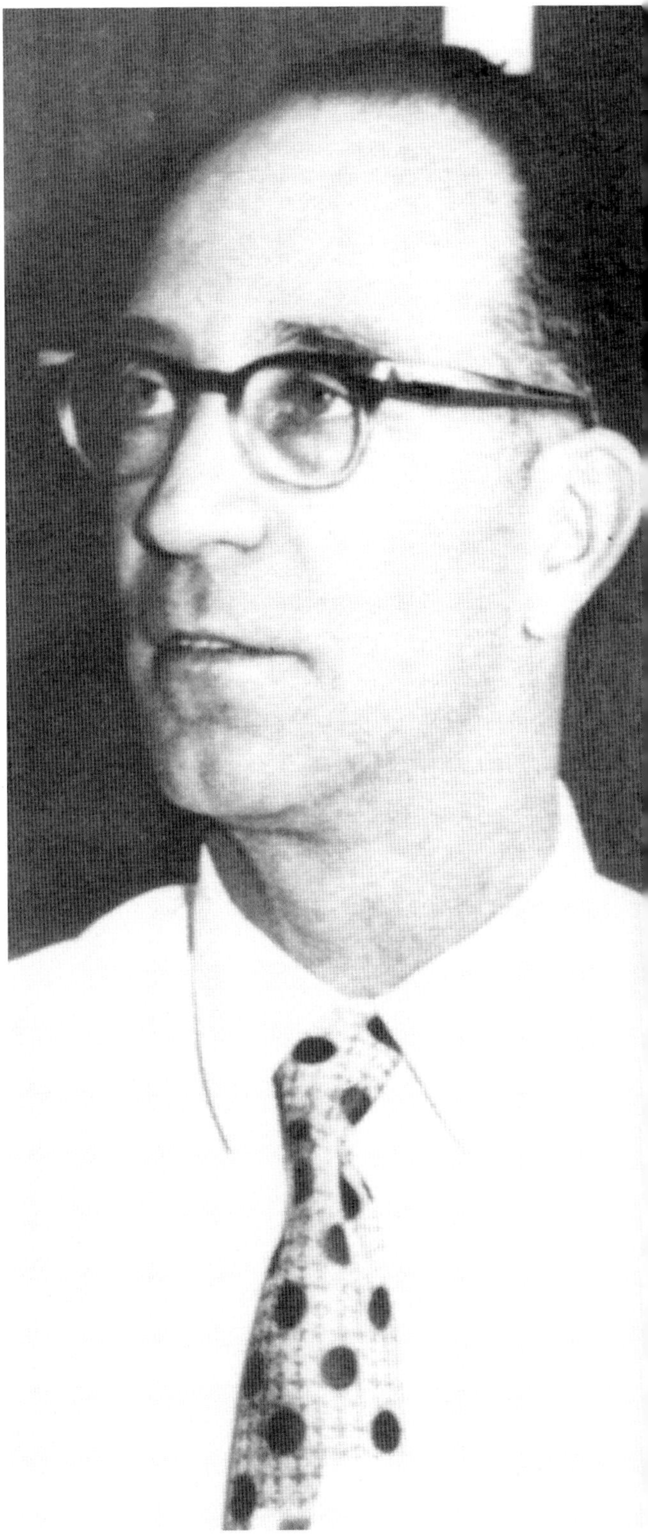

Thomas L. Kane III

Tom Kane was born on June 28, 1920, in Elyria, Ohio. As a young man, he attended the Hudson Academy in Hudson, Ohio. After graduation, Kane continued his education at Antioch College, where he received his bachelor of science in engineering. In 1943, he joined the US Army Engineering Office. He would remain in the Army through the end of World War II.

After his service, Kane returned to Dover where he embarked on a series of successful business ventures. He partnered with his father in the Black Bird Coal Mines, and later, he served as president of both Better Value Homes and Dover Cable Television. Although he was successful, Kane was not content.

In the 1950s, Kane decided to continue his education by earning his bachelor of arts in psychology and math from Muskingum College and then his master's degree in psychology from the Ohio State University. Armed with his new degrees, Kane began his second career by entering the education field in 1960. That year, Kane was hired by Dover High School as a teacher. He remained in the classroom for two years before accepting the position of school counselor in 1962. Tom Kane would remain with Dover City Schools until his retirement in 1978.

In addition to his professional interests, Kane was an active member of his community. He was deeply involved with Dover First Methodist Church and the Wilderness Center, where he served on the board of trustees. Kane also served the community through Dover Kiwanis. For 24 years, he chaired the scholarship committee. Perhaps Kane's greatest gift, though, was his work with Family and Children First Council of Tuscarawas County. For three years, he served as president of the organization, which allowed more than 25 organizations to collaborate and better serve the community.

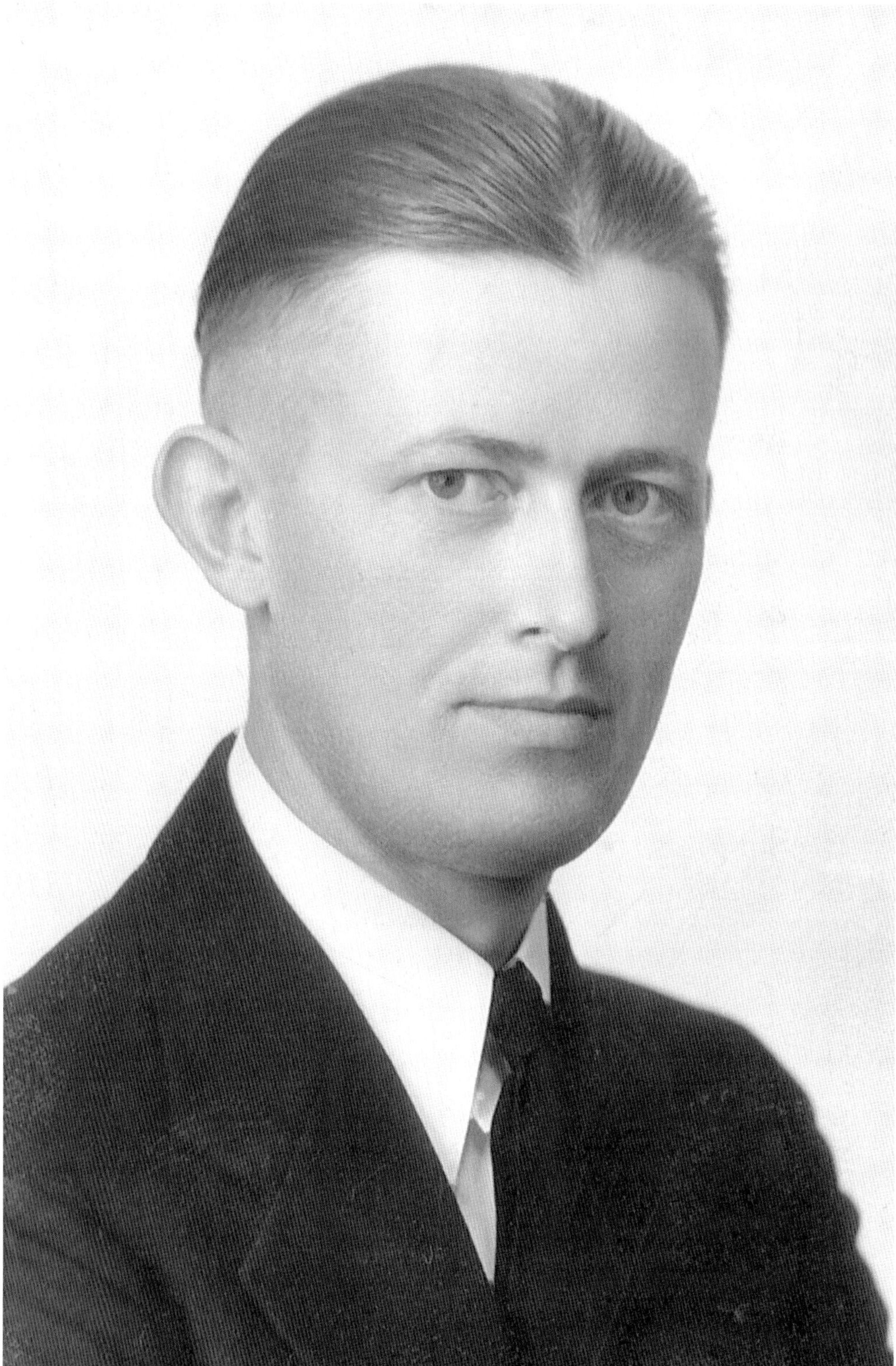

John Toland (BELOW AND OPPOSITE PAGE)
John Toland was born in the small village of New Cumberland, just outside of New Philadelphia, in 1900. He grew up in the town of Coffeyville, Kansas, where his father opened the town's first movie theater. After finishing high school, Toland would work for a year as a rural mail carrier before deciding to attend mortuary school. Toland attended the Worsham College of Mortuary Science in Illinois, graduating in 1923. After graduation, he returned to the area in which he was born. He began working at the Boyd Funeral Home in Dover. In 1929, Toland left Boyd's and set up his own funeral home. The Toland Funeral Home would eventually grow to become the Toland-Herzig Funeral Home.

Away from the business, John Toland devoted himself to the community. He served as the YMCA director from 1931 to 1935 and was an active advocate for the Salvation Army. During World War II, Toland was an important figure in the Dennison Canteen. He also worked to plan for the building of Interstate 77. In 1963, he was appointed by Gov. James A. Rhodes to the Ohio Board of Embalmers and Funeral Directors, a post he held for 10 years. For his many accomplishments, the Dover Exchange Club recognized John Toland with its Golden Deeds Award in 1956. (Courtesy of John Herzig.)

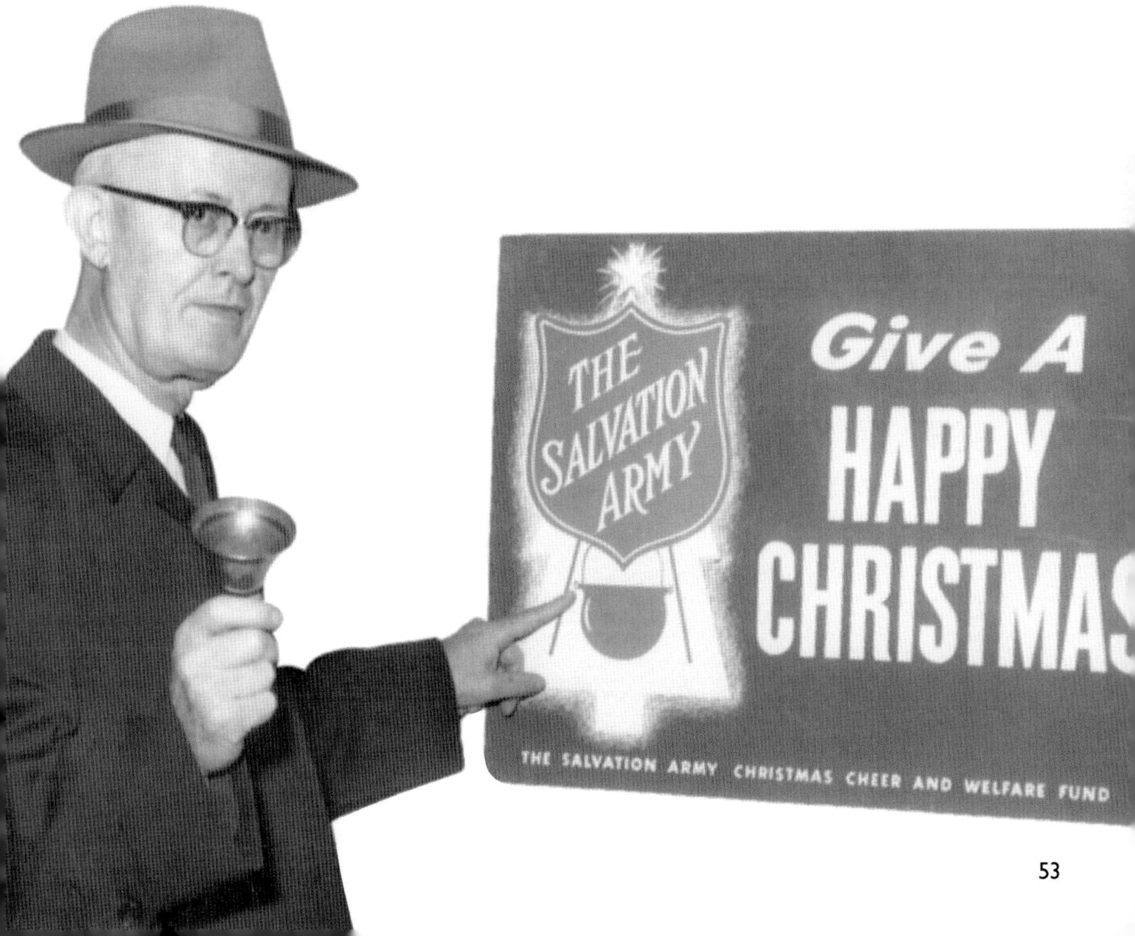

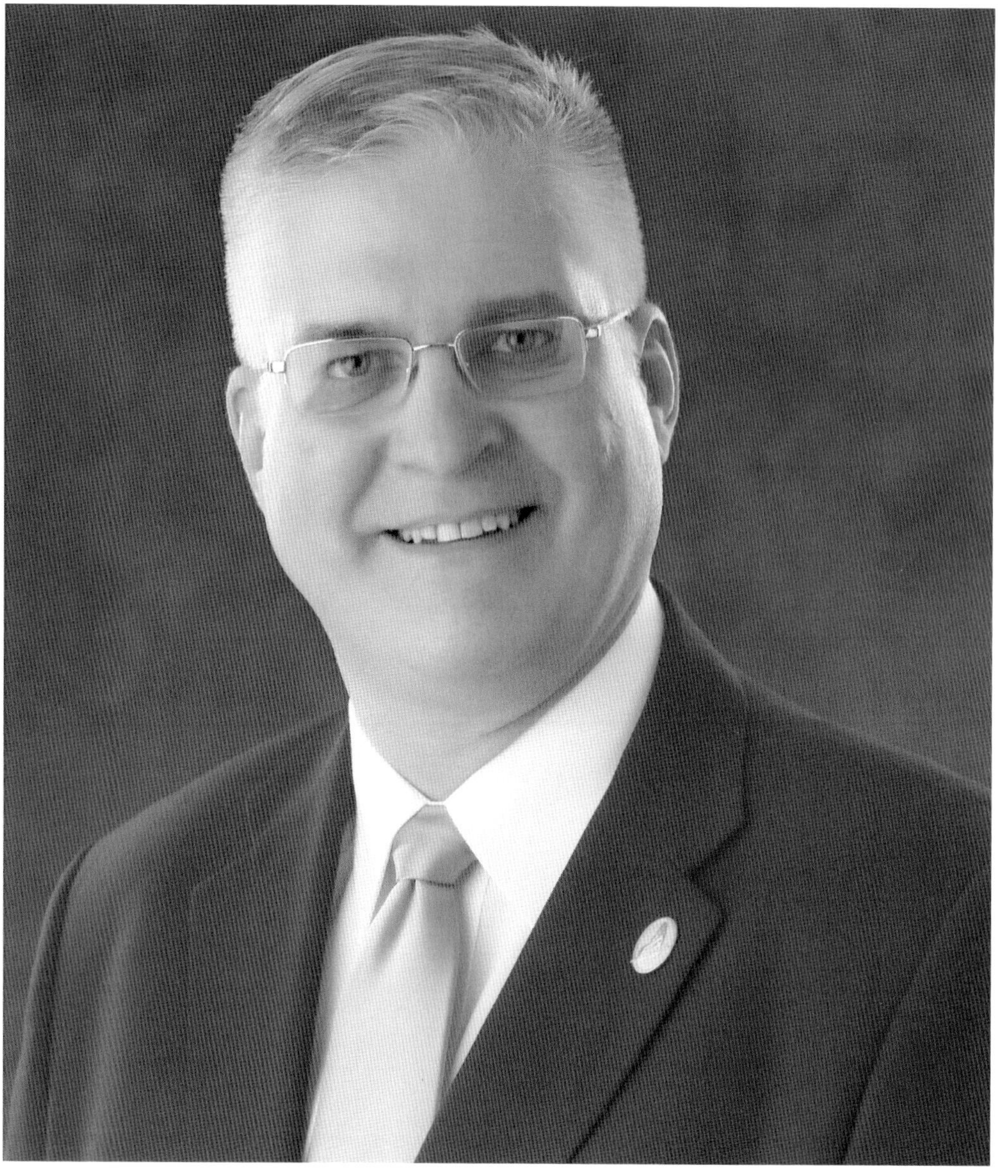

John Herzig

John Herzig is the third generation of his family to operate the Toland-Herzig Funeral Home. As a funeral professional and civic leader, he has garnered numerous awards including earning a prestigious Academy of Professional Funeral Services Practices recognition. This made Toland-Herzig one of the first funeral homes in the United States to win this distinction.

Beginning in 1996, John began collecting all manner of funeral memorabilia. This collection included anything from standard fare like programs and memory cards, to the more elaborate gifts circulated by the wealthy, famous, or just plain eccentric. John's hobby has now grown to become the largest collection of funeral memorabilia in the world. Today, his collection is organized and displayed at the Famous Endings Museum located inside the Toland-Herzig Funeral Home. Famous Endings has been featured on *Ripley's Believe It or Not!* and in numerous other media outlets like *USA Today*, NBC, and prominent tourism publications and websites. (Courtesy of John Herzig and Solid Rock Photos.)

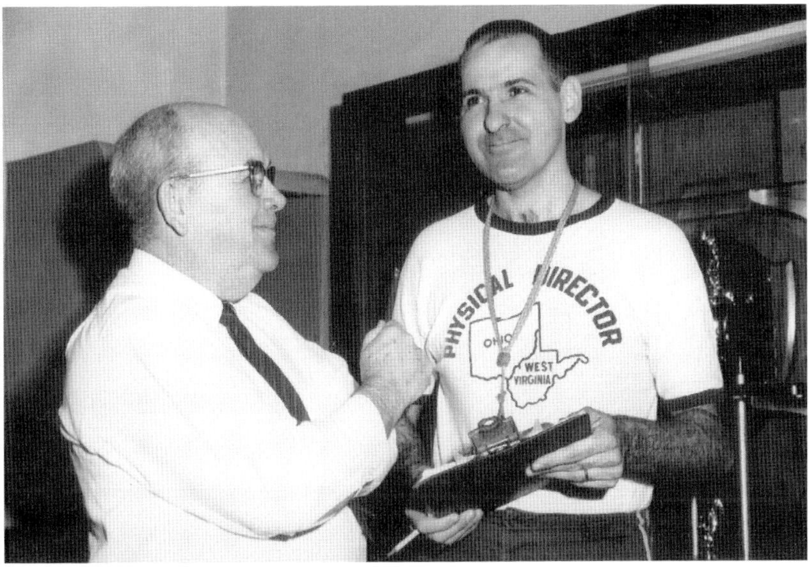

Tom Patton and Miles Durr

Tom Patton was born on his grandfather's farm just outside the small village of Trail, Ohio. He attended Dover schools, graduating in 1944. With World War II still raging, Tom took his first job with Shenango Penn Mold. When the war ended, Tom lost his job. Around this time, he heard from a friend that the local YMCA was looking for a janitor. He applied for the job and was hired by then-director Miles Durr. Durr would act as a mentor to Patton. After only a few months at the YMCA, Durr encouraged Tom to go to college. He enrolled at Miami (Ohio) and left in the fall of 1945.

Four years after his brief stint with the YMCA, Patton returned to Dover. He was a newly minted college graduate with a degree in health, physical education, and industrial arts. For the second time, Durr hired him. This time, though, he was not pushing a broom. Tom Patton was named the new physical director. He remained in this position for 17 years before being named the YMCA's director in 1966.

Tom (pictured at the right in the above image and pictured below) would spend the rest of his career as the YMCA's director, overseeing a wealth of change and expansion. This included the construction of a new building in 1971. After 39 years with the YMCA, Tom retired in 1989.

In addition to his work at the YMCA, Tom Patton has served as a trustee with the Reeves Foundation since the early 1990s and has worked with hospice, the Salvation Army, Kent State Tuscarawas, and various other community organizations.

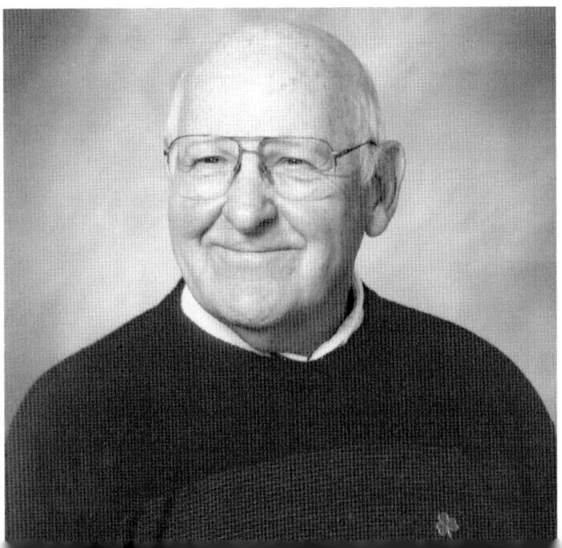

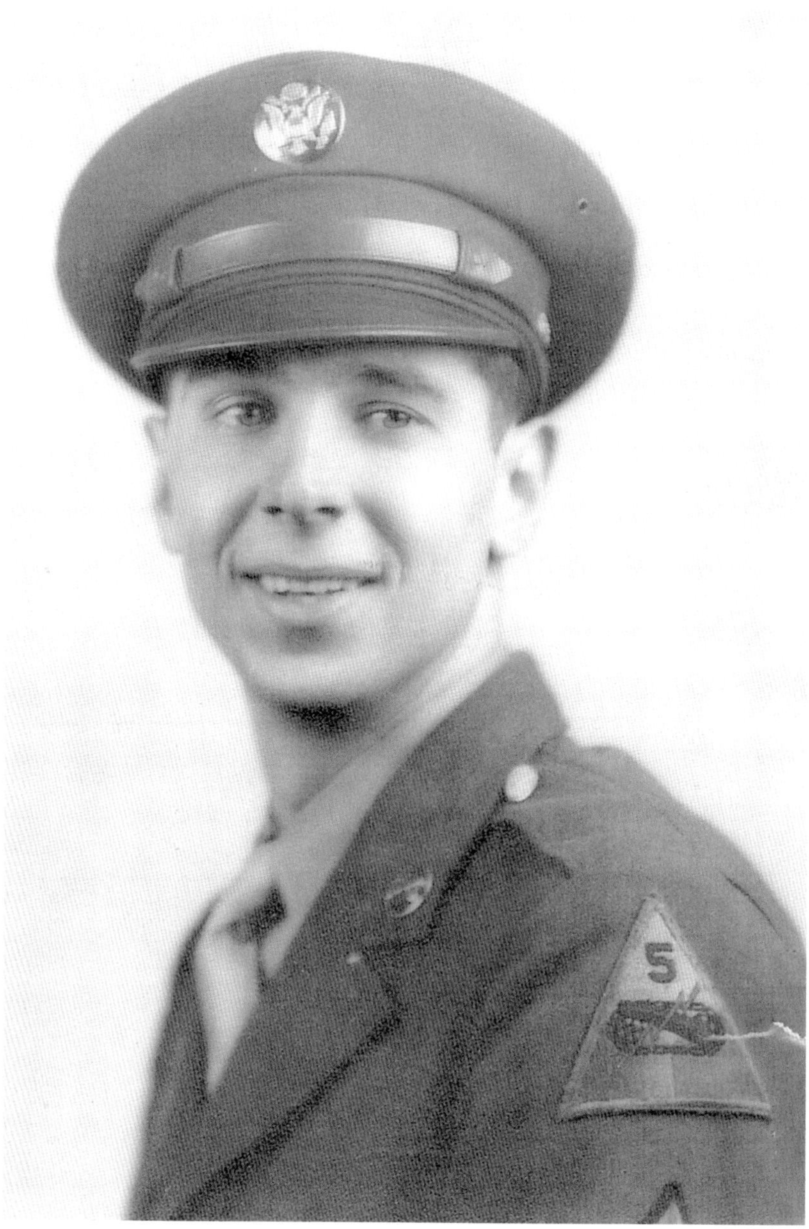

Guy Smith

Guy Smith was Dover's second-longest serving mayor. After graduating from Barnesville High School in 1940, Smith enlisted in the Army. He served in Europe as part of the 95th Armored Field Artillery Battalion of the 5th Armored Division. After his discharge from the Army, Smith returned to Tuscarawas County and worked for the *Times Reporter* in display advertising. Later, he would get his real estate license and found Smith Realty in Dover.

In 1972, Smith was elected mayor of Dover for the first time. It was the first of five consecutive terms he would serve. Under his guidance, the city accomplished many worthwhile projects. Among these are the construction of a city swimming pool, expansion of the city's parks system, and key improvements to Dover's electric generating facility. Smith remained Dover's mayor until his retirement in 1992.

Police Chief Frank Javens

Frank Javens was born in Wellsville, Ohio, on July 8, 1896. In 1926, he joined the police force at Dover when he was hired as a traffic officer. He would remain in this position, until he was promoted in 1929 to the rank of captain. It is possible he would have remained a captain for quite awhile if it were not for a very unusual situation involving Sunday movies.

At the beginning of 1930, there was a great debate over whether or not Sunday movies should be permitted in Dover. Former mayor Groh had first permitted the movies but then closed the theaters after anti-movie forces took the operators to court. In the spring of 1930, the issue came up at a city council meeting. Council voted 4-3 to close the theaters on Sundays despite the fact that many other towns in the county offered Sunday movies. Agreeing to abide by council's decision, newly elected mayor Stucky ordered the theaters closed on Sundays. When the Bexley Theater attempted to ignore the proclamation, a near riot ensued, and the theater's owners and six employees were arrested. Interestingly, the raid was made without Police Chief Byers, who objected to the use of tear gas at the theater and to the idea of cutting power to the Bexley.

After the near riot at the Bexley and Byers's subsequent resignation, Javens was named acting police chief. The position was made permanent on June 30, 1930. He would remain in this position for the next 27 years, retiring from the post in 1957. Under his guidance, Dover's police force doubled in size. Javens died in Massillon at the age of 77 in 1974. To this day, he remains Dover's longest-serving police chief.

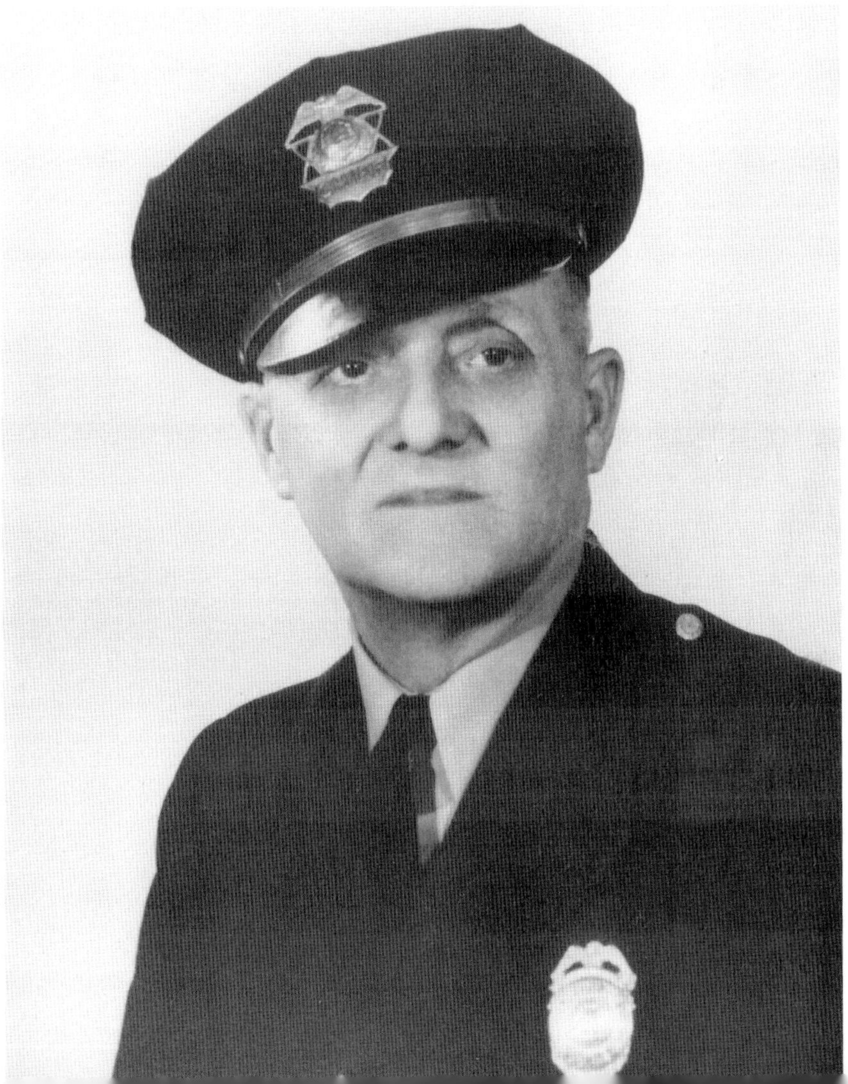

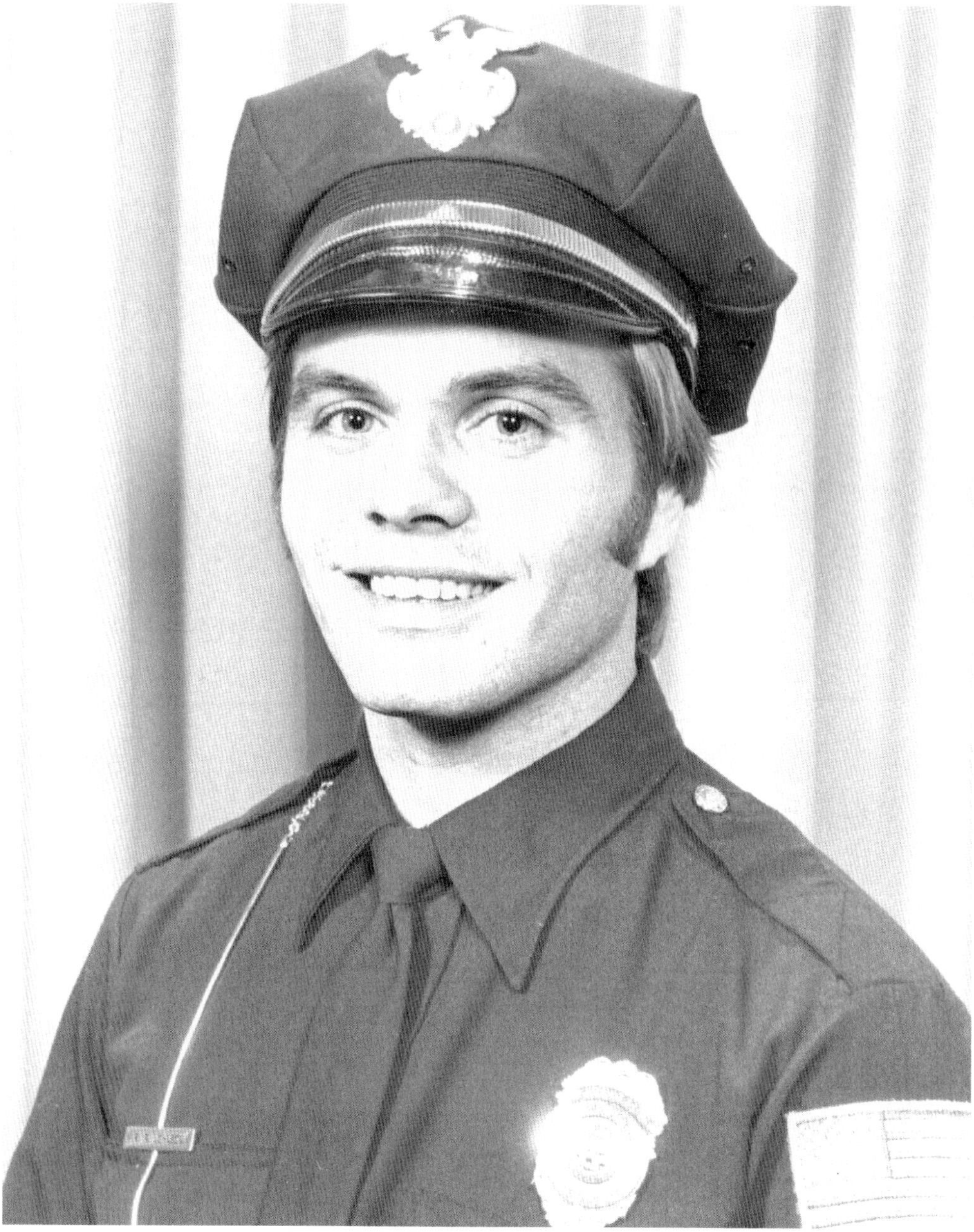

Chief Ron Johnson

Born in Cambridge in 1955, Ron Johnson attended the Lawrence Township Police Academy. After finishing the police academy, Johnson was hired by the City of Dover as a patrolman in 1977. While working as a patrolman, Johnson thought it was important to continue his education. He received an associate's degree from Kent Tuscarawas in 1981 and a bachelor's degree from the Kent main campus in 1983. Johnson's work paid off, and in 1985, he was promoted to captain. After seven years as a captain, Johnson was promoted to chief in 1992. He would later receive a master's degree in public administration in 1999. He remained Dover's police chief until his retirement in April 2011. (Courtesy of Ron Johnson.)

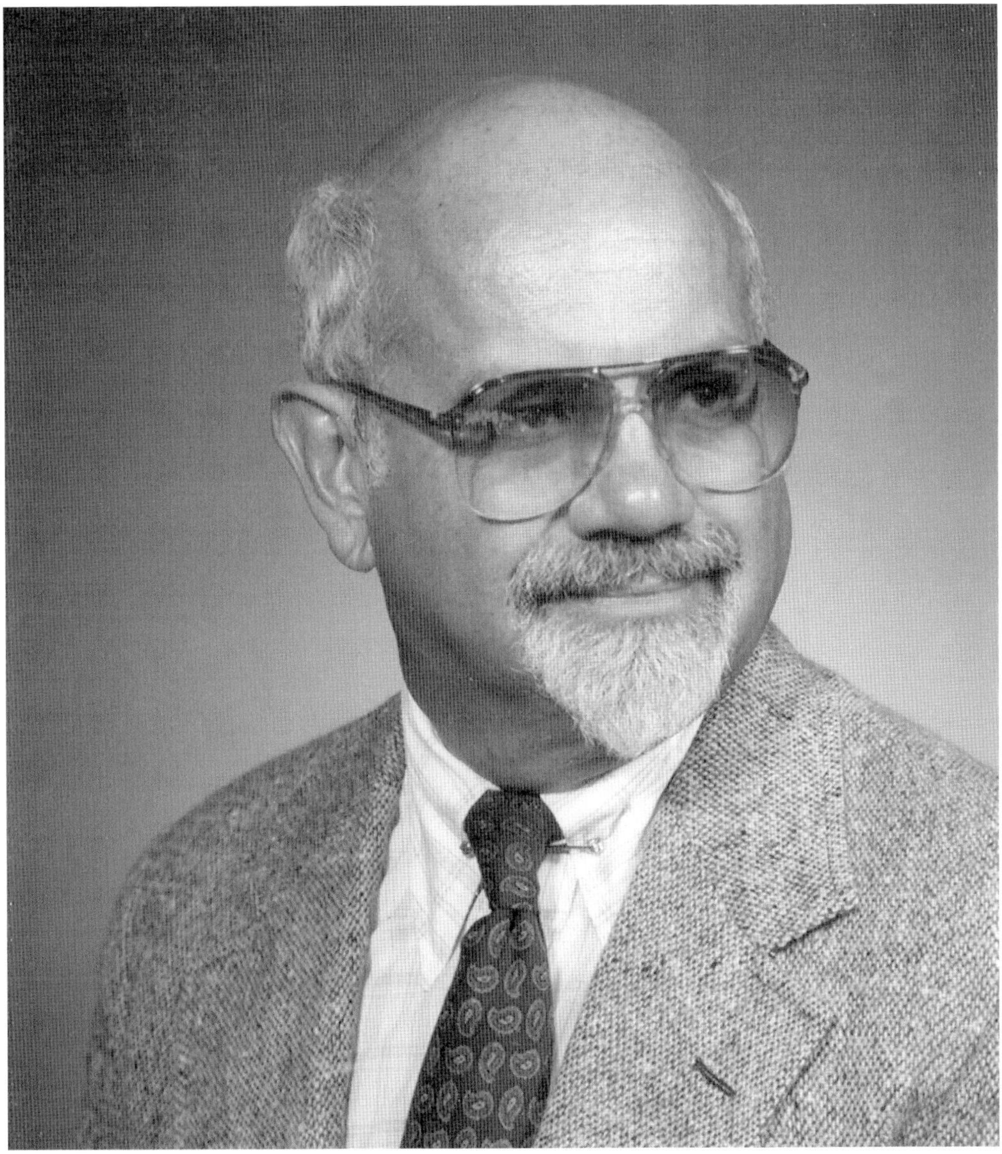

Harry Humphries

Harry Humphries was born in Charleston, West Virginia, in 1933. Not long after he was born, his father moved the family from West Virginia to the Ohio town of Delaware. In Delaware, he opened a car dealership. At this successful Ford dealership, Harry learned the trade of his father. As a young man, Humphries was an amateur boxer. After high school, he attended Babson College in Wellesley, Massachusetts. In 1956, Harry Humphries opened his first automobile dealership. Later, Humphries Auto City would move to Dover. In addition to his dealership, Harry helped to found Humphries-McKnight Trucking with his friend Joe McKnight; he later sold his interest, and the business is known today as McKnight Trucking.

After his retirement in 1984, Harry's sons took over operation of the dealership, and he was able to embrace his passion for travel. He traveled extensively and lived in the British Virgin Islands, London, Bahamas, North Carolina, and the Dominican Republic. (Courtesy of Mike Humphries.)

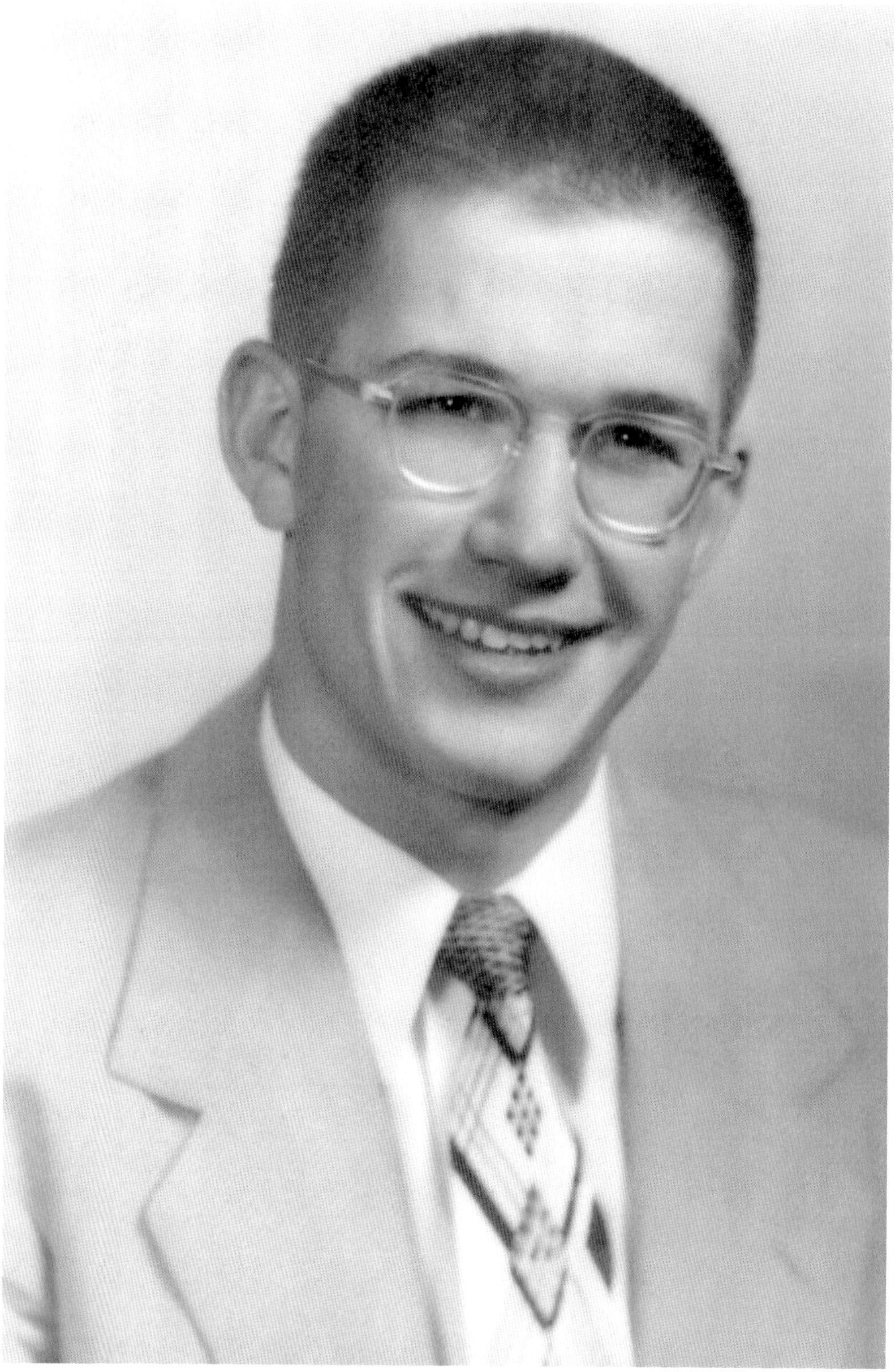

Charlie Deeds (BELOW AND OPPOSITE PAGE)
Charlie Deeds was born in Zanesville, Ohio, and grew up in the small town of Newark, just outside of Columbus. As a high school athlete, Charlie showed a natural gift for basketball and was named Second Team All-Ohio in his senior season. After graduation, he attended Baldwin-Wallace College, graduating in 1956 with a bachelor's of science degree.

Immediately after college, Charlie went to work for Owens-Corning. Those early years saw him transferred several times as he worked in production, quality control, and service. In 1961, he went to work for Snyder Manufacturing in New Philadelphia. He worked hard, and by the time of the company's transition in 1977, he was serving as the executive vice president. In 1977, Zimmer, Inc., of Warsaw, Indiana, purchased Snyder Manufacturing. When the dust settled, the business became the Zimmer Patient Care Division, and Charlie was named the new president. Zimmer Patient Care produces disposable medical surgical equipment. Today, they have plants located in New Philadelphia, Dover, and Statesville, North Carolina.

Perhaps the only thing that trumps Charlie's impact on the community through his business interests is the shared interest for the community of he and his wife, Virginia "Ginni." Among the many charitable causes that Charlie has championed are numerous volunteer organizations, board positions, and campaigns. Some of the more prominent of these are his service on the board of trustees with Union Hospital, the Tuscarawas County YMCA, Tuscarawas County Community Improvement Corporation (CIC), and United Way. He has also been very active with his alma mater, Baldwin Wallace, where he received an honorary doctoral degree in business in 2000.

Among the many honors bestowed upon Charlie are the Zeisberger-Heckewelder Medal, which he received with his wife; the Vic Marsh Medal for Volunteerism; and his induction into the Tuscarawas County Chamber of Commerce Hall of Fame. (Courtesy of Charlie Deeds.)

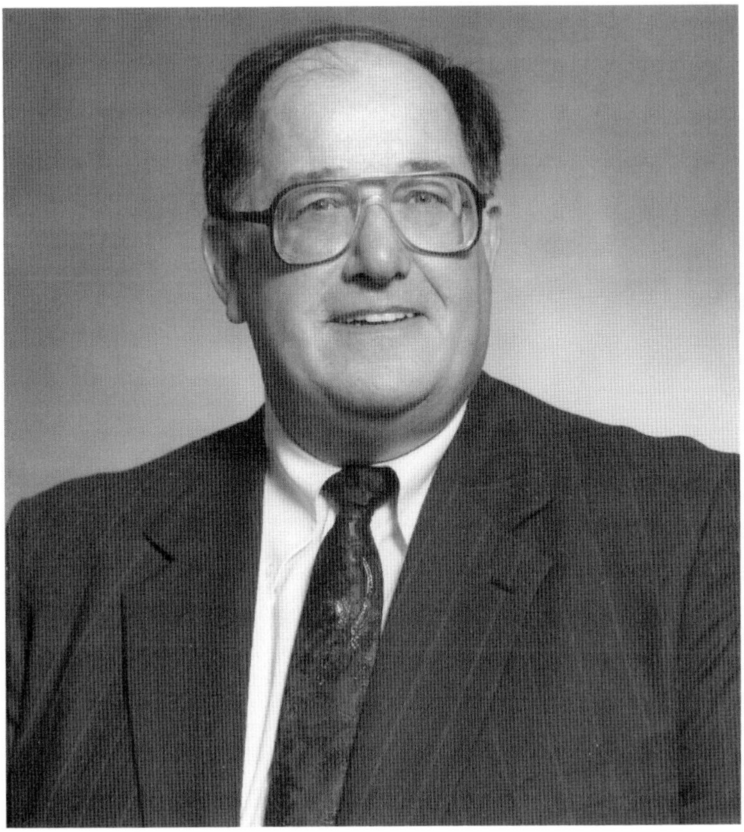

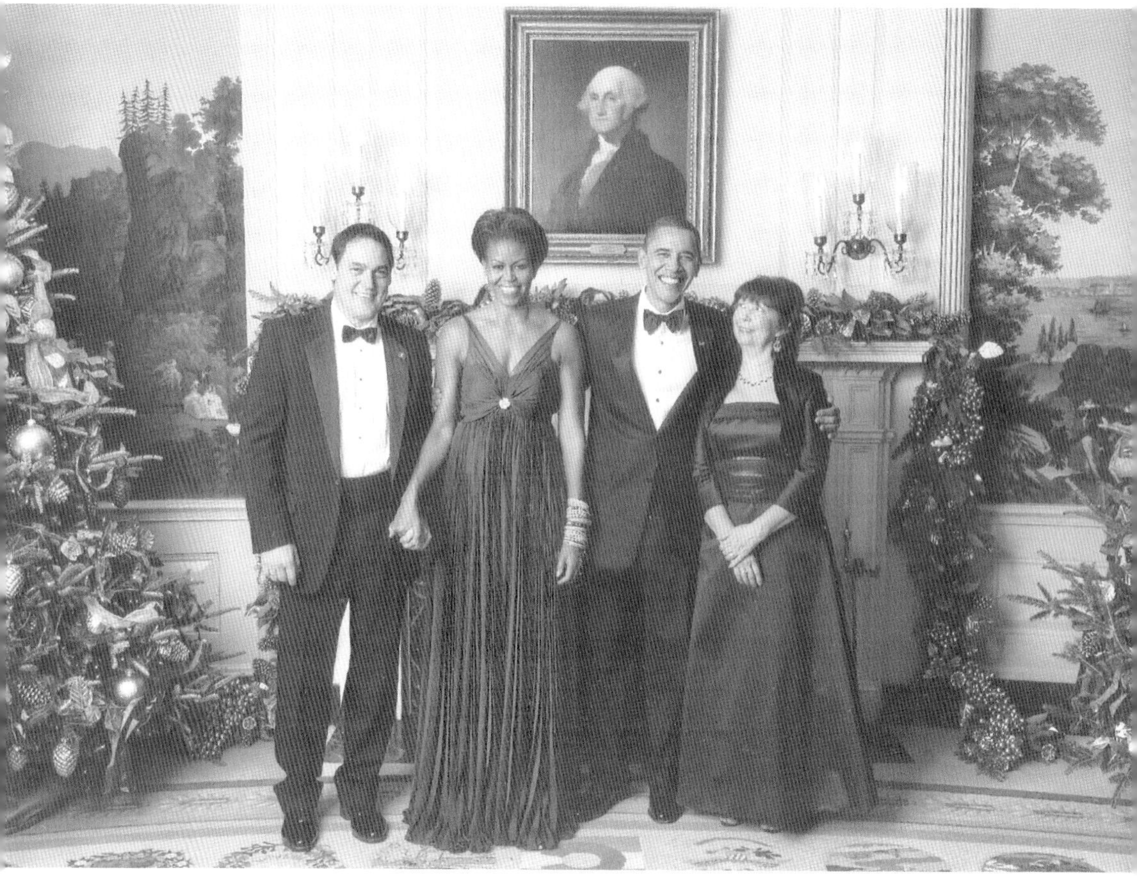

Zachary T. Space

Zack Space was born in Dover on January 1, 1961. The grandson of Greek immigrants, he attended Dover High School, where he excelled at football. After graduating from Dover in 1979, he pursued his bachelor's degree at Kenyon College. He also continued his football career. He was named a Division III All-American in his senior season. After college, Space attended Ohio State University where he pursued a law degree. Upon receiving his juris doctorate in 1986, Space returned to Dover and joined his father's law practice. In 2001, Space was named law director after the tragic death of Tom Watson. He would later be elected to this position in 2002 and reelected in 2004.

In 2006, Space's political aspirations grew as he decided to run for the congressional seat for Ohio's 18th District. Despite having very little name recognition outside of Tuscarawas County, Space won the election convincingly over Ohio State senator Joy Padgett. Space was reelected to the position in 2008. He would serve a total of four years in Congress before he was defeated during the "Republican Wave" election of 2010. During his tenure in Congress, Space served on the energy and commerce committee and committees for transportation, agriculture, and veteran's affairs. Through his committee work, Space had a hand in shaping the Affordable Care Act and the American Clean Energy and Security Act. (Courtesy of Zach Space.)

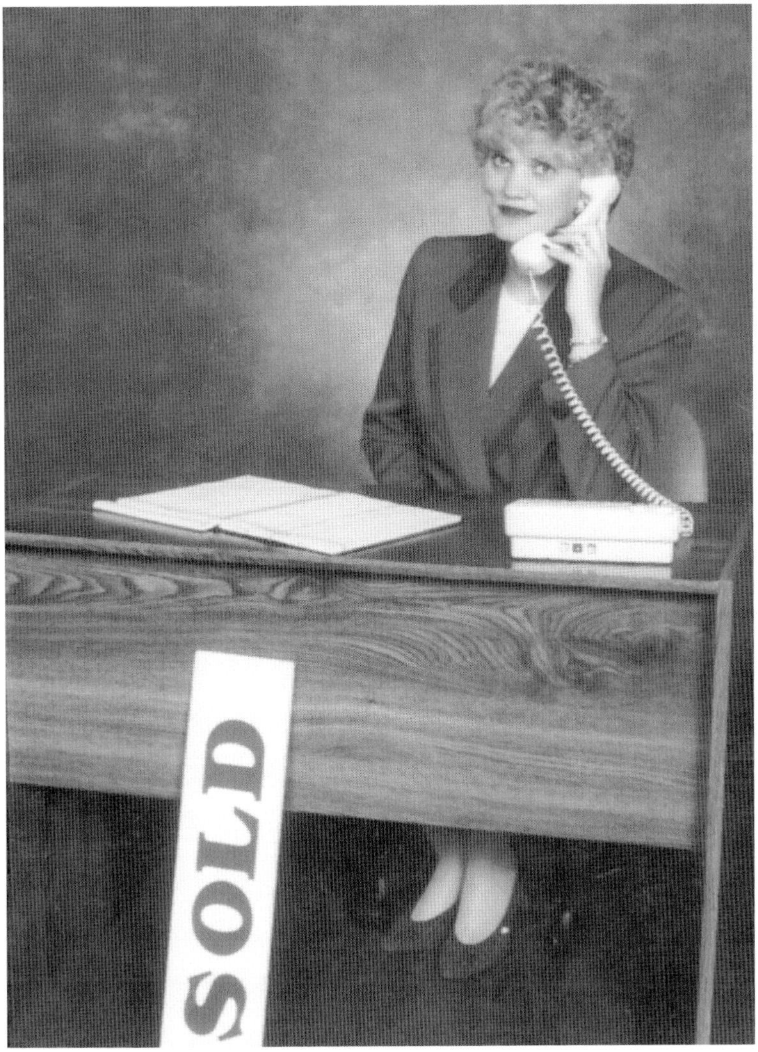

Kathy Pietro

Born and raised in New Philadelphia, Kathy Pietro has worked her way up from humble beginnings. After graduating from New Philadelphia High School, Kathy spent 14 years waitressing at local restaurants. In her early thirties, Kathy made a decision that would change her life forever. In 1985, she became a licensed realtor and began work with Pissocra-Mathias Realty. She spent eight years learning the ropes before breaking out on her own in 1993. That year, she founded the Remax Experts Realty. Success came quickly, and in 1995, she was awarded the National Association of Realtors award for the Best Small Real Estate Company in the United States.

Kathy parted ways with Remax in 2004 and became Experts Realty. At her busiest, she sold more than 300 homes per year and employed 40 people. She also became a national voice in the real estate field, partnering with Howard Brinton and helping to establish "Star Power Universities" to train realtors all over the United States.

Today, Kathy continues to oversee operations at Experts Realty in Dover. She is also active with a number of local community organizations, including Harbor House, the Tuscarawas County Senior Center, the Catholic Foundation at Tuscarawas Central Catholic, the Tuscarawas County Center for the Arts, and the Tuscarawas County Board of Realtors. (Courtesy of Kathy Pietro.)

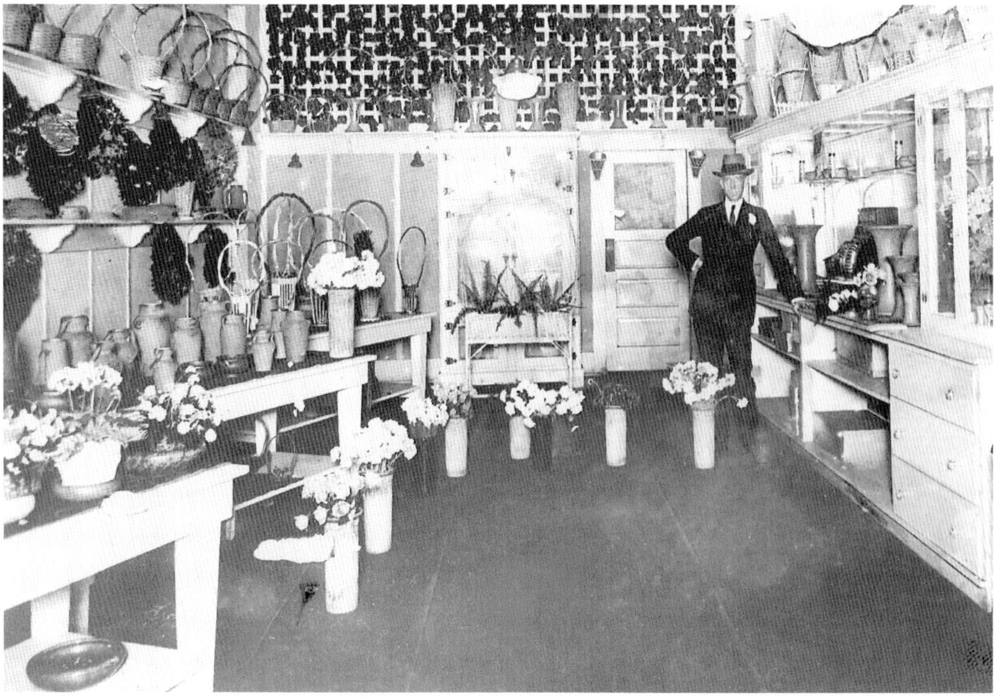

Roy Fulton Baker

Roy Fulton Baker was born on March 10, 1886. He worked as a streetcar conductor on the Northern Ohio Traction & Light (NOT&L) Railroad. His job took him primarily on the Cleveland to Canton route. Occasionally, Baker would be called on to do the run from Canton to Dover. In his spare time, Baker worked part-time for a Canton florist. What changed Baker's life was the 1923 NOT&L strike. The strike crippled the company, and it was forced to fold, leaving Baker unemployed. In 1924, he opened his first floral shop in the back of the Reeves Banking and Trust Company building. Two years later, he moved his shop to the garage of his North Walnut Street home. From this humble beginning grew Baker Florist, which continues to operate in Dover. (Both, courtesy of Baker Florists.)

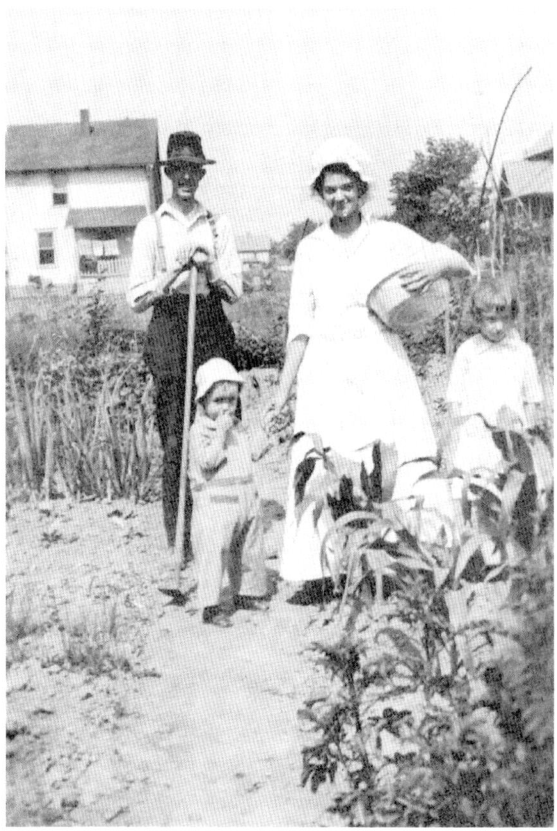

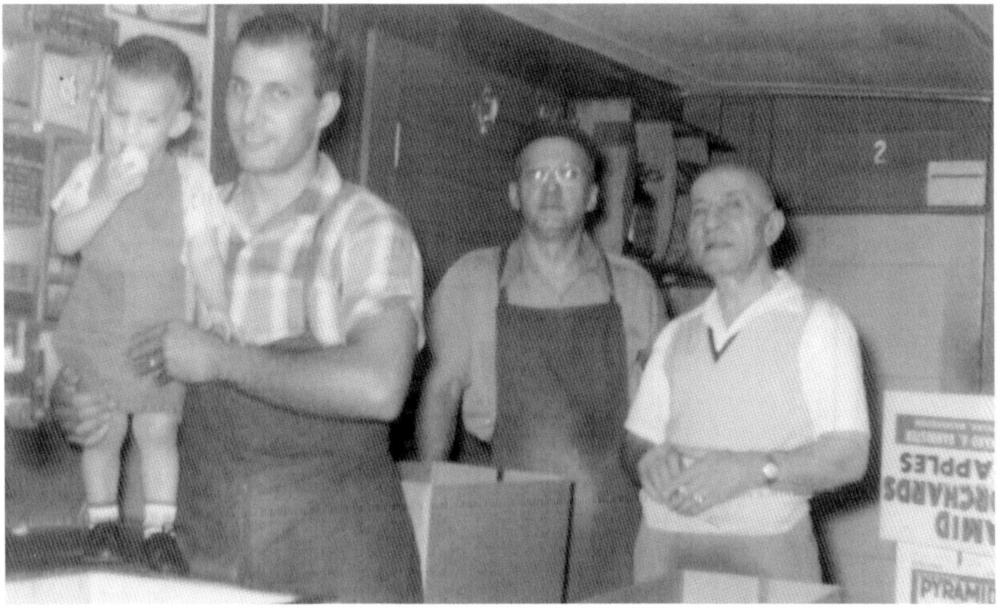

William Barkett

Born in Cleveland in 1932, William "Bill" Barkett began working in the family business at the age of eight. After spending his early career working to better the local community through Dover's St. Joseph's High School, Barkett returned to the family business after his father's death in 1975. Over the next 35 years, the Barkett Fruit Company increased its business 50 times over. Away from the business, Barkett is active in the Jaycees, and since he passed the company to his sons, he has worked diligently to grow Dover's Food Pantry. The Food Pantry distributes 17,000 to 20,000 items per week to those in need. Pictured above are four generations of the Barkett family. Below, from left to right, are Ron, Bill, and Jim Bartlett. (Courtesy of William Barkett.)

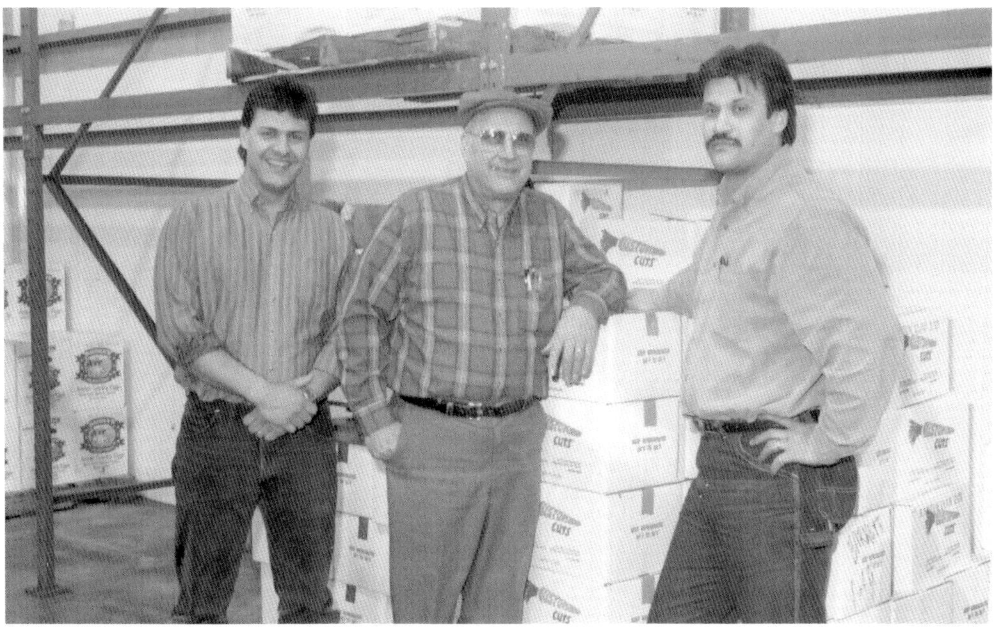

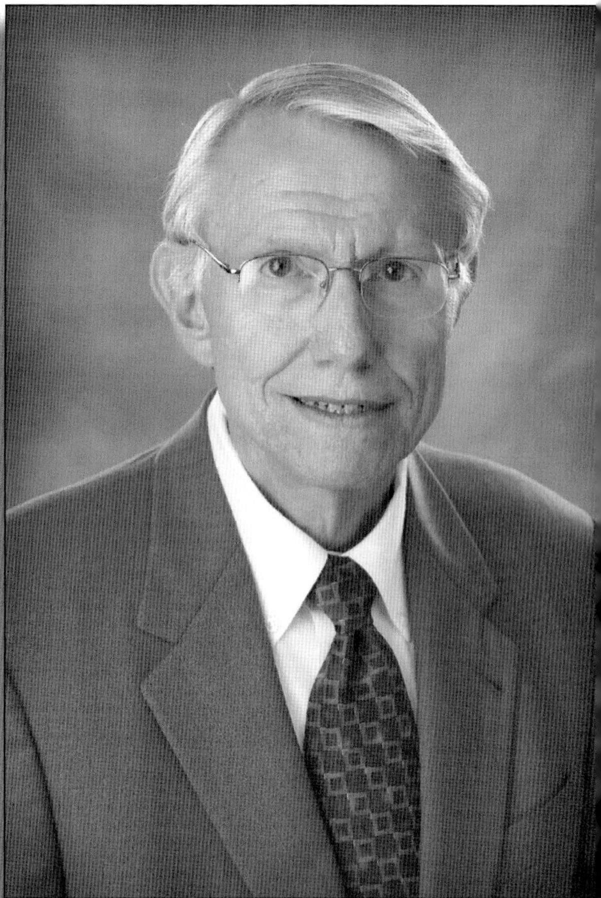

Gary Petricola

Born in Dover on May 18, 1950, Gary Petricola developed an interest in radio during high school. His first job in radio was as a part-time announcer with WJER. He continued in this capacity during his senior year and on-and-off throughout college. He was fortunate to work at several local Columbus stations in college, including WOSU. After graduation, Gary and his wife, Alison, moved to Dover and pursued their respective careers. For Gary, this meant a full-time position at WJER as the public affairs and public services director. In 1975, Gary was approached about purchasing WJER. Two years later, the deal was final, and Gary became one of the youngest station owners in the United States. (Courtesy of WJER and Solid Rock Photos.)

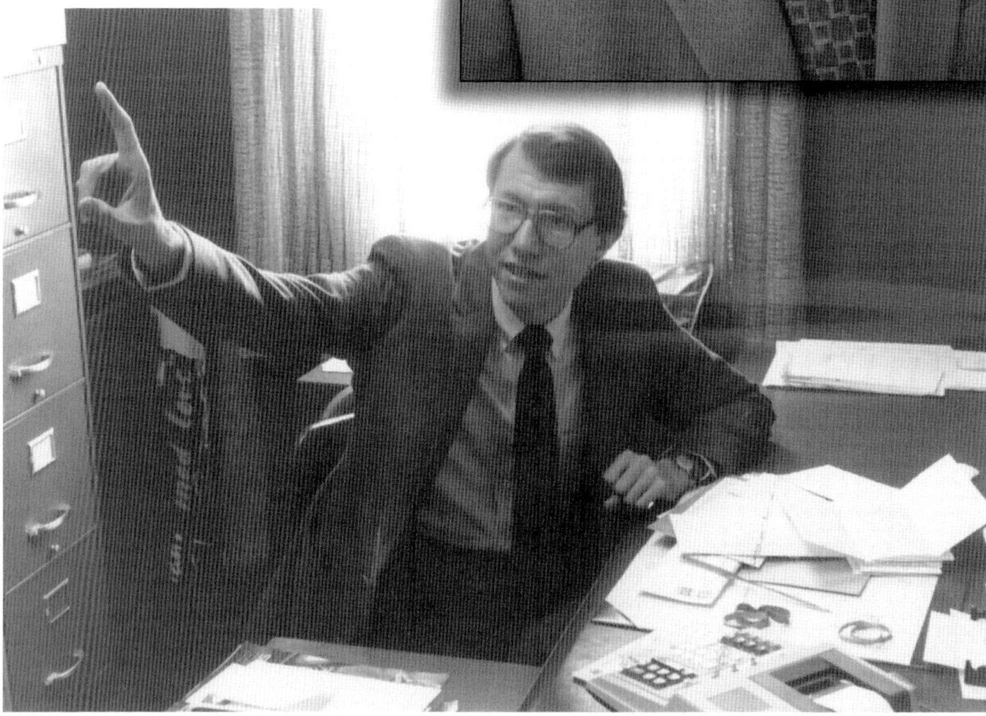

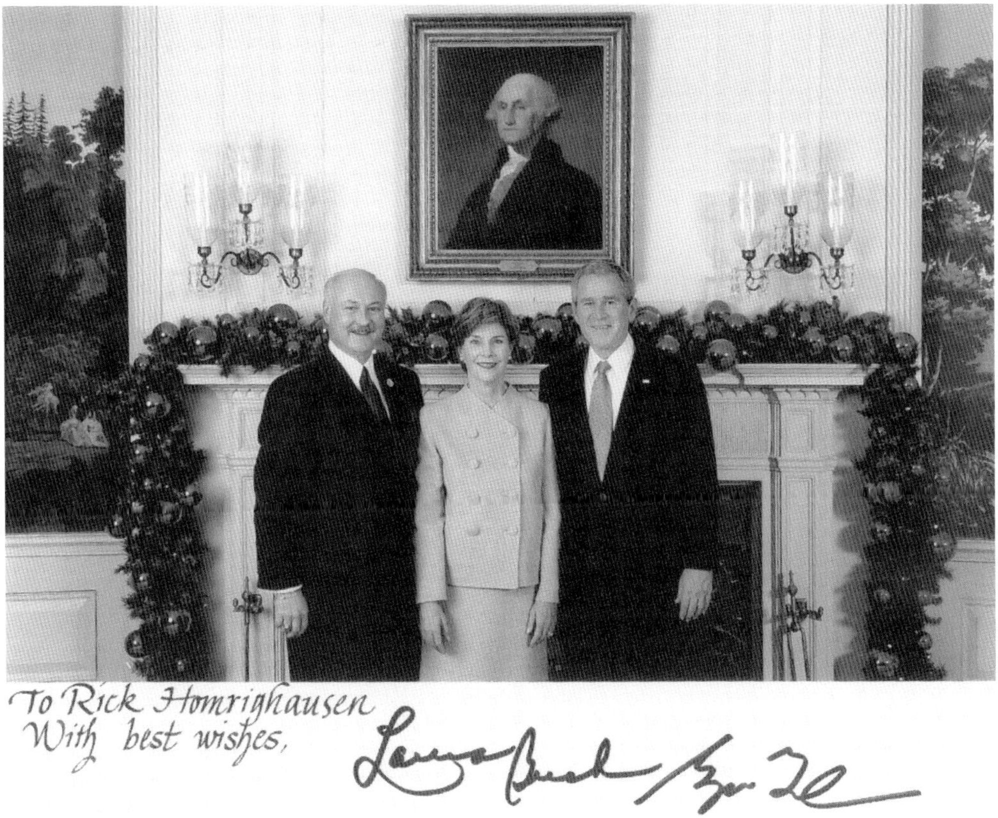

Mayor Richard Homrighausen

Richard Homrighausen was born on July 3, 1948. He was educated in Canton, graduating from Lincoln High School in 1966. After graduation, he began working for the Reed Funeral Home. He also continued his education at junior college and, later, at Northland College in Ashland, Wisconsin. He graduated from Northland in 1972 with a degree in business administration and economics and also an English degree. After graduation, he decided to pursue mortuary science, and in 1973, he graduated from the Cincinnati College of Mortuary Science.

After completing his education, Homrighausen returned to Canton and the Reed Funeral Home. He would remain there through 1977. In 1978, he moved to Dover and opened the Homrighausen Funeral Home. He operated the business until 2005. In addition to his work in the funeral industry, Homrighausen has dabbled in a number of small businesses with forays into novelties, wood products, and golf.

Most know Homrighausen for his political career. He was elected to Dover City Council in 1990 and mayor in 1992. He continues to serve as mayor as of 2013, making him Dover's longest-serving mayor. Politics have taken Homrighausen many places, and he has used his position to give back to his community. He has been very active with the Jaycees on both a state and local level. In 1980, he was elected president of the Dover Jaycees, and in 1984, he was elected to the same post on the state level. Homrighausen has also served on the Union Hospital Board of Directors. Outside of the community, Homrighausen has been very active with the American Public Power Association since his election in 1992. This involvement has led to his testifying in front of Congress on several occasions. (Courtesy of Richard Homrighausen.)

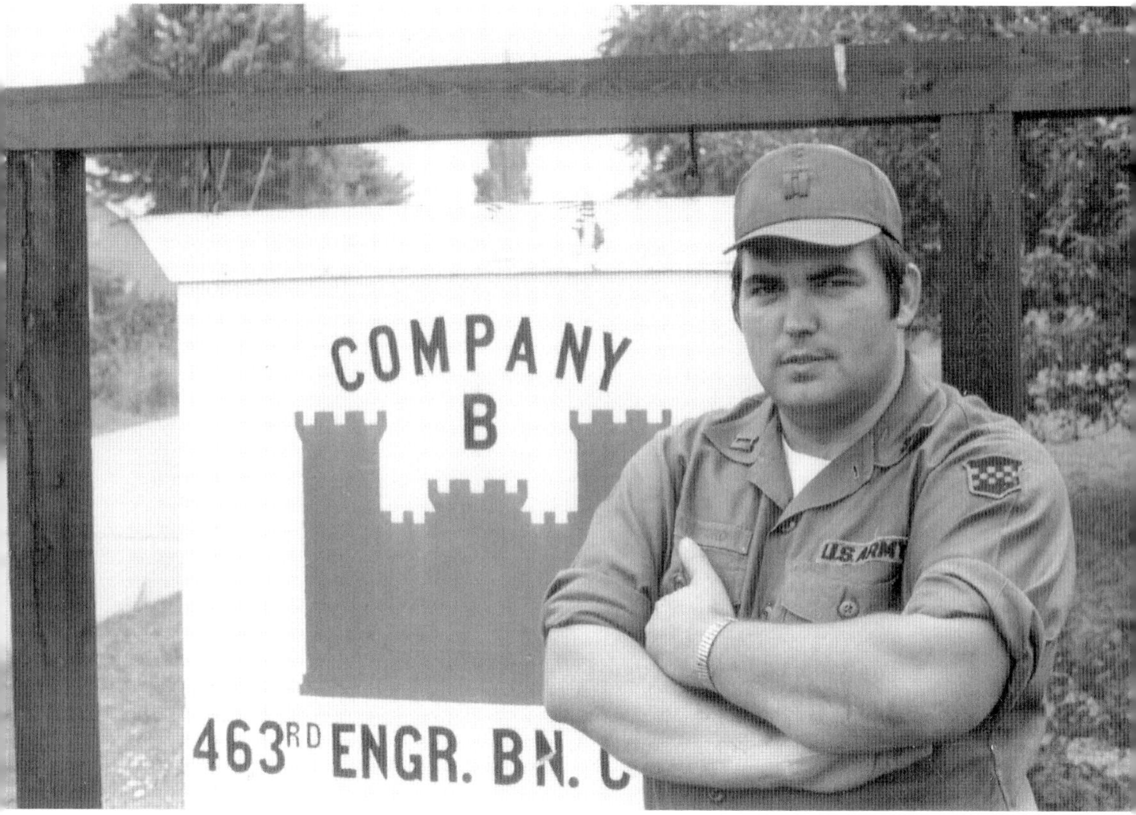

Roy Crawford

Roy Crawford was born in Steubenville, Ohio, where he attended public schools and graduated in 1965. After high school, Roy enlisted in the US Army and spent two years in Korea as an officer. In the military, Roy worked within the Army Corps of Engineers discovering a passion for engineering that would shape his career path. He took many lessons from his service to his country that defined his character and leadership abilities. In addition to his three years service, he also remained a part of the Army Reserve for 16 years.

After his time in the Army, Crawford attended Franciscan University where he majored in engineering. The G.I. Bill made his education possible. In 1973, following graduation, Crawford moved to Dover where he accepted a position with W.E. Quicksall and Associates remaining there through 2008. When he left, he had risen to the position of vice president. Crawford also made a difference in local politics. He was elected to Dover City Council in 1981 and was president of the council in 1996. He held this post until 2008.

In 2008, everything changed for Crawford. He retired from Quicksall and accepted a job with the state. Just a few months after beginning his new position, Crawford was diagnosed with mantle cell lymphoma. As he always had, he decided to face cancer head on. He chose the most aggressive form of treatment that meant a complete stem cell transplant and over two years of chemotherapy. Today, he remains cancer free. He credits his positive attitude and the lessons he learned in the military with his lifetime of success and with giving him the strength and will to beat cancer. (Courtesy of Roy Crawford.)

CHAPTER THREE

Sports Heroes

There is something special about sports in a small town. Unlike a big city, distractions of endless entertainment options, professional teams, and neighborhood rivalries do not exist in a small town. People in small towns have a sense of belonging. Nowhere is this more evident than with high school athletics. Sports give a sense of togetherness in a way that the entire community can relate to despite economic status, race, or political affiliation.

The other great aspect and one especially true in Dover are the opportunities that athletics provide young people. While it may only be for a short time, athletes get to feel the support of an entire town around them. They get to revel in the cheers of an entire community. Anyone that doubts this just needs to attend a Friday night football game or a basketball game on a cold Ohio day. Out of this support has grown a tradition of exceptional coaches, athletes, and teams.

Another great aspect of athletics is the impact these experiences have on individuals and how they continue to influence them for many years to come. Many of the legendary locals in this book were high school athletes at on time. They learned valuable lessons from their playing days, lessons about winning and losing, hard work, and dedication. Men like Charlie Deeds, Dick Klar, Bill Beitner (basketball), Zach Space (football), and Harry Humphries (boxing) all were active participants in high school sports. These experiences impacted their lives, and their participation taught them things that helped them succeed later in life. Athletics will continue to help produce leaders in the years to come.

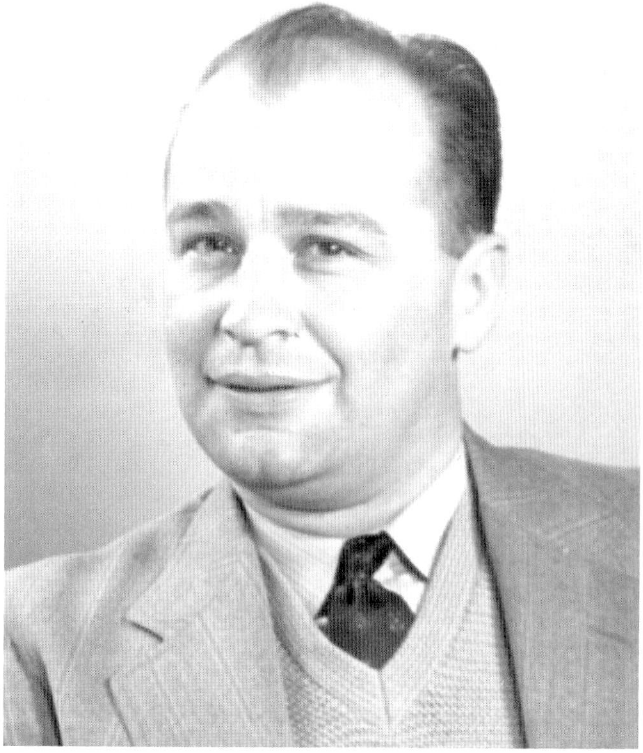

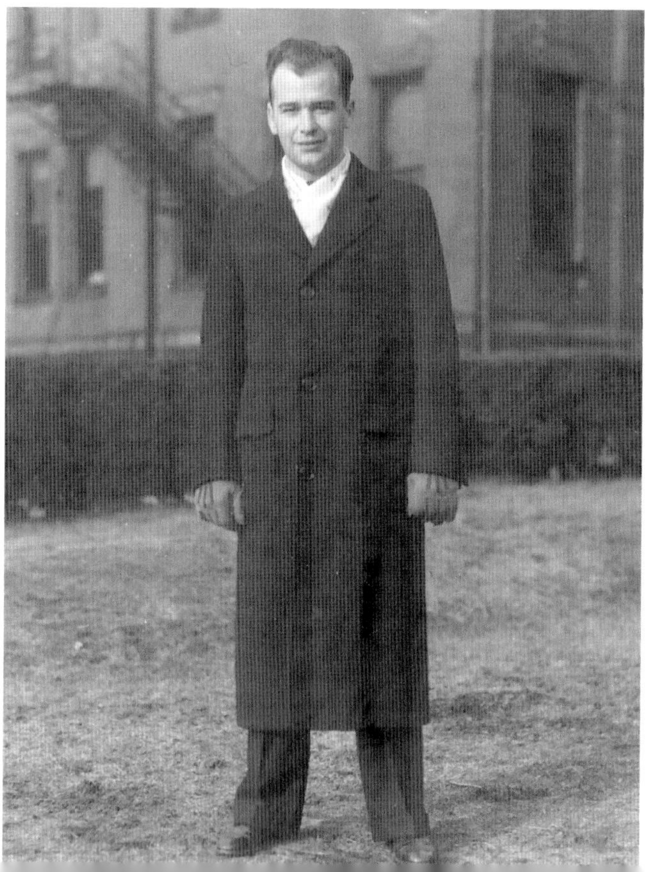

Herman "Bup" Rearick

Herman "Bup" Rearick was born on March 11, 1909. He attended Dover High, excelling at sports. He captained the 1926–1927 state championship basketball team and was the quarterback of the 1926 football team that went undefeated.

After high school, Rearick attended Wittenberg College, where he played three sports. His greatest athletic accomplishment at Wittenberg was as a member of Wittenberg's 1931 basketball team. That year, Bup's team went 18-1 with their only loss coming against a semiprofessional Akron team. Rearick graduated from Wittenberg in 1931 with a bachelor of arts degree in education and arithmetic.

After graduation, Rearick returned to Dover and was named the head coach for football and basketball. In only his second year back home, Rearick's football team went 10-0 with an 18-0 win over Massillon, and the basketball team won the 1933 state championship. Among Rearick's many accomplishments at Dover, his football teams had a 29-game winning streak, and he twice beat Massillon, once against legendary coach Paul Brown. Rearick's overall record at Dover was an outstanding 51-13-4. (Courtesy of Denny Rubright.)

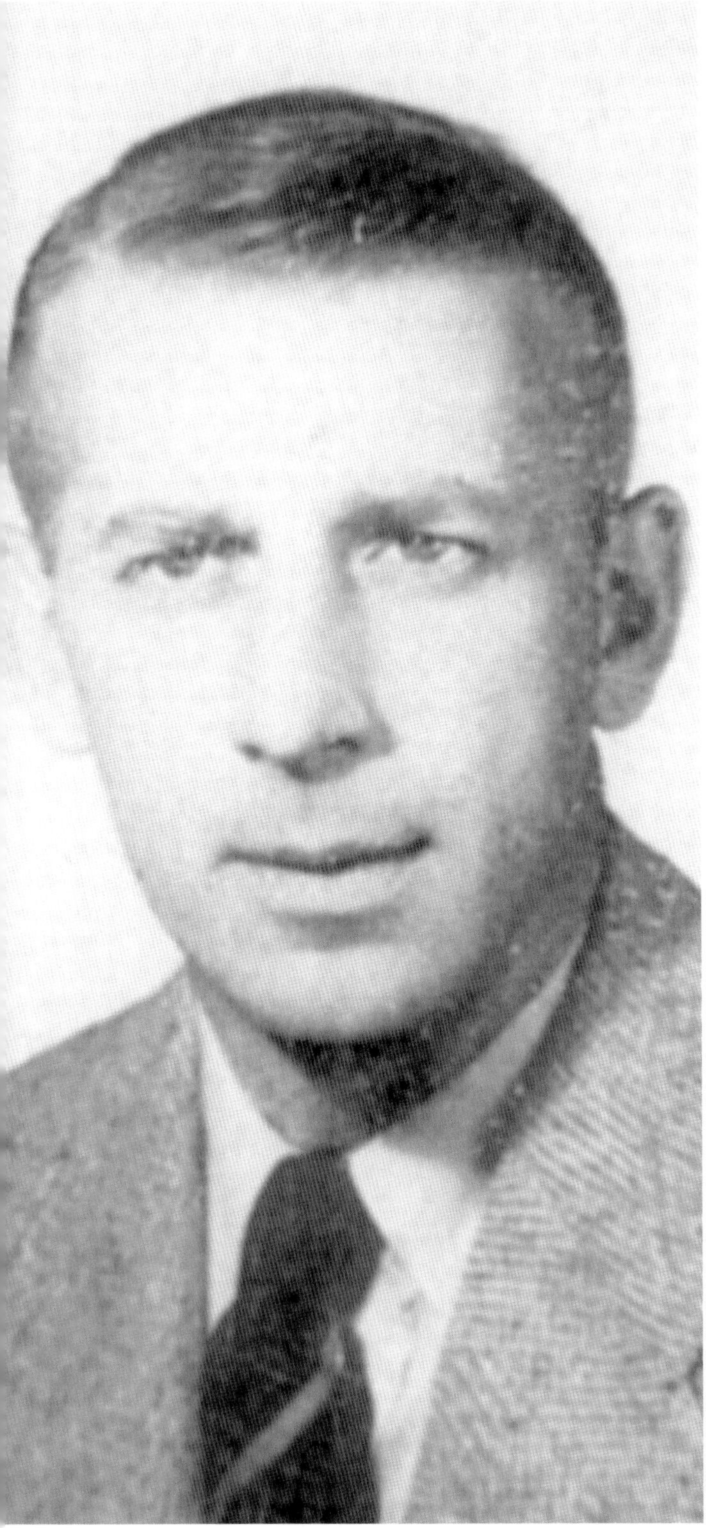

Glen "Dutch" Furbay
Born on August 5, 1912, Glen Furbay was a graduate of Uhrichsville High School. After high school, Furbay attended Muskingum College and got interested in sports. After graduation, he took a position as head coach at Chandlersville High School. His stay at Chandlersville lasted only one year (1934) before he moved on to Dennison High School.

Furbay must have been pleased to return to Tuscarawas County. At Dennison, he assumed the head coaching duties for both the football and basketball programs. He remained at Dennison as the football coach through the 1940 season and the 1940–1941 basketball campaign.

In the fall of 1941, Furbay left Dennison to become an assistant football coach at Dover. That first year, he was working under coach Richard Roberts. In 1941, Dover enjoyed a fine 7-3 record. After the season, Roberts resigned his position to enter the service during World War II. Furbay was promoted to head coach. During the 14 seasons from 1942 to 1955, Dutch Furbay would become one of Dover's winningest head football coaches. He compiled a record of 85-50-4 at Dover, including a 10-0 record in his first year. At the time he retired in 1955, he had more wins and a longer tenure than any coach in Dover's history. Although both of those marks have now been eclipsed, Furbay is still regarded by many as one of Dover's greatest coaches.

In addition to his work on the gridiron, Furbay also coached the school's basketball team from 1942 to 1951. Glen "Dutch" Furbay retired from coaching in 1955. (Courtesy of Denny Rubright.)

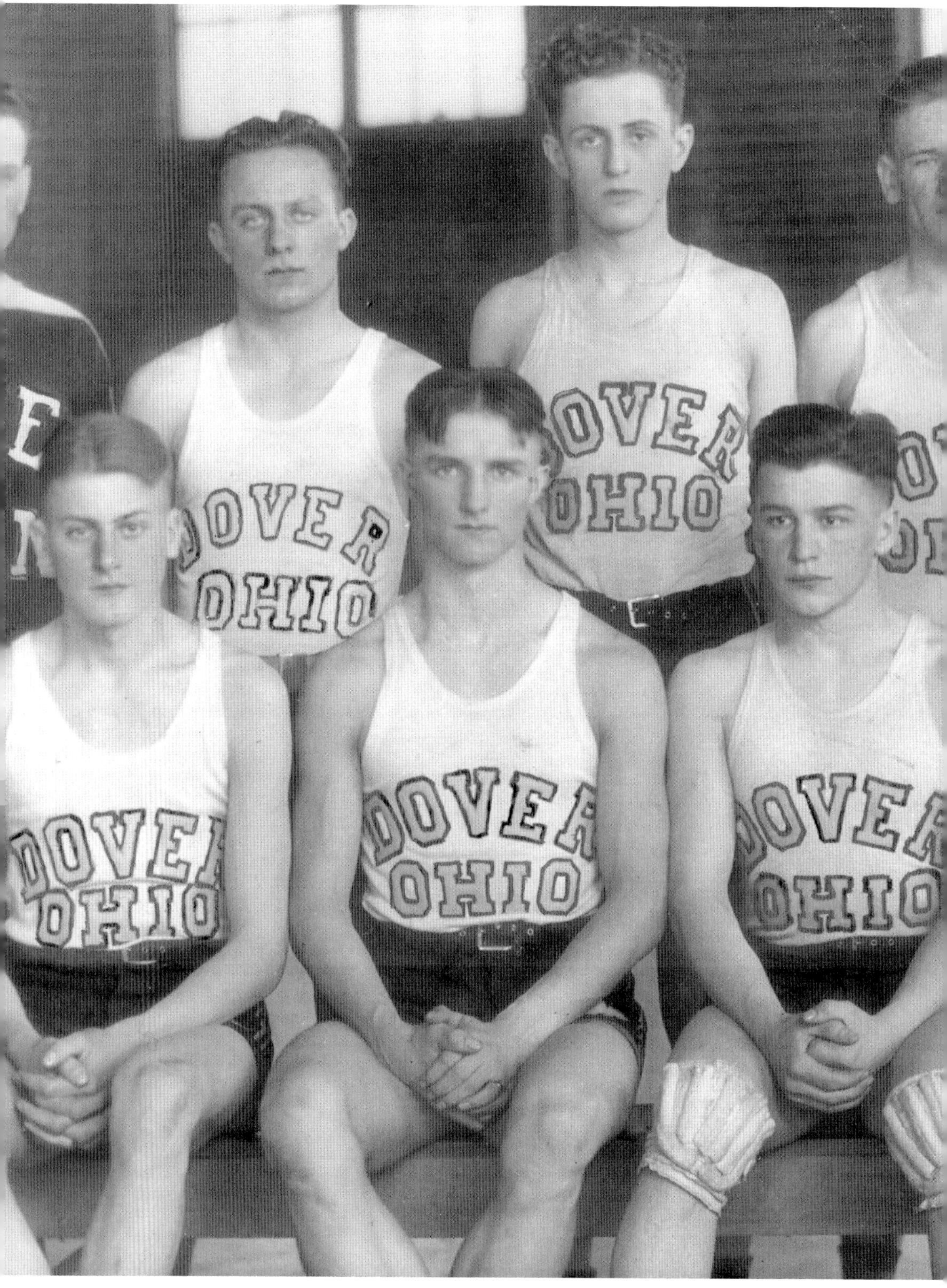
DOVER
OHIO
DOVER
OHIO
DOVER
OHIO
DOVER
OHIO
DOVER
OHIO

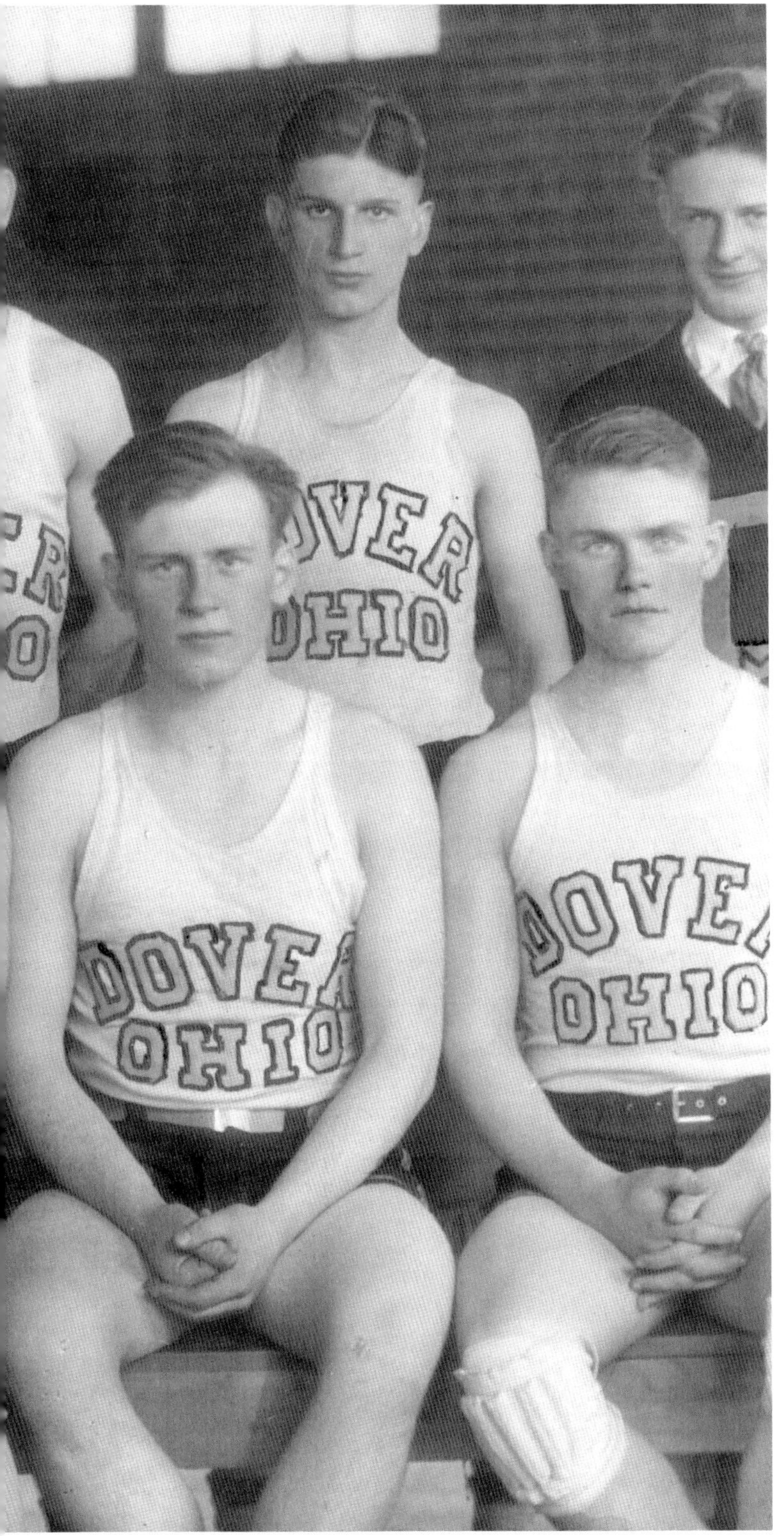

1927 State Basketball Champions
Dover's first state championship team was the 1927 basketball squad. The legendary Joe Herman coached them. At the state tournament, Dover played Mansfield and Portsmouth to set up a finals matchup with Toledo. The final was closer than the previous two games, but Dover squeaked out a 23-21 victory to win its first state championship. Following the game, Dover participated in a national championship tournament, winning its first game but being knocked out by a Colorado team in the second round.

Ernest Godfrey

Dover native Ernie Godfrey (first row, center) graduated from the Oak Grove School in 1911. After high school, he attended Ohio State University. There, he continued an outstanding athletic career as a member of both the football and basketball teams.

After finishing his education at Ohio State, Godfrey was hired as head football coach at Wooster High School. His stay at the school, and tenure as a high school coach, would be short. In 1916, he accepted a job with Wittenberg College. He was named the college's first full-time football and basketball coach. He remained at Wittenberg until 1929, enjoying great success with the Tigers. This included several undefeated seasons.

In 1929, Godfrey jumped at the chance to return to his alma mater, Ohio State. He would remain at the university for the next 33 years as an assistant coach. During his time at OSU, he was responsible for coaching Buckeye legends Lou "The Toe" Groza and Vic Janowicz. After retiring from Ohio State in 1962, Godfrey helped out Paul Brown during the 1968 preseason. He worked with the Bengals' kickers and punters.

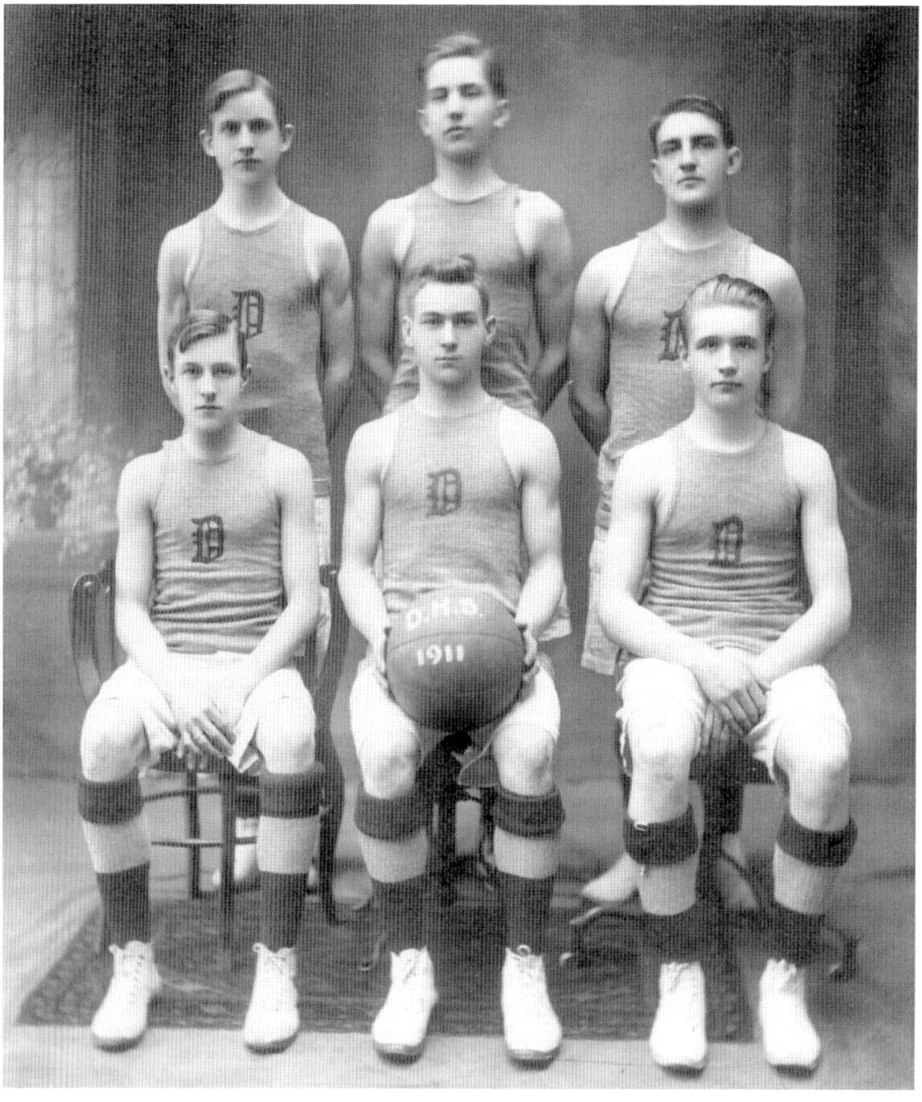

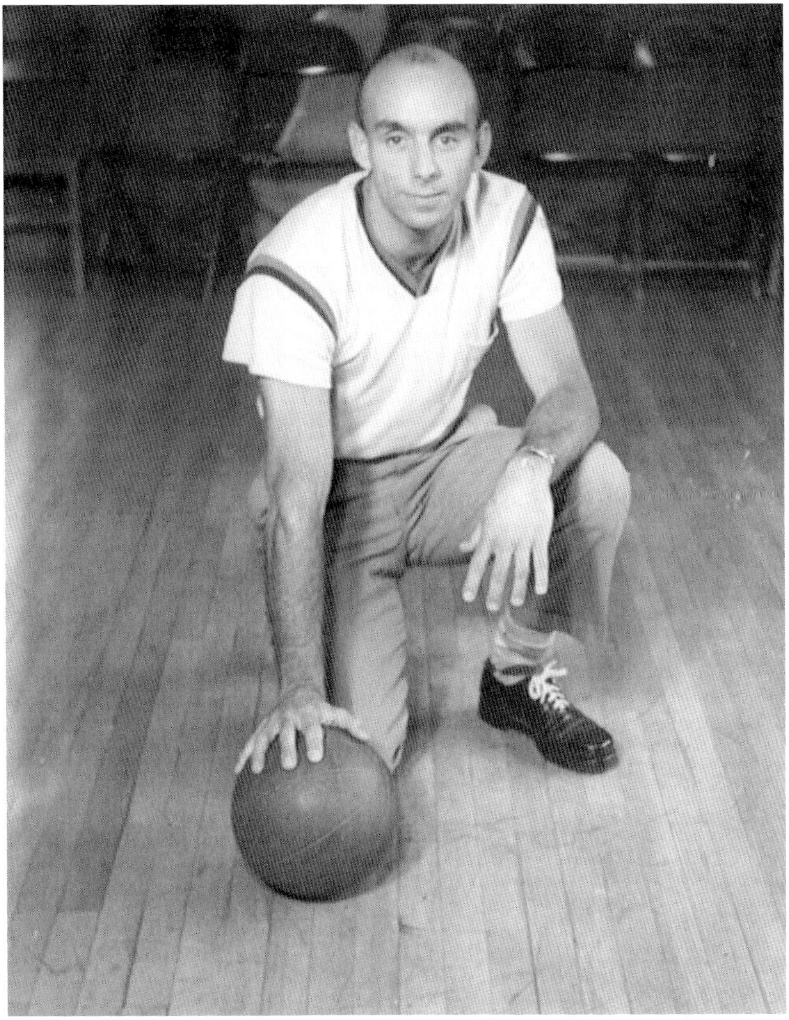

George J. Elford Jr.

George Elford spent his life living in and giving back to the community he loved. He was born on February 3, 1926, attended Dover City Schools, and served his country in the Navy during World War II. Perhaps he is best known, though, for the role he played on the local sports scene. He was a fixture on the Crater Stadium "chain gang" for more than 50 years and the founder of Dover's most famous group of young men, the Basketeers.

Elford's founding of the Basketeers happened nearly by accident. In the early 1950s, a young Elford stopped into the office of head football coach Glen "Dutch" Furbay and offered his service to help with the football team. While Coach Furbay did not have a place for Elford with football, he suggested a spot as a basketball coach with the Sixth Street Elementary (the Sixth Street wing of Dover High School). Despite the fact that Elford knew very little about basketball, he accepted.

Elford coached the Sixth Street Elementary team for five years. During his fifth year, he noticed a couple of the boys doing Globe Trotter–style tricks. This gave Elford an idea, and in 1955, the Basketeers were born. Elford and his troop of boy wonders would eventually gain national recognition, appear in three movies, and perform in front of thousands of people nationwide. Elford and the Basketeers remained active until March 1963, when working full-time and the travel got to be too much. In 1997, Elford and the Basketeers were featured on the annual Canal Dover Days plate.

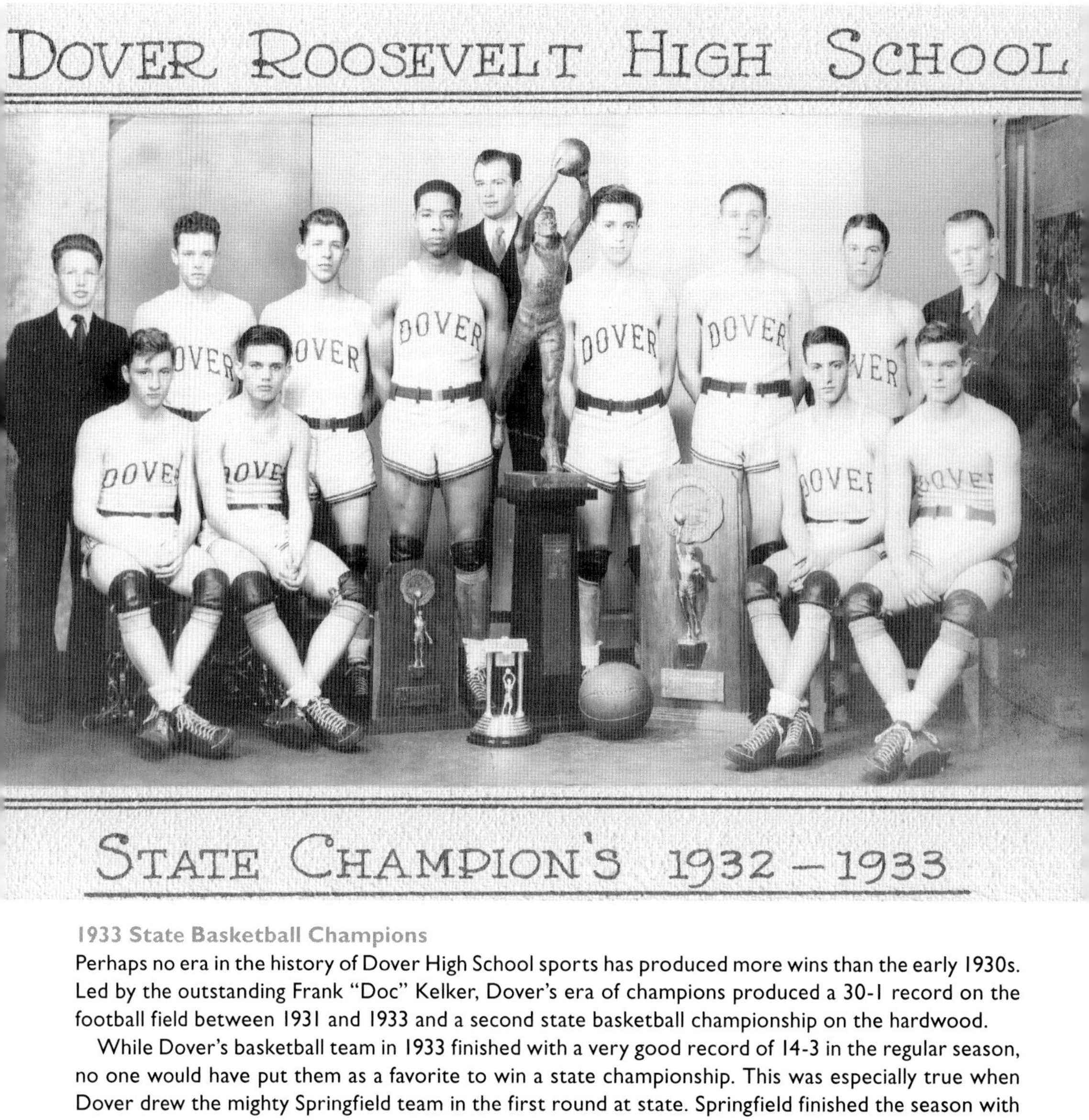

1933 State Basketball Champions

Perhaps no era in the history of Dover High School sports has produced more wins than the early 1930s. Led by the outstanding Frank "Doc" Kelker, Dover's era of champions produced a 30-1 record on the football field between 1931 and 1933 and a second state basketball championship on the hardwood.

While Dover's basketball team in 1933 finished with a very good record of 14-3 in the regular season, no one would have put them as a favorite to win a state championship. This was especially true when Dover drew the mighty Springfield team in the first round at state. Springfield finished the season with a remarkable 26-1 record. Despite very few believers, Dover shocked Springfield 26-17, setting up a second-round showdown with Massillon. Up against a mighty Massillon team, Dover struggled its way to a 24-24 tie at the end of regulation. Rallying in the overtime period, with a winning shot by Harold Braun, Dover triumphed.

The state final game proved the least interesting of the three games played at state. Dover pulled away and easily won over Marietta. The players on the 1933 state championship team were Dick Klar, Edgar Davis, Frank Kelker, Harold Braun, Earl Maurer, Dale Andreas, Don Godfrey, Robert Boyd, Donald Goettge, Harry Seibert, and Thomas Homrighausen. The coach, and captain of the 1927 championship team, was Herman "Bup" Rearick.

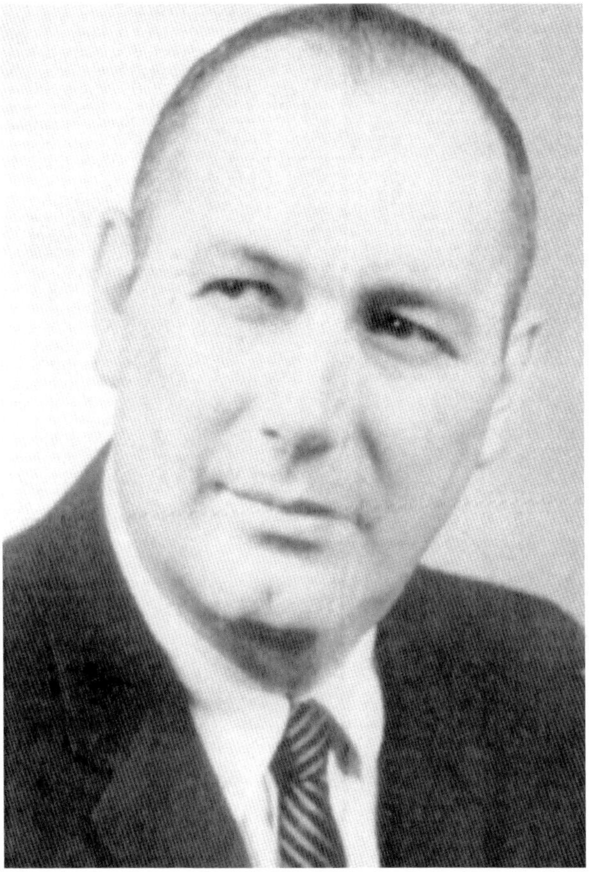

Ben Wilson
Although his birth certificate lists Cadiz as his place of birth, Ben Wilson always thought of Dover as his hometown. He attended Dover High School while being raised by his grandparents on Union Avenue. From seventh grade on, Ben Wilson dreamed of football. In high school, he played under coach Glen "Dutch" Furbay and was part of the 1942 undefeated team. Alongside Wilson in the class of 1944 were other recognizable names from Dover's past, men like Tom Patton, George Elford, and Bill Ellwood.

After high school, Ben joined the Navy and its V-12 program. While in the Navy he was able to pursue his education, studying at Dennison University during the 1944–1945 school year, and at Kansas State the following year. After an honorable discharge from the Navy, Wilson took up his studies full-time at Heidelberg College. After graduation, he remained at Heidelberg and joined the football coaching staff from 1949 to 1951.

In 1951, Wilson joined the ranks of Ohio's high school football coaches. He started at Wellston, before moving on to Mount Vernon, Sandusky, and, eventually, Warren Harding High School. In all, he was a high school coach from 1951 to 1964. His overall record was 95-35-3. In 1957, he was selected as the Ohio High School Coach of the Year when he led Mount Vernon to its second consecutive undefeated season.

Moving to the college ranks in 1965, he became the offensive coordinator at the University of Virginia. In 1968, his Virginia offense broke or tied 19 ACC records. This fine finish propelled Wilson to his first college head coaching position at Wichita State University. Only a year and a half after taking the job at Wichita State, things ended tragically for Wilson, his wife, and many of his players. On October 2, 1970, the football team's plane crashed near Silver Plume, Colorado. Thirty-one coaches, players, and staff were killed in the accident. (Courtesy of Denny Rubright.)

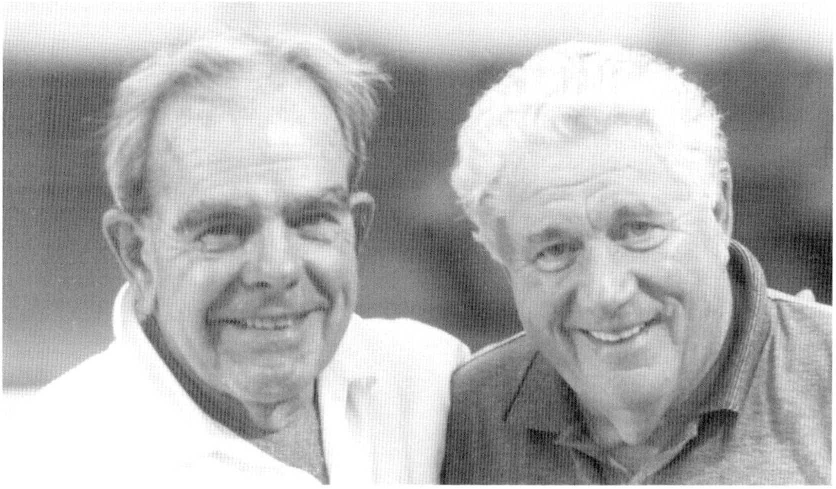

Ray Mears

Raised in Dover, Ray Mears fell in love with basketball and coaching at a young age. As a young man, Mears suffered from what doctors misdiagnosed as tuberculosis. Because he was unable to play, Dover coach "Dutch" Furbay asked the young Mears to coach an elementary school team. The team performed well, and Mears was hooked.

After high school, Mears attended Miami (Ohio) where he was able to play basketball, lettering twice. While attending Miami, he earned his tuition by working at the Reeves Mill. After college, Mears spent a period of years coaching at the high school level before serving his county for two years beginning in 1950. After his stint in the service, he again returned to coaching while working on his master's degree at Kent State University. Mears's first college coaching job came at Wittenberg College. During a six-year stint there, Mears compiled a stellar record of 121 wins to only 23 losses. The real highlight of his tenure at Wittenberg was the 1961–1962 season. That year, Wittenberg won the small college national championship.

Mears success soon drew the attention of larger programs, and at the age of 35, he was hired to coach the University of Tennessee Volunteers. In a 12-year run at Tennessee, Mears led the Volunteers to a 278-112 record. He won three Southeastern Conference Championships and seven times finished second. Perhaps Mears number of championships would have been much higher if it were not for legendary coach Adolph Rupp. Rupp was the coach at the University of Kentucky from 1930 to 1972.

Mears retired in 1977 after 21 years as a college head basketball coach. He never had a losing season. (Courtesy of Denny Rubright.)

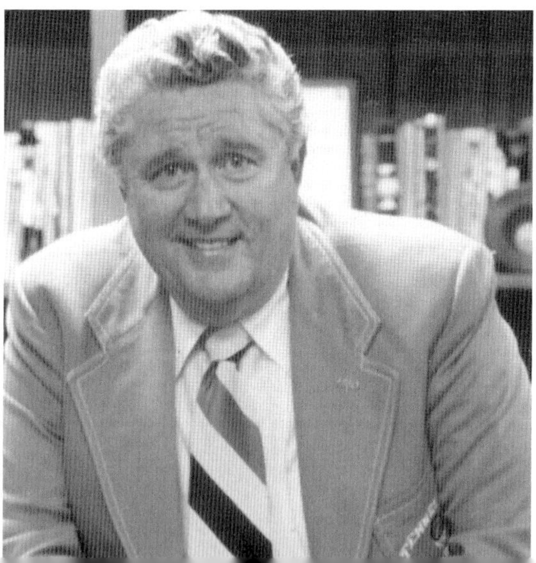

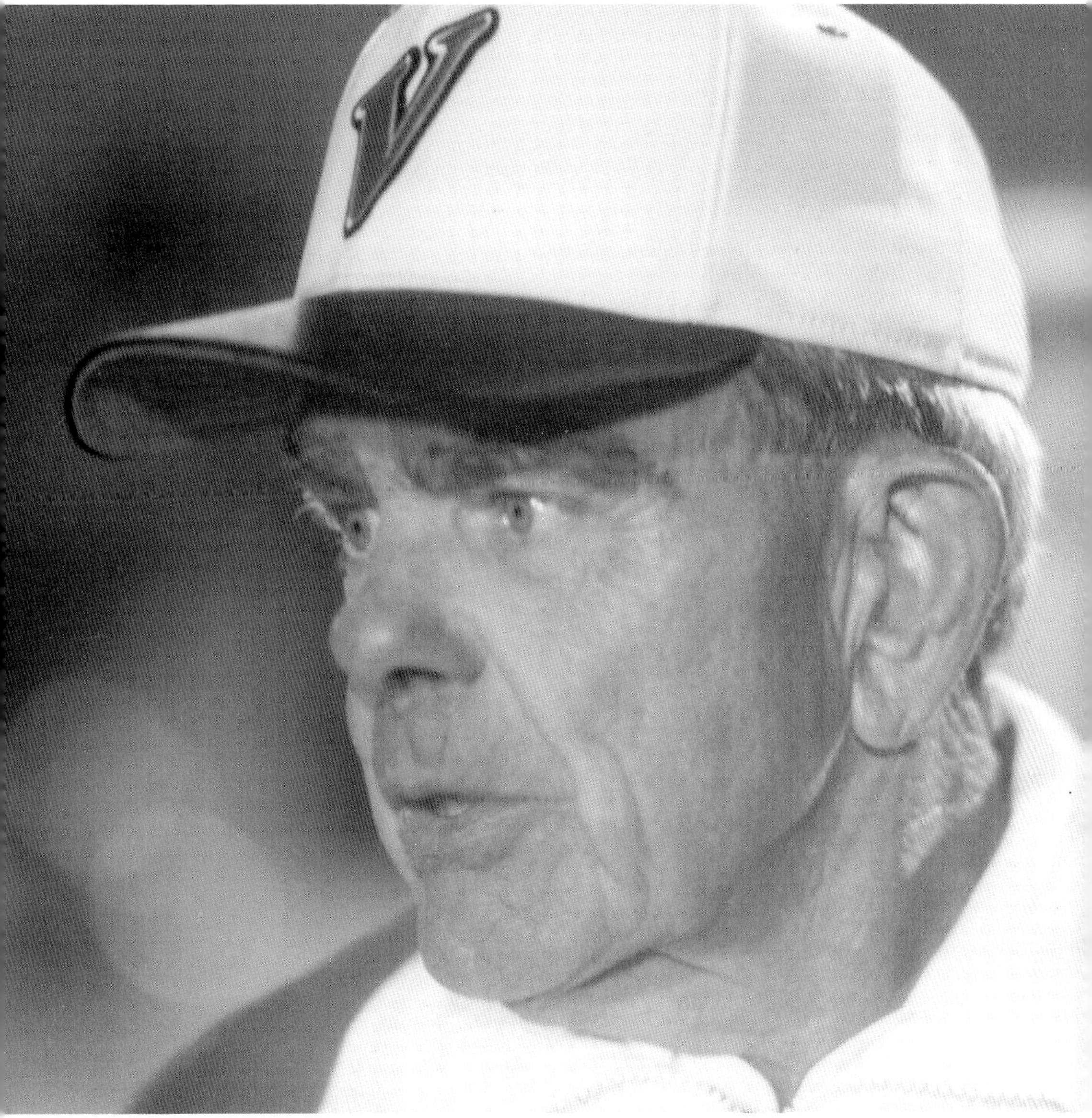

Dick Haines
Born in West Virginia, Dick Haines played his college football at West Liberty. After college, Haines bounced around several Southern Ohio schools before arriving in Tuscarawas County in 1958. Hired as Dover's head football coach, Haines struggled in his first year while laying the groundwork for success. The 1958 Tornadoes went 4-5-1, but the tide was turning. Between 1959 and 1970, Dover grew into a perennial power. Twice, Haines's teams were undefeated at 8-0-2 in 1961 and 10-0 in 1967. The 1967 season was perhaps Haines's greatest. That year, running back Colby Byrom secured Haines's only 10-0 season as Dover squeaked by rival New Philadelphia 6-0 in the season's final game.

In 1970, Haines left Dover so his wife could be closer to her family in California. He resumed his coaching career at Vista High School near San Diego. While at Vista, Haines led his teams to two California State Football Championships, 1974 and 1985. He retired from coaching in 1995. (Courtesy of Denny Rubright.).

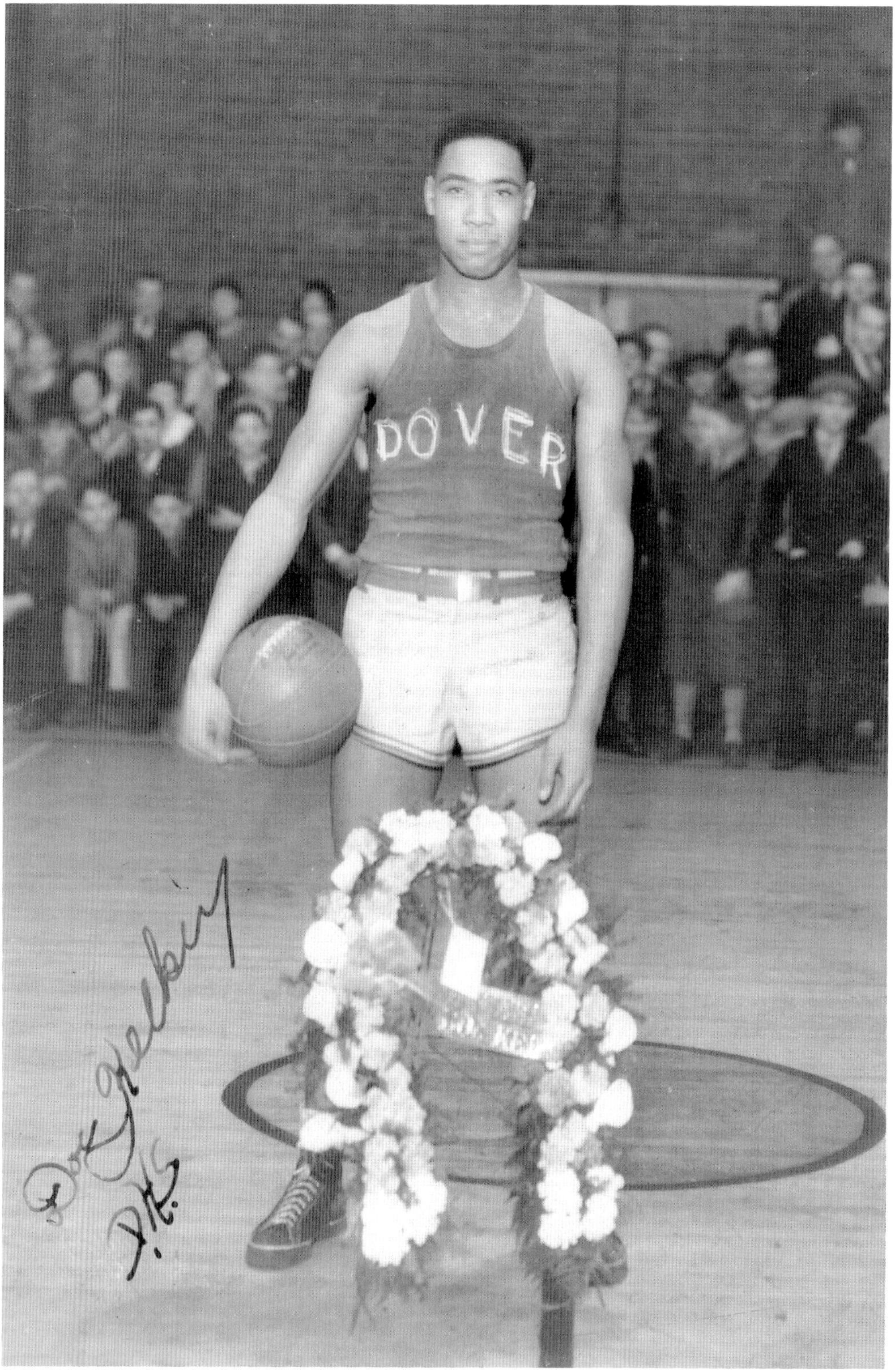
DOVER

Frank "Doc" Kelker (OPPOSITE PAGE)
Although he played for Dover 80 years ago, many still consider Frank "Doc" Kelker one of the greatest athletes ever to come out of Dover High School. Doc, and his twin brother, Spider, were born in the small Florida community of Woodsville. In the 1920s, Kelker's father moved his family to Dover to take advantage of the opportunity to work at the Reeves Mill and to escape racial tensions in the South.

The Kelker boys, especially Frank, excelled early in sports. Frank was a three-sport star at Dover, leading his teams to the most successful athletic years in the school's history. Kelker's Dover football team compiled a 30-1 record during his three years, the basketball team in 1933 won a state championship, and he batted .521 for a very good baseball team.

After high school, Kelker attended Western Reserve University (Case Western), where he was named to five All-American teams. After graduating from college, Kelker remained in Cleveland where he became director of the Cedar Addison Branch of the YMCA. The Cedar Addison YMCA is located in Cleveland's Hough neighborhood, which was racked by violence during the summer of 1966. Over six nights, more than 240 fires were set. Miraculously, the YMCA remained completely untouched by the riots. Many attribute this to Kelker's involvement, leadership, and respect in the community. (Courtesy of Denny Rubright.)

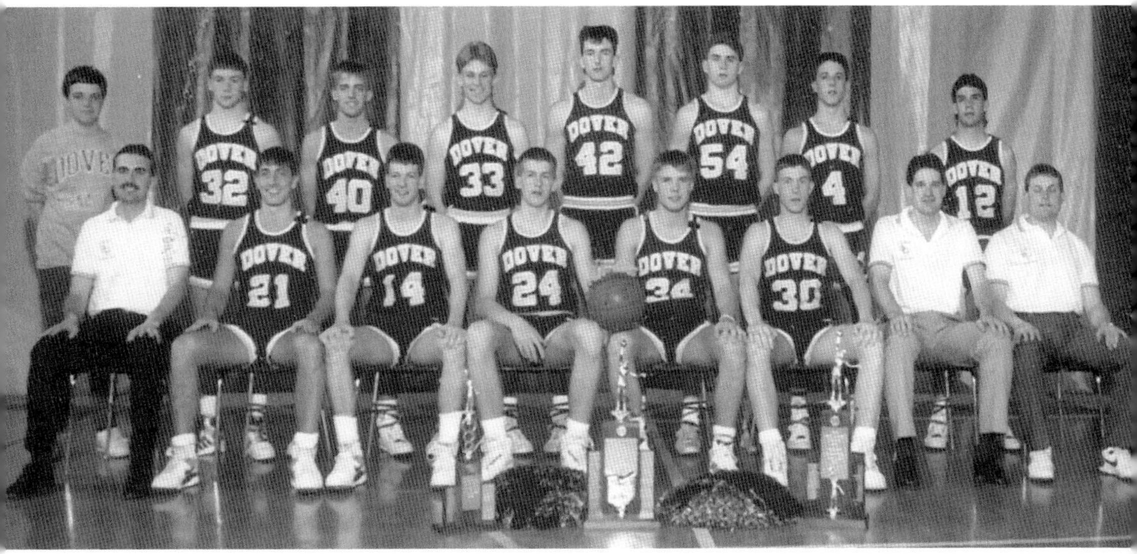

The Bomb Squad
In 1989, the Dover High School basketball team and its improbable run to the state final four captivated Dover. Led by first-year head coach Jud Compton, many expected the team to be pretty good, but no one outside of Dover's locker room would have predicted the success the team would enjoy. Compton, who graduated from Indian Valley South, was only 31 years old at the time of his hiring. Prior to his stint as Dover's head coach, he worked as the eighth-grade coach (1980–1982) and then as a junior varsity coach (1982–1988). In 1988, after the departure of coach Dan Rosenberry, Compton was given the top job at Dover. During the 1988–1989 season, the Tornadoes started a disappointing 6-4 before undertaking a seven-game winning streak. Although the winning streak, as well as a chance at a league title, ended with a second loss to Tusky Valley, the Tornadoes still felt confident going into the tournament.

When the tournament began, Dover started five seniors: Kevin Frye, Matt Kinsey, Kent Beal, Dave Tidrick, and Tom Luthy, with sixth man, Don Watson, coming off the bench. With a high-energy offense and an exceptionally high shooting percentage, Dover rolled through four state-ranked opponents to get to the final four. Although the run would end at the hands of 25-0 West Geauga in the state semifinals, the 1989 team achieved Dover's best finish since 1937. (Courtesy of Jud Compton.)

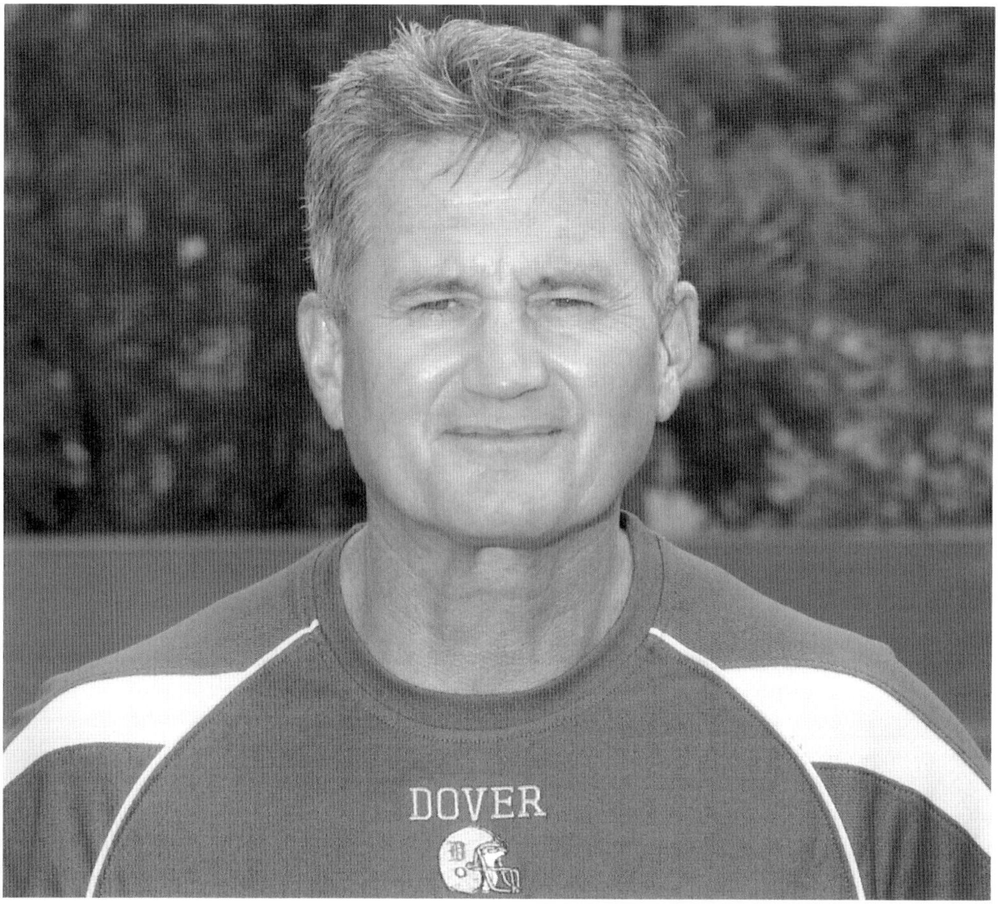

Dan Ifft

April 9, 1995, was one of the most important days in the history of Dover High School football. The reason this date will forever be remembered by Tornado fans is that was the day Dan Ifft was hired as Dover's head football coach. Since April 1995, Coach Ifft has gone on to become the winningest coach in the program's long history. Although he may not have been raised locally, Coach Ifft has adopted the community in a way that few would have thought possible back in 1995.

Dan Ifft was a standout in both track and football at Warren JFK High School where he competed at the state level in the 120-meter high hurdles. As a boy, he dreamed not of gridiron glory but of courtroom glory. This dream lasted into his collegiate career at Kent State University before his love of football and coaching won out. Graduating from Kent in 1978, he was hired as a teacher and coach at Austintown Fitch High School. After four years at Fitch, Ifft moved to Stark County to work under coach Keith Wakefield at Massillon Perry. From 1983 to 1984 and again from 1986 to 1994, Ifft remained a part of Wakefield's staff, learning and growing as a coach.

In 1995, he applied for the Dover job, not really expecting to get it but for the experience. To the shock of Coach Ifft, he was chosen from a pool of over 50 other candidates, many with prior experience. At the time of his hiring, Ifft was 38 and had never served as a head coach at any level.

His hiring immediately changed the football landscape of the Dover Tornadoes. He demanded more from his players but delivered more as well. What he delivered were wins. Since Ifft's hiring, the Tornadoes have never suffered a losing season. In addition, the team has made many appearances in the state football playoffs and, in 2012, became the first Tuscarawas County team to ever appear in the state football final four. (Courtesy of Miller Studios.)

2012 State Final Four Football Team

Before coach Dan Ifft arrived in Dover, no Tuscarawas County High School football team had ever won a state playoff game. Since Coach Ifft's arrival, Dover has become a perennial power on the state playoff scene. Despite this, the Tornadoes have struggled to move beyond the regional level. That is until 2012, when the Tornadoes finally broke through and became the first local team to reach the state final four.

Dover's season in 2012 was not unlike many of the previous seasons under Coach Ifft. Senior quarterback Mason Mamarella, who proved a double threat, led the team. He ran for 1,253 yards and passed for another 3,011. The Tornadoes finished 8-2 with a dramatic three point win over the New Philadelphia Quakers to end the regular season.

Once in the playoffs, Dover accomplished the same feat in the first round as Felipe Bravo hit his second game-winning field goal in as many weeks to lead the Tornadoes to a 27-24 win over Granville. This was followed by a win over Poland Seminary, setting up a regional finals match-up with West Holmes. Dover would roll over West Holmes, 48-21, to make its first-ever appearance in the state final four. Although the team fell to an incredibly talented team in Akron, St. Vincent–St. Mary, Dover's season was one for the ages. (Courtesy of Mitchell's Studio.)

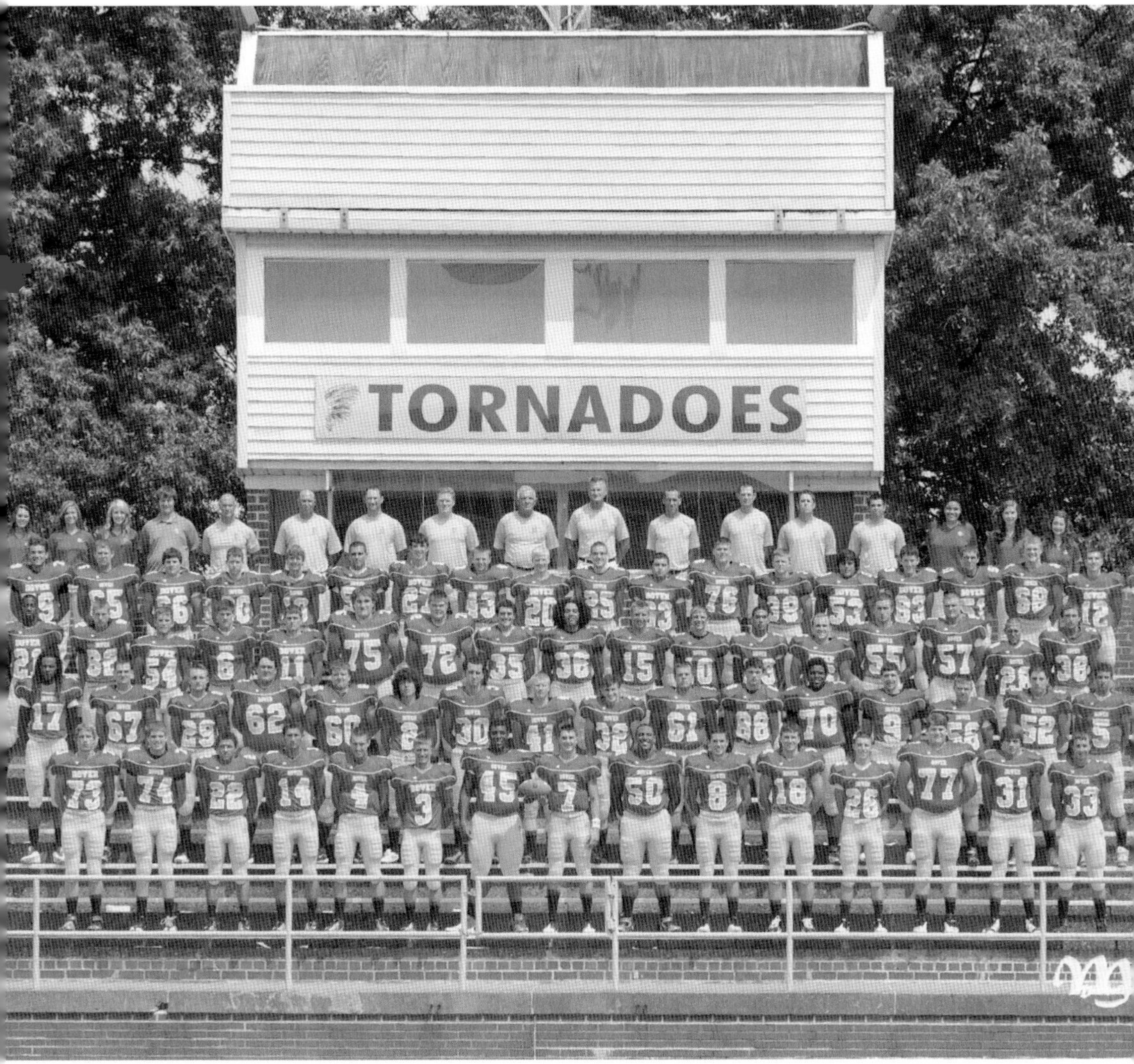

Bob Von Kaenel

A 1973 graduate of Strasburg High School, Bob Von Kaenel developed a love for sports at a young age. While in high school, he played four sports: football, basketball, baseball, and track. Also during his years at Strasburg, he had the opportunity to learn from, and later play against, legendary basketball coach Charlie Huggins. Huggins was Strasburg's coach while Von Kaenel was in junior high, and he played against Huggins's teams once he made varsity.

After high school, Von Kaenel attended Alderson-Broadus College, graduating in 1977. His first chance to coach came at his alma mater, Strasburg. He coached the girls' reserve for two seasons and the boys' reserve and seventh grade for a season before moving on to Tusky Valley High School in 1989. He was again relegated to the junior high during the 1979–1980 season, but in 1980, he received his first big opportunity. That year, he was hired to be Tusky Valley's head boys' basketball coach. Over the next 11 seasons, he compiled a steady 142-103 record and lead the Trojans to the 1988 state championship game.

Just a few years removed from his best season at Tusky Valley, Von Kaenel decided to make the move to neighboring Dover. This proved a great move for not only Von Kaenel but also for the entire Dover basketball community. Since coming to Dover, coach Bob Von Kaenel has compiled a stellar 395-112 record in 22 seasons. His best seasons came in 1998 and 2004 when his teams went to the state final four.

Among his many awards, Coach Von Kaenel was named Associated Press Coach of the Year in 1988, 1995, and 1997 and Ohio High School Basketball Coaches Association Coach of the Year in 1995 and 1997. He was also presented the prestigious Paul Walker Award. The Paul Walker Award is presented for outstanding coaching and service to Ohio high school basketball. (Courtesy of Bob Von Kaenel.)

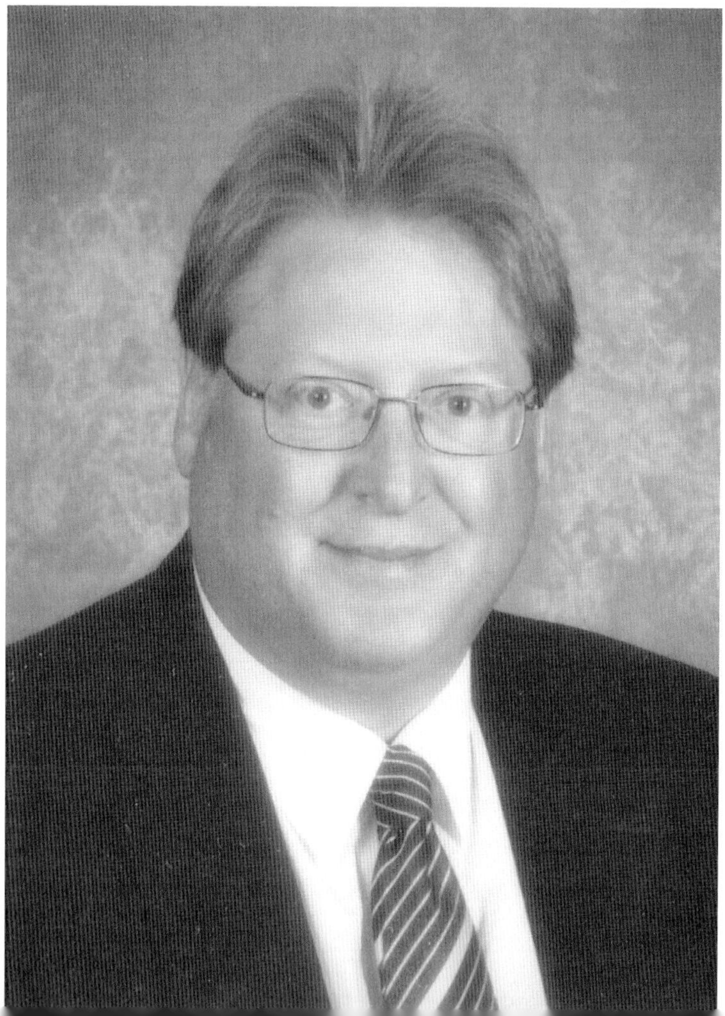

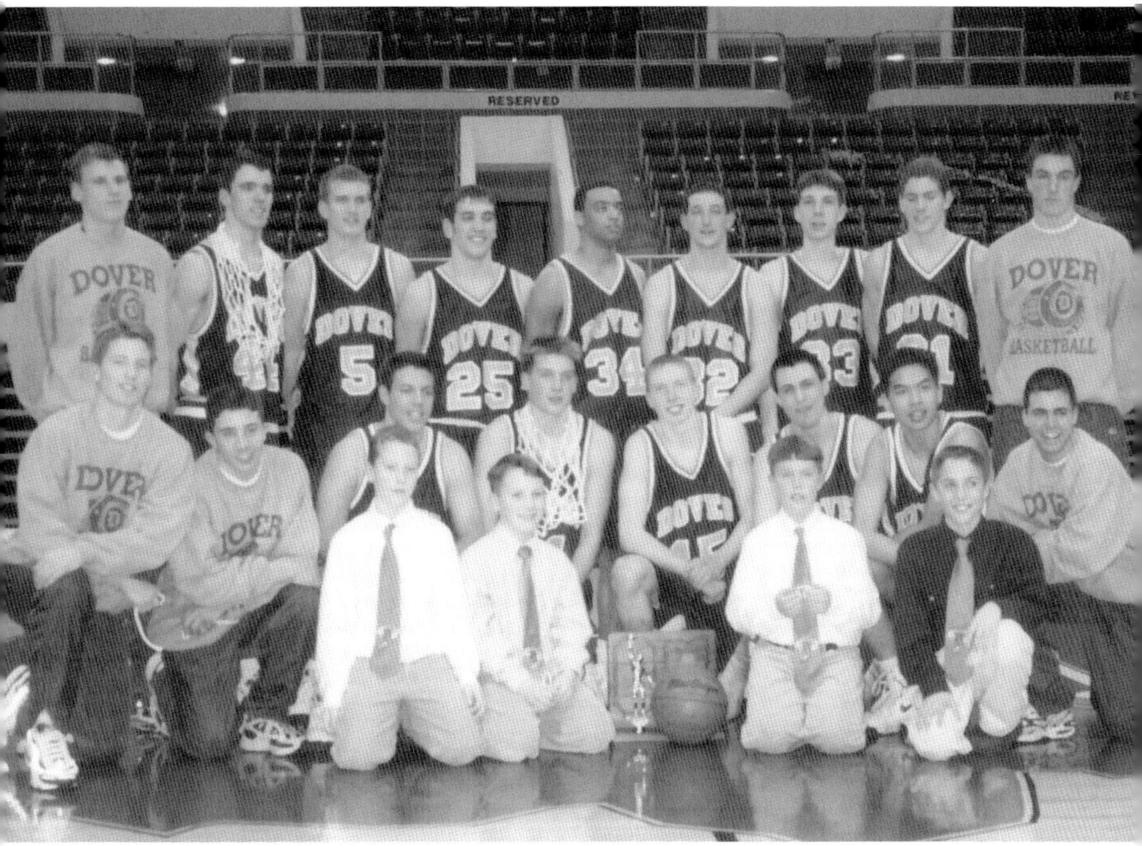

1998 Dover Basketball Team

The 1998 Dover Tornadoes put together a magical season. They posted a remarkable 24-3 record and finished second in the state tournament. Among the many highlights in 1998 was a buzzer-beater to top Massillon and an unforgettable finish in the state semifinal game. Battling a tough Akron Hoban team, Dover trailed with only seconds remaining. A full-court pass from Marc Von Kaenel to Ben Swartzwelder for a layup gave Dover a thrilling victory. Although they would fall in the championship game to Cleveland Benedictine, Dover's run was the school's best since 1937. (Courtesy of Bob Von Kaenel.)

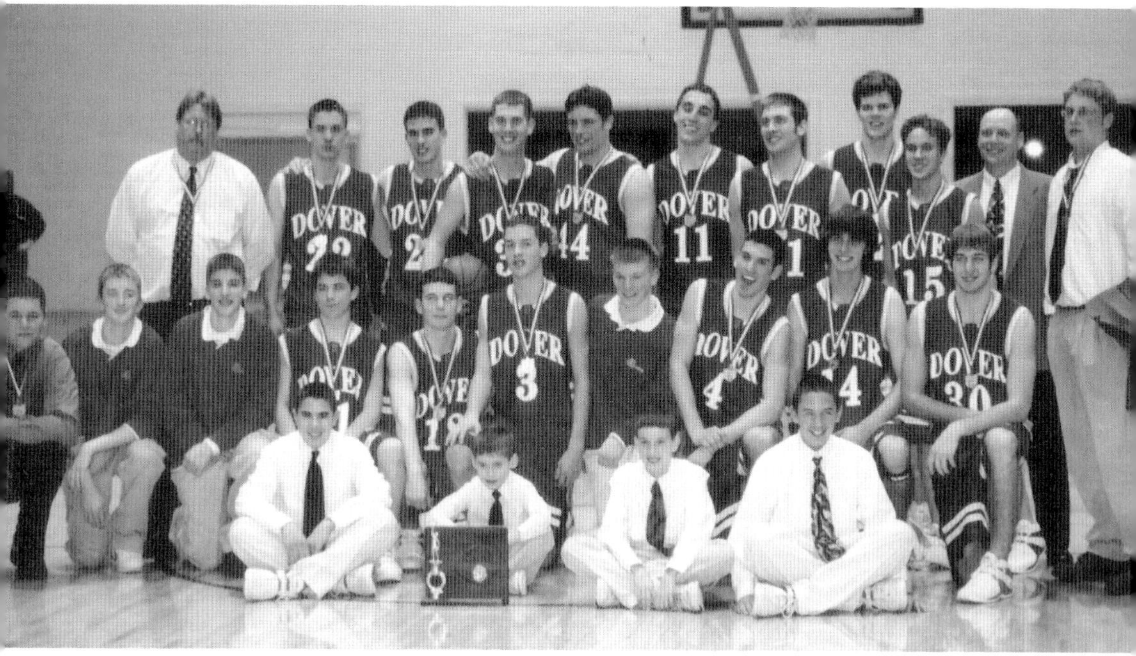

2004 Dover Basketball Team

The 2004 Dover basketball team, led by Jeremy Ady and Todd Lisowski, played an exciting brand of basketball. After an outstanding 17-3 regular season and a league championship, the team stormed into the 2004 playoffs. A string of wins propelled them into the region final, where Dover put together a thrilling victory over Columbus Beechcroft 57-54 to reach its second state final four under coach Bob Von Kaenel. At state, they lost a close game to Ottawa-Glandorf, 61-60. Ottawa-Glandorf would go on to win the 2004 state championship. (Courtesy of Bob Von Kaenel.)

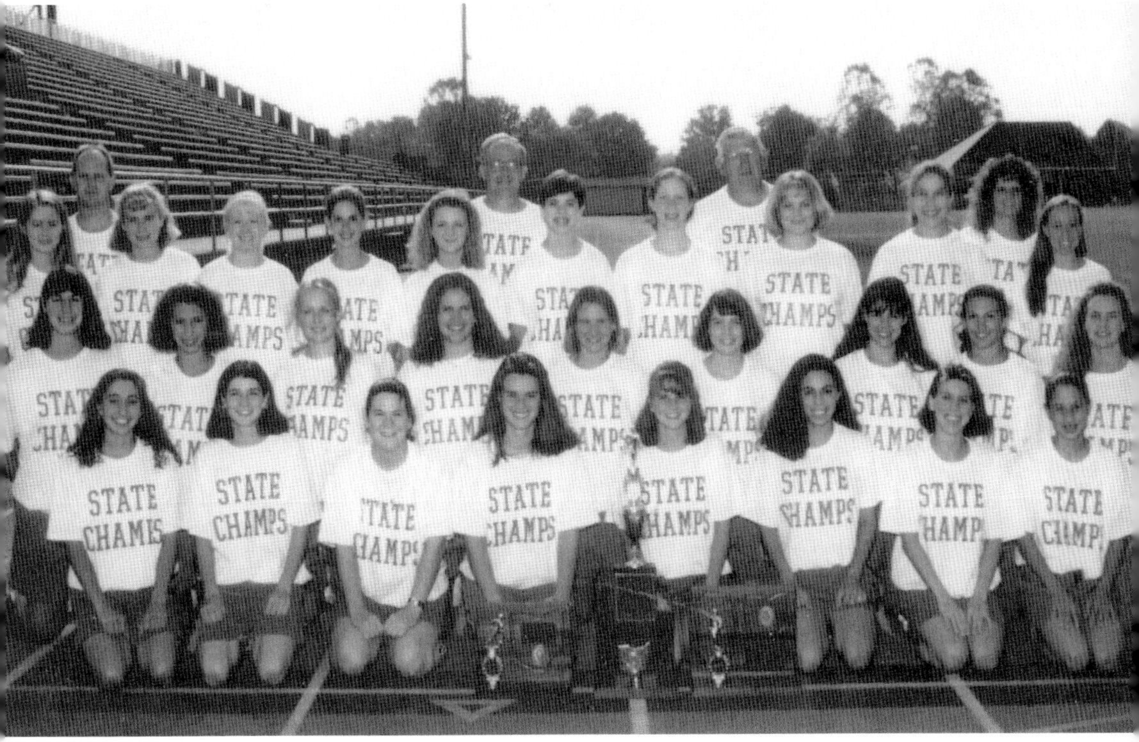

1995 State Championship Track Team

The year 1995 was a magical one for coach Rick Staley's girls' track team. Because of the success of the cross country team in the fall, he knew he had a special group of young women. This included standouts Rikki Cerrett and Sarah Monteleone. Coach Staley had taken over the girls' track program in the early 1980s. He was also a football coach with the Tornadoes for many years. In 1995, everything came together for the Tornadoes at the state meet. Led by distance coach Mark Albaugh's outstanding distance runners, Dover took first in the 3,200 relay (Julie Klar, Jessie Hunt, Liz Murphy, and Rikki Cerrett). In the 1,600 relay, they finished as the state runner-up (Jesse Hunt, Liz Murphy, Ellen Nixon, and Rikki Cerrett). Individually, both Rikki Cerrett (800 meters) and Sarah Monteleone (3,200 meters) were state champions. When the final numbers were tallied, Dover easily outdistanced the competition to win the school's first state championship since 1933. (Courtesy of Susan Hunt.)

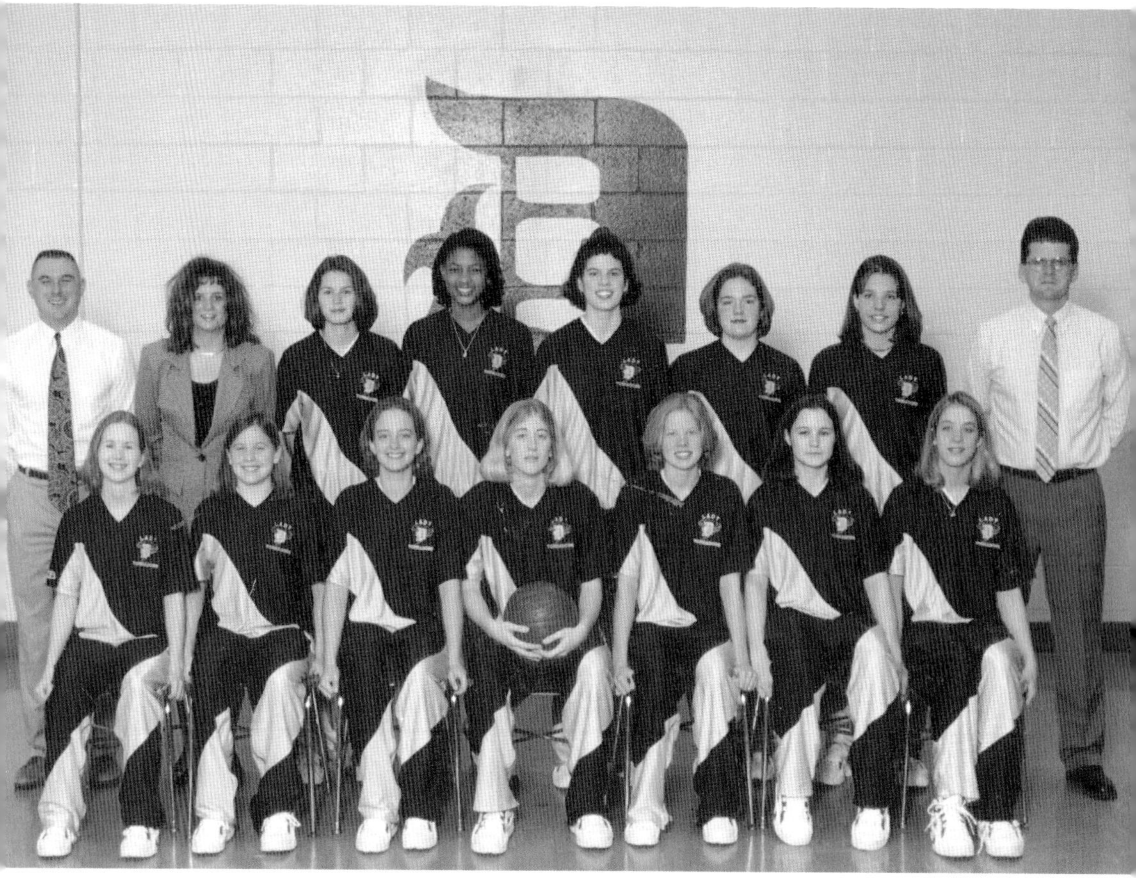

1998 Girls' Basketball State Runner-Up

Not a lot was expected of the Dover girls' basketball team in 1998. After the 1997 season, longtime coach Tom Andreas retired, and the team graduated seven seniors from a regional semifinal team. First-year head coach Terry Immel led Dover. The team started 8-5, before winning six out of its final seven games. The team ended up third in its conference, the East Central Ohio League (ECOL).

Everything changed once the Lady Tornadoes began tournament play. After a tough first-round matchup with Buckeye Local, Dover went on a roll. The highlight came when Dover defeated Vincent Warren in the regional final. Vincent Warren was the 1997 state runner-up. They had nearly all of their starters returning and had two additional players who had moved in from another school. Dover won the game by 20 points to advance to the state final four.

Once at state, Dover faced its toughest competition yet. The team played top-ranked Wasseon. Wasseon came into the game as the defending state champions riding a 53-game winning streak. The game was hard fought, and Dover tied the contest with only 50 seconds to go. With only 30 seconds remaining, Dover's Kate Fishley stole the ball and was fouled with only 0.3 seconds left. Fishley hit both free throws, and Dover was propelled into the state championship game. Although the team lost to Hamilton Badin in the finals, the Dover girls' remarkable run in 1998 is one of the most memorable in school history. (Courtesy of Terry Immel.)

CHAPTER FOUR

Celebrities

In the same way that every community needs builders, businessmen, and the civic minded, every community also needs dreamers. These are the people whose talent is too good not to share with the rest of the world. Whether they find success elsewhere and return to the area later or whether they seek their fortune elsewhere and never return to home, they will always be part of our story. Just like each and every one of the legendary locals within this book, these celebrities and their talents were shaped and molded by their experiences in Dover. They were educated here, raised here, and in some cases received their inspiration by someone they met here.

All of those in the following chapter have enjoyed incredible success in their lifetimes. They have gotten to do things that most only dream of. The most important part of their stories is not the money or the fame; it is what they represent to the next generation. These individuals are proof that with hard work, commitment, and talent, anyone can go on to do great things. One can be an actor on a high school stage and dream of starring in a Broadway play; one can also write stories or doodle cartoons and dream of someday getting an Academy Award. One can even pick up a pocketknife and use it to carve his way to New York's Grand Central Station. All of these are true stories, and all of these feats were accomplished by Doverites.

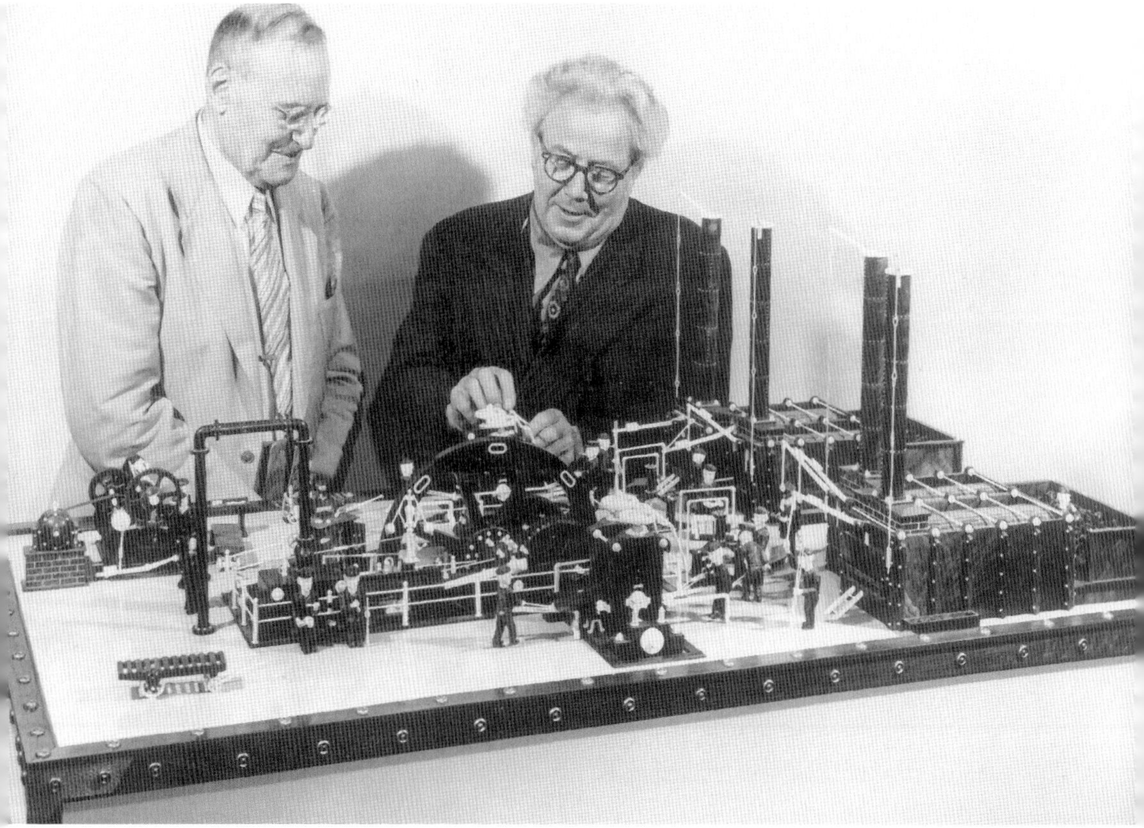

Ernest "Mooney" Warther

Ernest "Mooney" Warther (right) was born in Dover on October 30, 1885. Forced to grow up quickly when his father passed away, Mooney quit school after second grade. To help the family's financial situation, he began work as a cow herder for a penny a day. It was during these early years that a chance encounter with a hobo changed Mooney's life. He passed his free time whittling, and the hobo taught him to carve a pair of pliers using a single piece of wood. Later, in 1913, Warther carved a "pliers tree." It took over two months to complete, required 31,000 cuts, and created 511 working pliers. The pliers tree was displayed at the 1933 World's Fair in Chicago. At the age of 14, Warther began his first full-time job at the American Sheet and Tin Plate Company. He began as a scrap bundler, eventually working his way up to become the head shears man.

In 1910, Mooney married Freida Richard. The couple built a modest home and, in 1912, a workshop followed. Around this time, Mooney quit whittling and started carving. His subject in those early years was a series of locomotives, titled the "History of Steam." This collection grew to 65 carvings including his masterpiece, "The Great Northern Locomotive," which he carved in 1933.

In 1923, thanks to the New York Central Railroad, Mooney traveled the country for six months and spent time displaying his trains at Grand Central Station in New York. The opening of a small museum in 1936 followed, providing for Mooney's most productive years. Today, that small museum has grown to become one of the premier museums in Ohio. Although Mooney retired in 1953, he began carving again in 1957. His son Dave suggested he focus on the great events in American railroad history. This collection saw nine new carvings, including his "Lincoln Funeral Train." Ernest "Mooney" Warther died in 1973 at age 87.

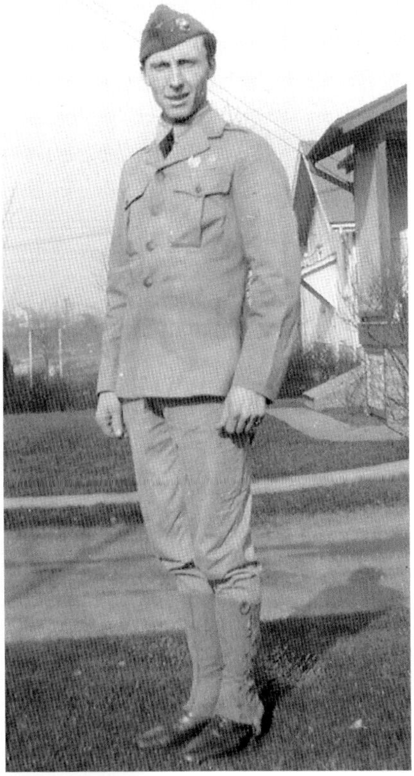

Marion W. Wallick

Marion Wallick (left) was born in Dover on April 25, 1904. At the age of 17, he began his show-business career when he became an acrobat with Dutton's Attractions. The promoter for Dutton's had noticed Wallick's work on the diving board at Summit Beach Park. He was hired and toured with the company until 1926. Later, after returning to Dover for a time, Wallick rejoined the circus and traveled again before partnering with Dave Gold to put on the show "Lights and Shadows" in New York City. The show would run for two years before Marion would again return to Dover. Back in Dover, he went to work with young people. After a while, Marion and some of the young men he had been training began to tour. They joined the Montana Meechy's Western Show and traveled throughout Ohio.

In the 1940s, Marion Wallick's life took another turn when he served in the Pacific during World War II. What changed Marion was the hardship and suffering he saw during the war. This was especially true in the case of the many children. After this experience, Marion vowed that he would dedicate himself to the benefit of children for the rest of his life. He did this by working to build a number of playgrounds at many local elementary schools. Wallick is pictured below with the Wallick Entertainers. (Both, courtesy of Sally Warner and Carolyn Dreher.)

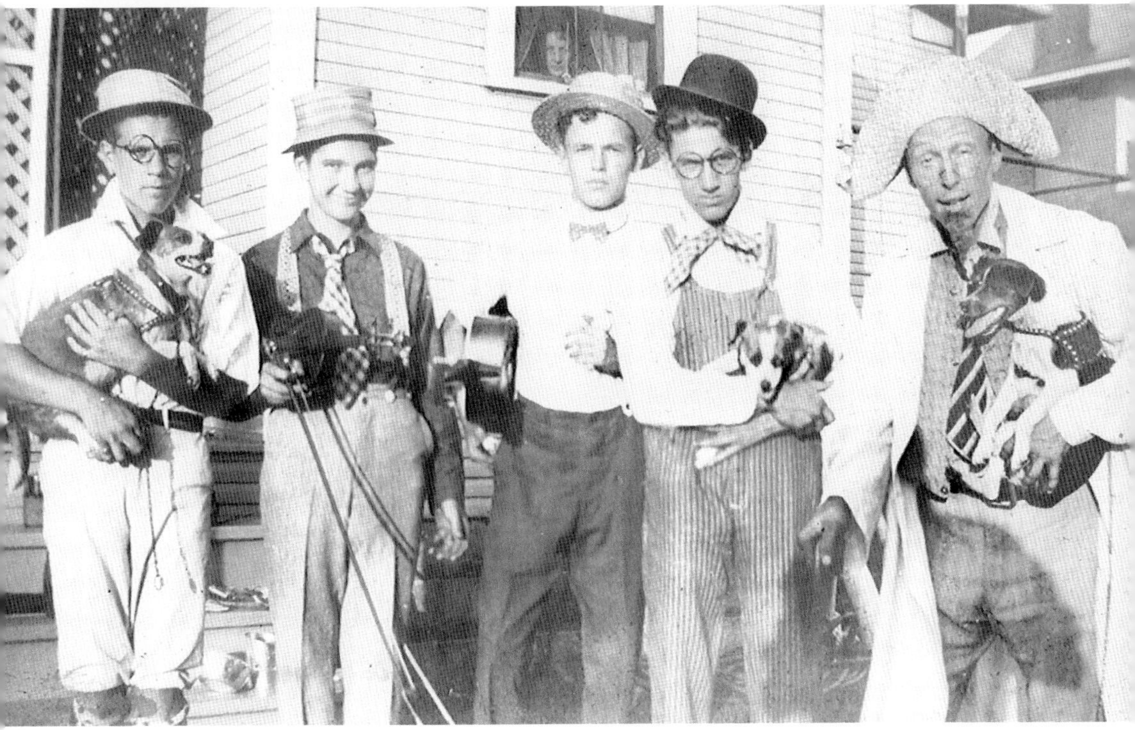

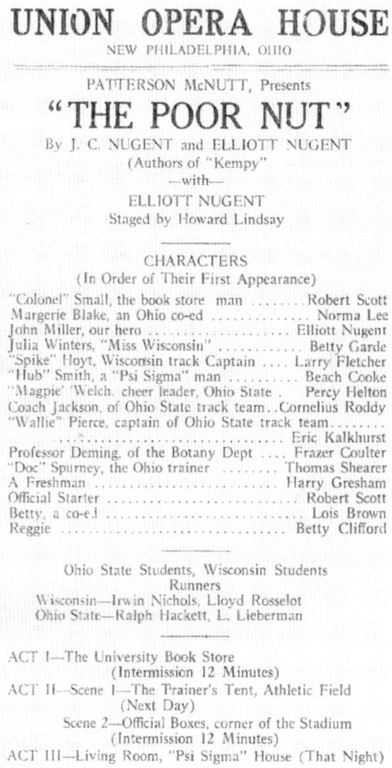

UNION OPERA HOUSE
NEW PHILADELPHIA, OHIO

PATTERSON McNUTT, Presents
"THE POOR NUT"
By J. C. NUGENT and ELLIOTT NUGENT
(Authors of "Kempy"
—with—
ELLIOTT NUGENT
Staged by Howard Lindsay

CHARACTERS
(In Order of Their First Appearance)

"Colonel" Small, the book store man .... Robert Scott
Margerie Blake, an Ohio co-ed .... Norma Lee
John Miller, our hero .... Elliott Nugent
Julia Winters, "Miss Wisconsin" .... Betty Garde
"Spike" Hoyt, Wisconsin track Captain .... Larry Fletcher
"Hub" Smith, a "Psi Sigma" man .... Beach Cooke
"Magpie" Welch, cheer leader, Ohio State . Percy Helton
Coach Jackson, of Ohio State track team..Cornelius Roddy
"Wallie" Pierce, captain of Ohio State track team........ Eric Kalkhurst
Professor Deming, of the Botany Dept .... Frazer Coulter
"Doc" Spurney, the Ohio trainer .... Thomas Shearer
A Freshman .... Harry Gresham
Official Starter .... Robert Scott
Betty, a co-ed .... Lois Brown
Reggie .... Betty Clifford

Ohio State Students, Wisconsin Students
Runners
Wisconsin—Irwin Nichols, Lloyd Rosselot
Ohio State—Ralph Hackett, L. Lieberman

ACT I—The University Book Store
(Intermission 12 Minutes)
ACT II—Scene 1—The Trainer's Tent, Athletic Field
(Next Day)
Scene 2—Official Boxes, corner of the Stadium
(Intermission 12 Minutes)
ACT III—Living Room, "Psi Sigma" House (That Night)

J.C. Nugent

As a young man, John Charles Nugent moved to Dover and married Grace Fertig. Although he worked as a millworker for a time, J.C.'s true passion was the stage. Throughout the first decade or so of the 20th century, the family toured the Vaudeville circuit where J.C. was a hit. After leaving Dover permanently in the 1920s, J.C. and his family split much of their time between Hollywood and New York City. Alongside his son Elliott, he wrote or cowrote 17 plays including *Kempy* and *The Poor Nut*, which both appeared on Broadway. J.C. also appeared as an actor on Broadway and in more than 20 motion pictures.

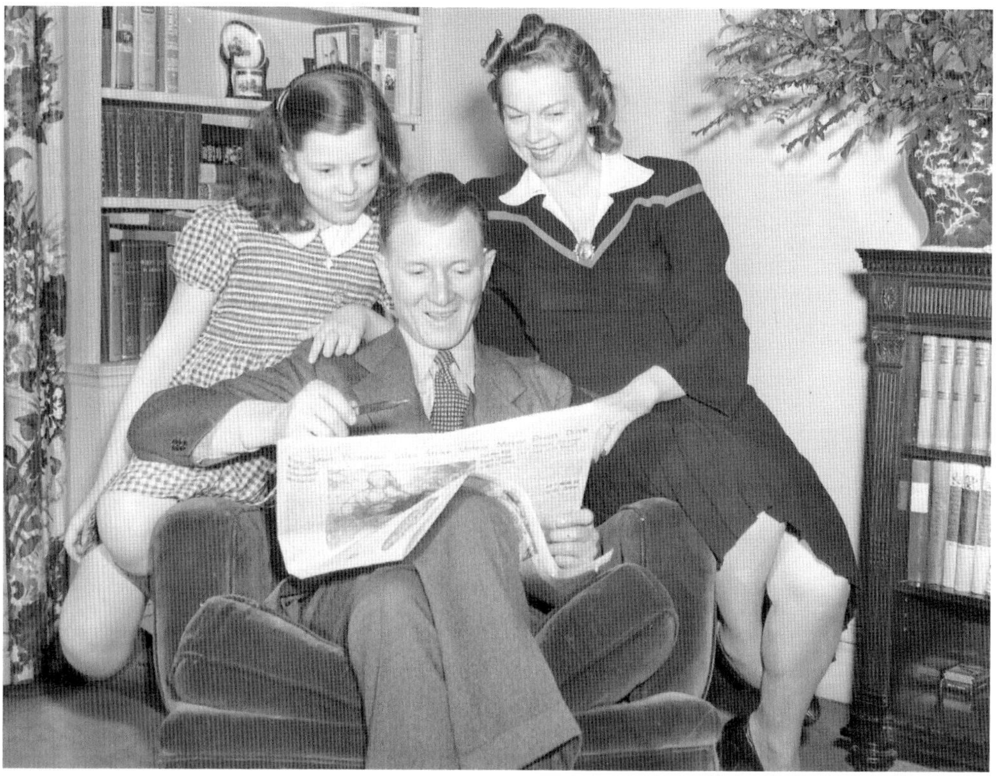

Elliott Nugent

Elliott Nugent was born on September 20, 1896, in the home of his grandfather on Factory Street (North Tuscarawas Avenue) in Dover. According to Nugent in his biography *Events Leading up to the Comedy*, his exact birthplace was in the library of the home. This is a fitting beginning for a man who would go on to pen many plays, screenplays, novels, and his own autobiography. Nugent's acting career began early as he was born into a very talented family. Elliott's father, J.C. (John Charles) Nugent was a fairly successful stage and screen actor who appeared in multiple movies and on Broadway. As a group, the family toured as a vaudeville act when Nugent was a boy.

After graduating from Dover High School, Elliot Nugent attended the Ohio State University where he roomed with and quickly befriended a talented young writer named James Thurber. Thurber would go on to become one of the best-known humorists of his era. His short stories and cartoons appeared regularly in the *New Yorker* magazine or in one of the many collected volumes of his work. It was this friendship that produced Nugent's best-know work, the play *The Male Animal*. *The Male Animal* appeared regularly on Broadway and was made into a 1942 movie starring Henry Fonda and Olivia de Havilland. Nugent acted in the Broadway version and was the director of the film. In addition to *The Male Animal*, Nugent directed 30 other films. Among these are three in which Nugent worked with fellow Ohioan Bob Hope: *The Cat and the Canary* (1939), *Never Say Die* (1939), and *My Favorite Brunette* (1947). Nugent retired from show business in 1957.

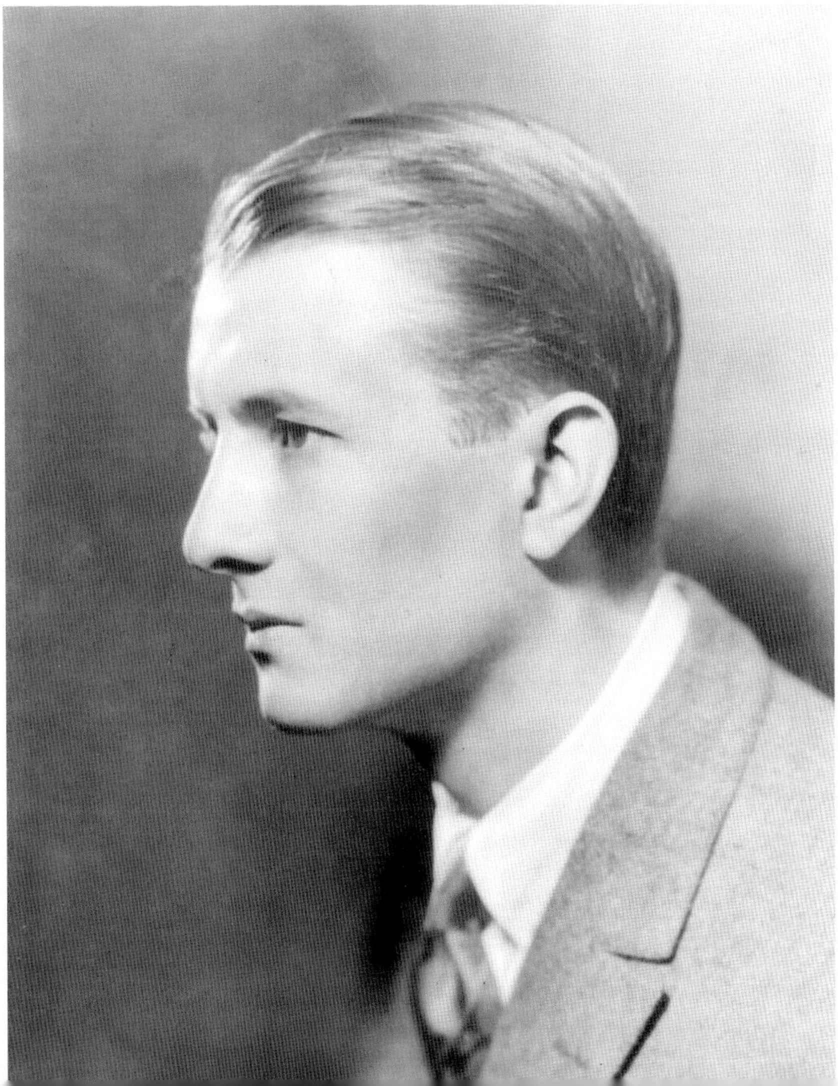

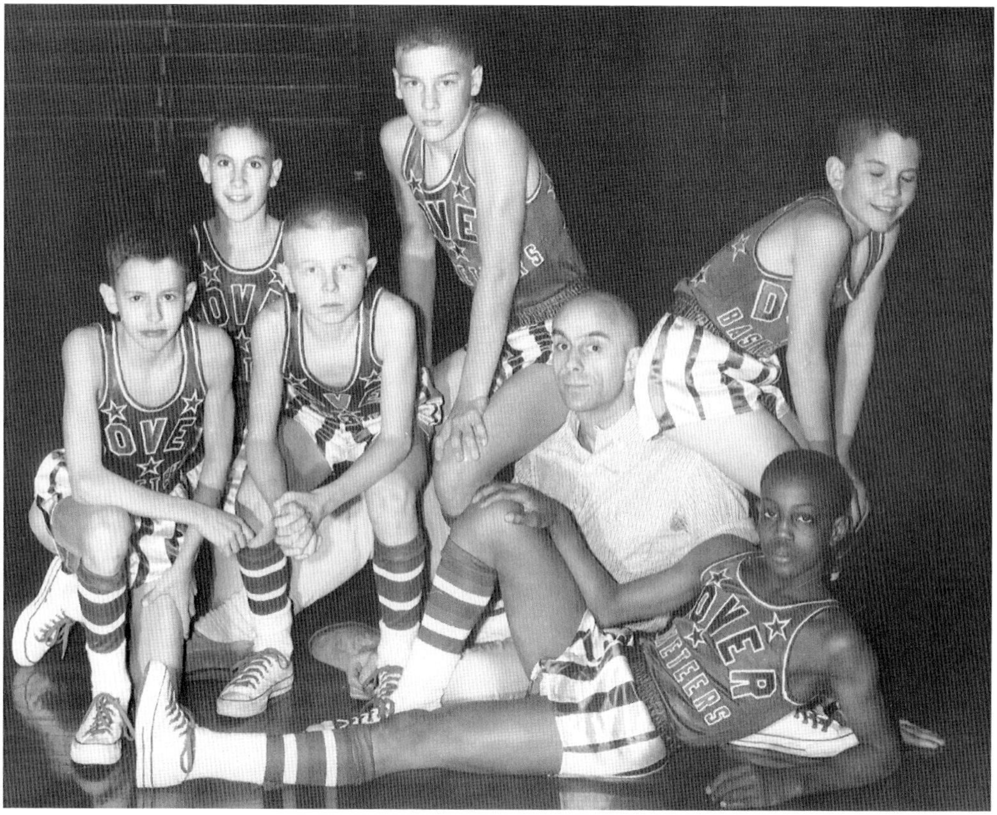

The Dover Basketeers

It is hard to believe but Dover, Ohio, once had its own version of the Harlem Globetrotters. The idea began when Sixth Street Elementary School coach George Elford watched a couple of his players doing tricks the last 15 minutes of basketball practice. This brief exhibition planted the seed of what would become a nationally recognized act.

During the fall of 1955, Coach Elford and a group of six boys approached the local Elks club for a donation to purchase uniforms. Although Elford was told not to expect a decision that night, all it took was a short program by the young men, and the Elks were happy to help with uniforms and also to offset the cost of travel in the early days. Over the next eight years, the Dover Basketeers performed for countless people and celebrities in famous venues like the Boston Garden. They even played for the Harlem Globetrotters themselves. Perhaps their crowning achievement, though, was an appearance in the 1961 movie *The Errand Boy*, starring Jerry Lewis. The young men and Elford spent five days in Hollywood filming and seeing the sites. When they returned home, they were greeted with another surprise—a caravan of 80 to 100 vehicles escorting them into town.

The Basketeers remained active through 1963 when all the travel and appearances began to take their toll on Elford. Over the course of their eight years, 24 boys took part in performances. Among these are a number of men who still call Dover home.

Bob Peterson

Bob Peterson was born at Wooster, Ohio, on January 18, 1961. As a boy, he spent time with family in Brooklyn, New York, before returning to Ohio where his family settled in Dover. He attended Dover schools, graduating from Dover High in 1979. After high school, Peterson attended Ohio Northern University for his undergraduate degree and Purdue University for a master's degree in mechanical engineering. During his time at Purdue, Peterson spent a great deal of time in the computer graphics lab. Also at Purdue, he wrote and illustrated a comic strip called "Loco-Motives." Both of these experiences would play a role in his future.

After graduation, Peterson worked for Wavefront Technologies and Rezn8 Productions before joining Pixar Studios in 1994. His first project while at Pixar was working on the smash hit *Toy Story*. Later, he worked on *A Bug's Life* and *Monsters, Inc.* Peterson's big breakthrough came when he began cowriting a screenplay for the adventures of a young clown fish. The movie *Finding Nemo* was another great success, and Peterson was nominated for an Academy Award for his work. Around 2004, Peterson and fellow Pixar writer Pete Doctor began bouncing ideas around about the story of a grumpy old man and a flying house suspended in the air by helium balloons. These conversations became the screenplay for the movie *Up*. Peterson wrote the script, codirected the picture, and even voiced the unforgettable character of Dug. Dug is the quintessential family pet. He is loyal, friendly, and easily distracted by the word "squirrel."

Presently, Peterson lives in San Francisco with his wife and three children.

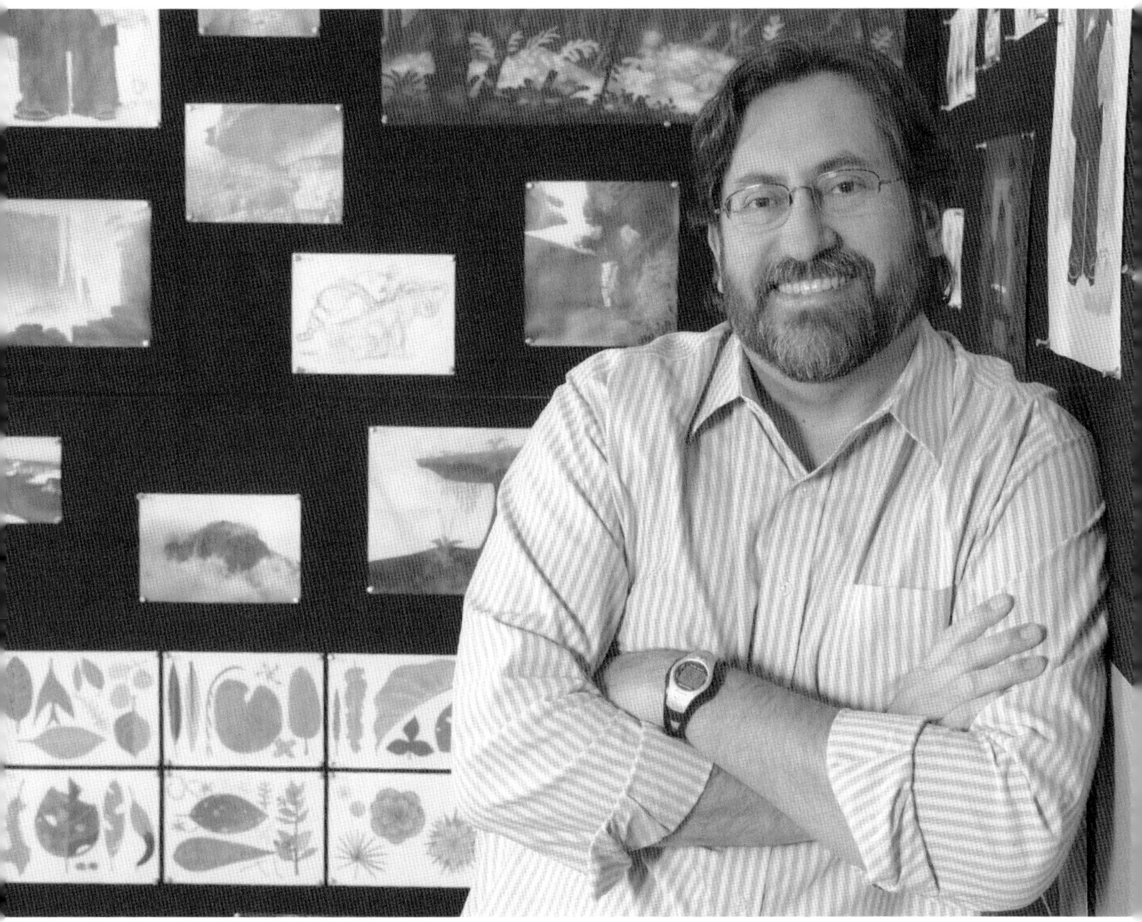

James R. Black

Born in Lima, Ohio, James Black is a 1980 graduate of Dover High School. Black excelled at sports, starring on Dover's undefeated 1979 grid team. After high school, he attended the University of Akron and played under the legendary coach Jim Dennison. There, Black was again a star, being named an All-American in 1982 and 1983. Later, he spent parts of two seasons as a member of the Cleveland Browns, being signed as a free agent. Black's football career also took him to the Canadian Football League, where he played for the Ottawa Rough Riders.

After his football career ended, Black embarked on a new challenge. He decided to try his hand at acting. His first big break came when he appeared alongside George Clooney and Jennifer Lopez in the movie, *Out of Sight*. Black has appeared in numerous movies and television series including *The Burning Zone*, *The PJ's*, *Godzilla*, *Universal Soldier*, in the HBO movie *Don King: Only in America*, *Bones*, *Navy NCIS*, *CSI: Miami*, *Charmed*, and *Will and Grace*. On the stage, James Black has appeared in the musical *Big River*. The role garnered him a nomination and Ovation Award for best actor in a musical. These are just a few of Black's credits on both stage and screen. When he is not acting, Black is a talented musician who plays both piano and guitar.

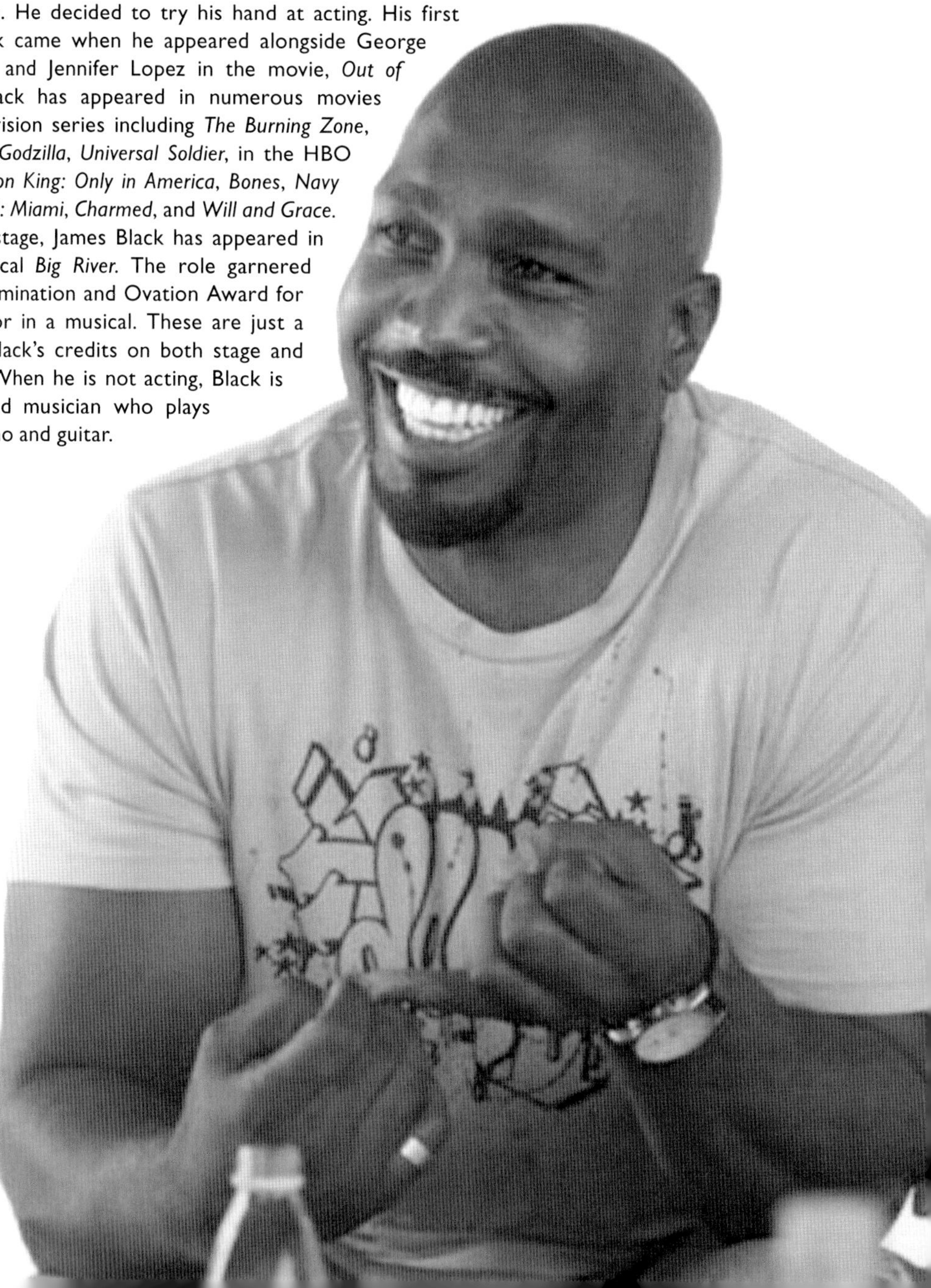

CHAPTER FIVE

Unforgettable Individuals

While every community has its founders, builders, and sports heroes, every community also has its characters. Without these people, life would be a little less interesting. If a community were a painting, these men and women would be the colors. Some are quirky, some talented, and some just unique, but all contribute to making a place special.

Included in this chapter are some of the community's unforgettable individuals. Whether one is talking about those who inspire others, like Adm. Herald Stout; those that move us, like L.H. Alexander; or those who bring the community unwanted attention, like William Clark Quantrill, no one would ever call these people uninteresting. This chapter is also the only one in the book where some of the subjects are not ones to look up to. Along with being unforgettable, two of the individuals here are not role models. Quantrill was a notorious Confederate guerilla best known for his bloody raid on Lawrence, Kansas. Ellen Athey was a mild-mannered housewife until she murdered her serving girl in a fit of rage.

On the other hand, the vast majority of those in this chapter were good people doing good things. They or their actions are responsible for so many good memories. Who could forget Max Krantz's gardens? Located on the corner of Tremont and Fourteenth Streets, the gardens were a popular place for people to have wedding photographs taken or to enjoy strolls on pleasant summer evenings. Fannie Marlowe was a working mom before working moms were commonplace. She balanced family with running a successful business. She raised her boys with the same generosity and work ethic. Her random acts of kindness still bring smiles to faces of many locals. Who could forget Dinolfo's after a Friday night football game? It was simply as good as it gets. While they may never have built a steel mill, employed hundreds, or brought home a state championships, these legendary locals are pure Dover.

William Clark Quantrill

Little in the childhood of W.C. Quantrill hinted at the future he was destined for. Born in Dover on July 31, 1837, he was raised in a household that valued education. He attended, and later taught at, Dover's public schools, where his father was the superintendent. After his father's death in 1854, his prospects locally declined, and he decided to look outside the area to make his way.

Throughout the mid-1850s and into the late 1850s, Quantrill bounced around the American West. There were stops in Illinois, Wyoming, Utah, Colorado, Kansas, and Missouri. As the 1850s came to a close, Quantrill found himself deeply involved in the border wars between Kansas and Missouri. In those days, the border between the two states was indeed the Wild West. Abolitionists and the like raided plantations in Missouri, and pro-slavery men led raids into the free Kansas Territory to recover their property. Tensions ran high, especially after Ohioan John Brown's 1856 Pottawatomie Massacre in Franklin County, Missouri. During Brown's raid, five pro-slavery men were pulled from their cabins and executed. By the start of the Civil War, the border region between the two states was a powder keg waiting to explode.

After the war broke out, Quantrill joined up on the Confederate side and led many raiding parties into Kansas. The most famous of these was the bloody raid of Lawrence, Kansas, in 1863. During the raid, Quantrill and his raiders burned the city to the ground killing 150 people.

Toward the end of the Civil War in the spring of 1865, Quantrill and his band were surrounded outside of Louisville, Kentucky, where Quantrill was mortally wounded. He was placed in a Union hospital where he died a month later on June 6, 1865.

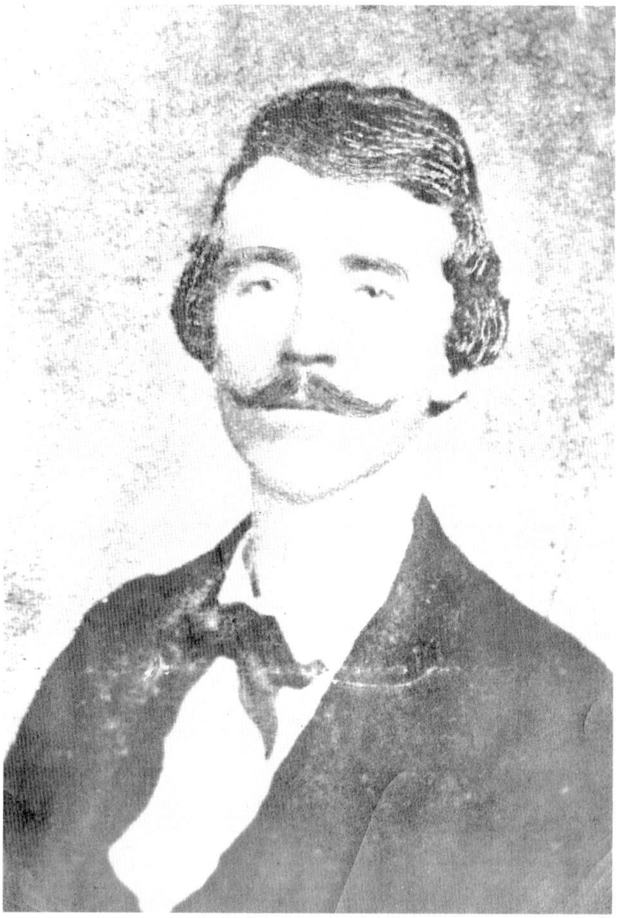

Mary Seneff and Ellen Athey

The night of May 28, 1880, would forever alter the lives of two women and their families in Dover. That night and the days that followed provided one of the most sensational murders and trials in Tuscarawas County history.

Prior to May 28, Mary Seneff (right) worked in the home of her employer and friend, Ellen Athey (left). She helped the overwhelmed Athey with her new baby and children and kept house. She also acted as a companion to Athey whose husband would occasionally be away for the night working in the local salt wells. That fateful night, something was different. Athey had begun to suspect that Seneff had an interest in her husband that was more than professional. When she confronted Seneff, the two women argued. In a fit of anger, Athey picked up an axe and attacked her helper. In a scene out of a horror movie, Athey murdered Seneff, striking her multiple times with the axe.

When she calmed down, Athey attempted to hide the body in the ash pile behind the family home. This solution proved only temporary as family members began to notice a foul smell after several days. Feeling desperate, Athey enlisted the help of her brother to move the body and toss it into the Tuscarawas River. Despite their efforts to weigh the body down, on June 15, it was discovered alongside the river. Athey, her husband, and her brother Alex Crites were all arrested for the crime.

Prior to the trial, Crites and Athey's husband were released, but Athey and her baby remained in jail. It was common in those days for a baby to be interred in a jail cell alongside its mother. In a bizarre twist, Athey escaped from jail at one point, leaving her baby alone, but was quickly recaptured. At the trial, Athey claimed self-defense, but the jury disagreed. Athey was found guilty and sent to the Ohio Penitentiary. She was later moved to the Ohio Asylum for the Criminally Insane, where she died in 1920.

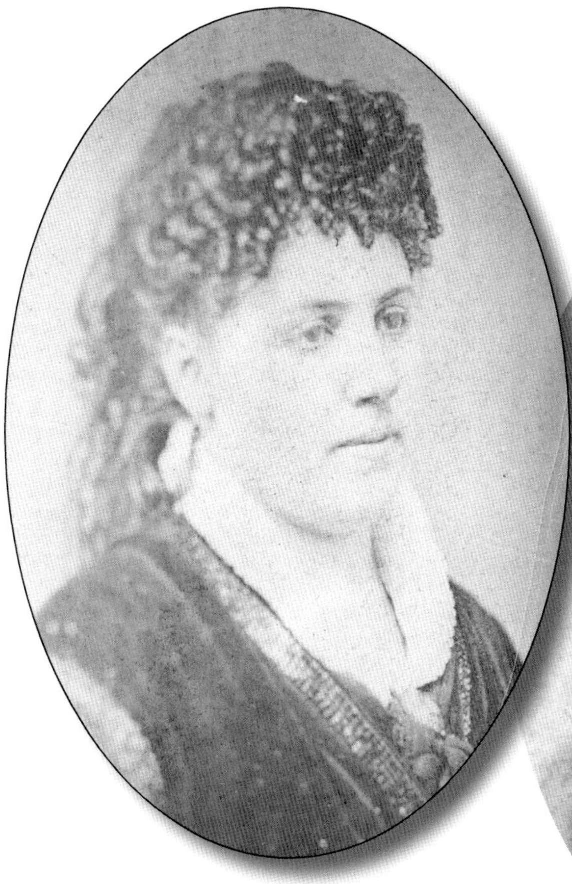

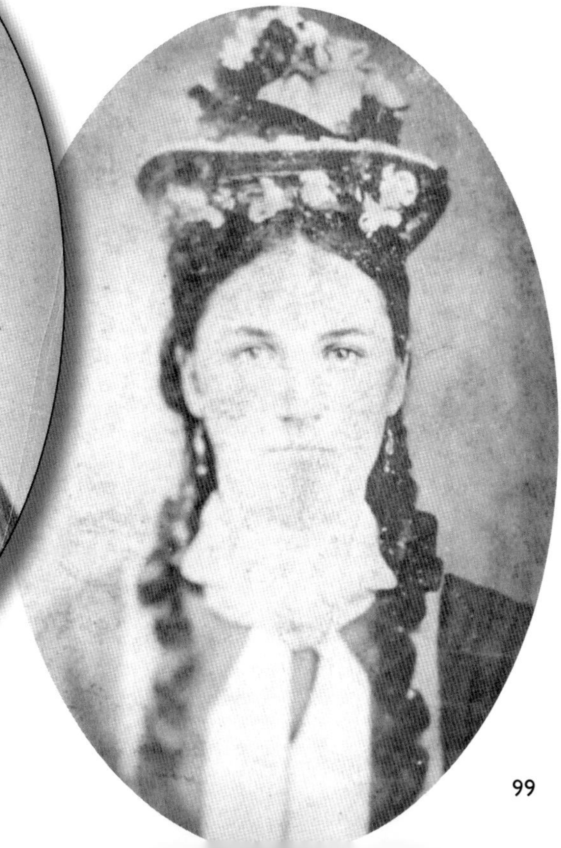

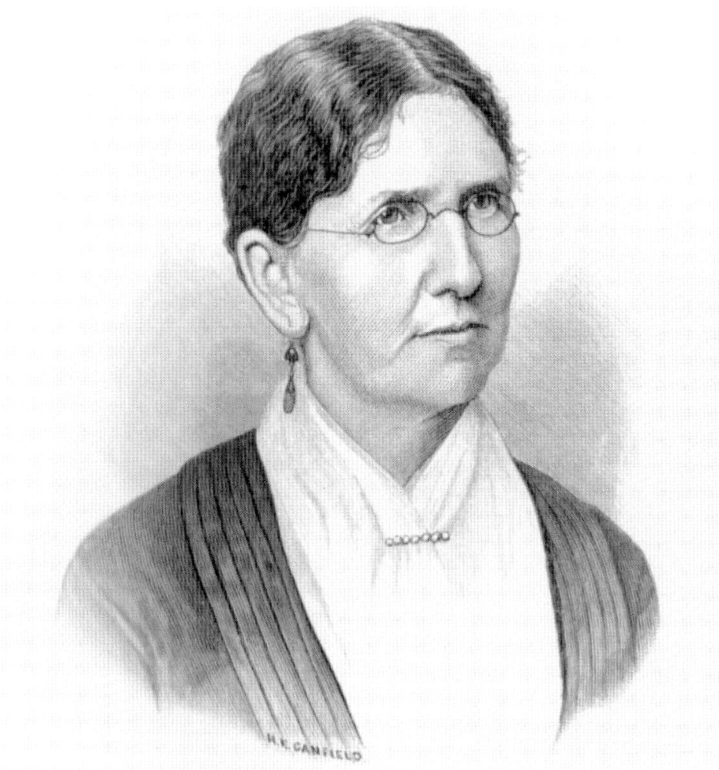

THE "MOTHER OF THE REGIMENT."

Catherine Whitacre Brashear

Catherine Whitacre was born in New Philadelphia on October 16, 1828. When she was just a girl, the family moved to Dover after the death of Catherine's father. While at Dover, Catherine's mother operated a boardinghouse.

After studying in Dover's public schools, she was trained as a teacher. She worked in this capacity until her marriage to Dr. B.B. Brashear in 1849. Dr. Brashear met Catherine while studying under her stepfather, a doctor, at Dover. The young couple spent the next 11 years in Dover, where Brashear had a successful medical practice.

In 1861, Dr. Brashear felt the calling of his country when war broke out with the rebellious Southern states. The couple put their children in the care of the Bethlehem Seminary in Pennsylvania and joined the war effort. Initially, Brashear was named the surgeon for the 19th Regiment, and Catherine was named the regiment's "matron." Like many Northerners, the Brashears assumed the war would be over by the end of their three-month enlistments.

When in the fall of 1861 the war showed no sign of a quick resolution, the couple made the difficult decision to reenlist. They were commissioned out of Camp Tiffin at Wooster, Ohio, in the late fall of 1861. Brashear was again asked to be the regiment's surgeon, with Catherine as its matron. Life in the 16th Ohio Volunteer Infantry (OVI) was difficult, and over the course of the next three years, Catherine suffered several illnesses and bouts of camp fever. Despite this, she showed an uncommon sympathy and caring for the soldiers of her unit. Over time, the men even began to refer to her as the "Mother of the Regiment."

After the 16th OVI was mustered out in October 1864, Catherine and her husband returned to Dover. Later, while living in Akron, Catherine Brashear took ill and died in May 1883. Her funeral was a grand event, and many of the former members of the 16th OVI turned out. She was buried at Akron's Historic Glendale Cemetery, where a monument was dedicated in honor of the "Mother of the Regiment."

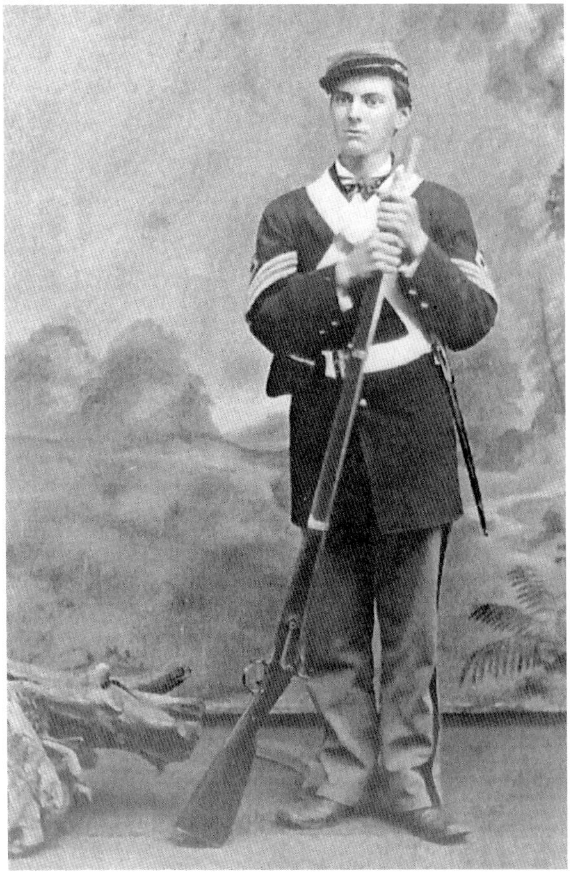

Rufus Ricksecker

Rufus Ricksecker was born on April 19, 1842, to Canal Dover jeweler Israel Ricksecker. As a boy, Rufus showed an aptitude for music and instruments, developing a talent for the violin. His family was deeply involved with the local Moravian church. They came to Ohio from Bethlehem, Pennsylvania, one of the two most important centers of the Moravian church in the United States.

When the Civil War broke out in 1861, Ricksecker joined the Dover Light Guards, serving as their orderly sergeant. Later, when the war did not end as quickly as many had thought, Ricksecker felt the call to greater service for his country. In June 1862, he mustered into Ohio's 126th Volunteer Infantry at Steubenville. Because of his education and strong writing ability and business sense, he was named commissary sergeant of the regiment.

Risksecker's time in service was not easy, and he struggled like many young men to deal with the sickness in camp. Twice between his enlistment and June 1864, he nearly died of disease. In June 1864, things seemed to be looking up for Ricksecker. That month, he was named first lieutenant of Company G 126th OVI. This promotion made him commander of his company. Three months later, Rufus Ricksecker led his company into action at the Battle of Opequan in Virginia's Shenandoah Valley. During the battle, Ricksecker was mortally wounded after being shot three times, once through the hand, once in the neck, and once in the abdomen. Although his men attempted to remove the injured man from the field of battle, Rufus asked them to leave him, as he knew that his wounds were fatal. Instead, the men took a number of his personal effects that could be sent home to his family. Ricksecker was buried where he fell on the battlefield, although many of the fallen were later exhumed and buried in the nearby National Cemetery at Winchester. Following the war, Dover's GAR Post was named in Rufus Ricksecker's honor. (Courtesy of Deborah Rinderknecht.)

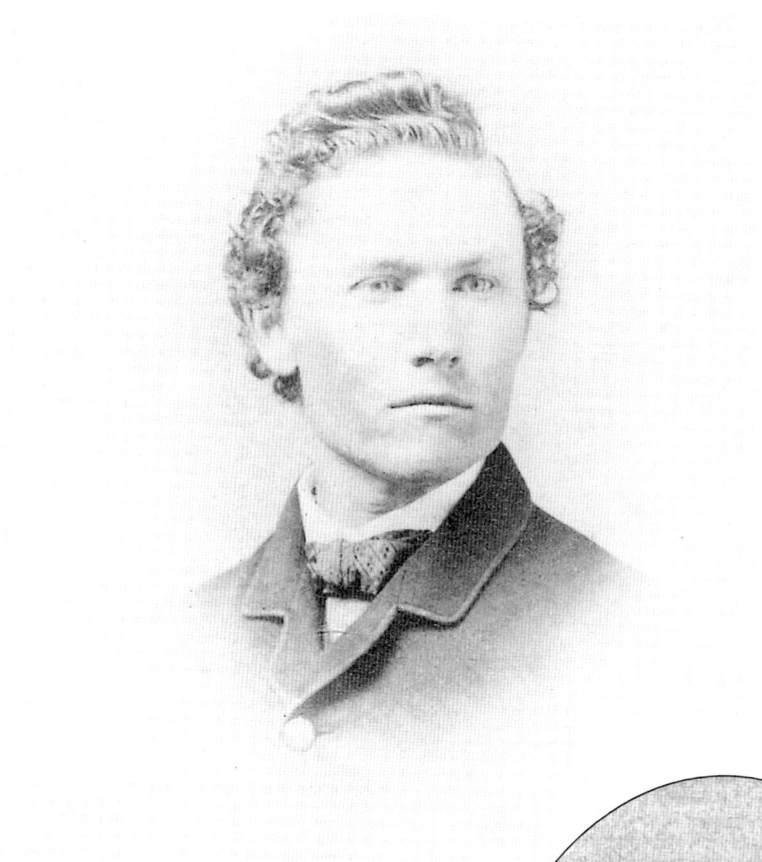

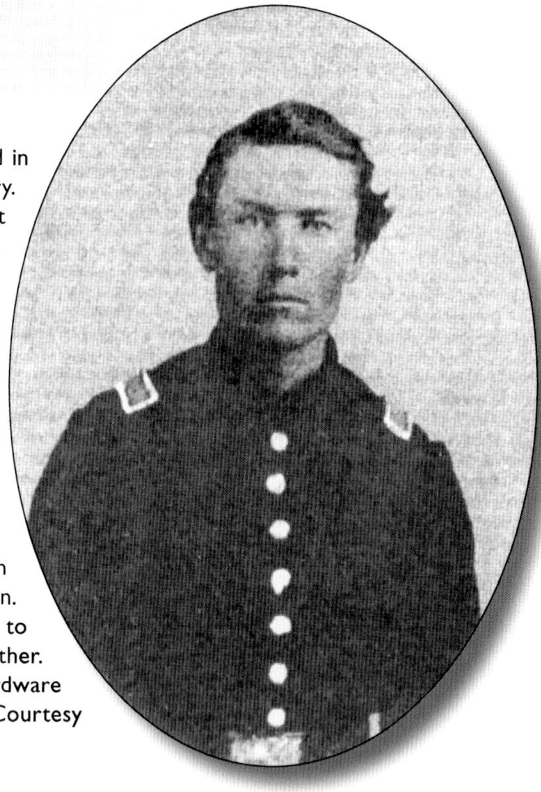

Capt. Charles G. Harger

Born July 20, 1839, Charles G. Harger enlisted in Company G of the 51st Ohio Volunteer Infantry. Mustered in on September 17, 1861, Harger spent his time as a private. After reenlisting for a three-year term at the end of October 1861, he was promoted to captain. After his service in the war, Harger remained in the South for a period of years. He formed an agricultural supply business and took advantage of the economic opportunities created by Reconstruction.

Most likely Harger was a carpetbagger. This was a derogatory term given to Northern businessman who worked in the South after the war. Whether it was the case with Harger or whether he faced any backlash from bitter Southerners, it will never be known. Nevertheless, he returned to Dover in 1873 to enter into the hardware business with his father. He continued in the Harger Brothers Hardware venture and also partnered in a planing mill. (Courtesy of Deborah Rinderknecht.)

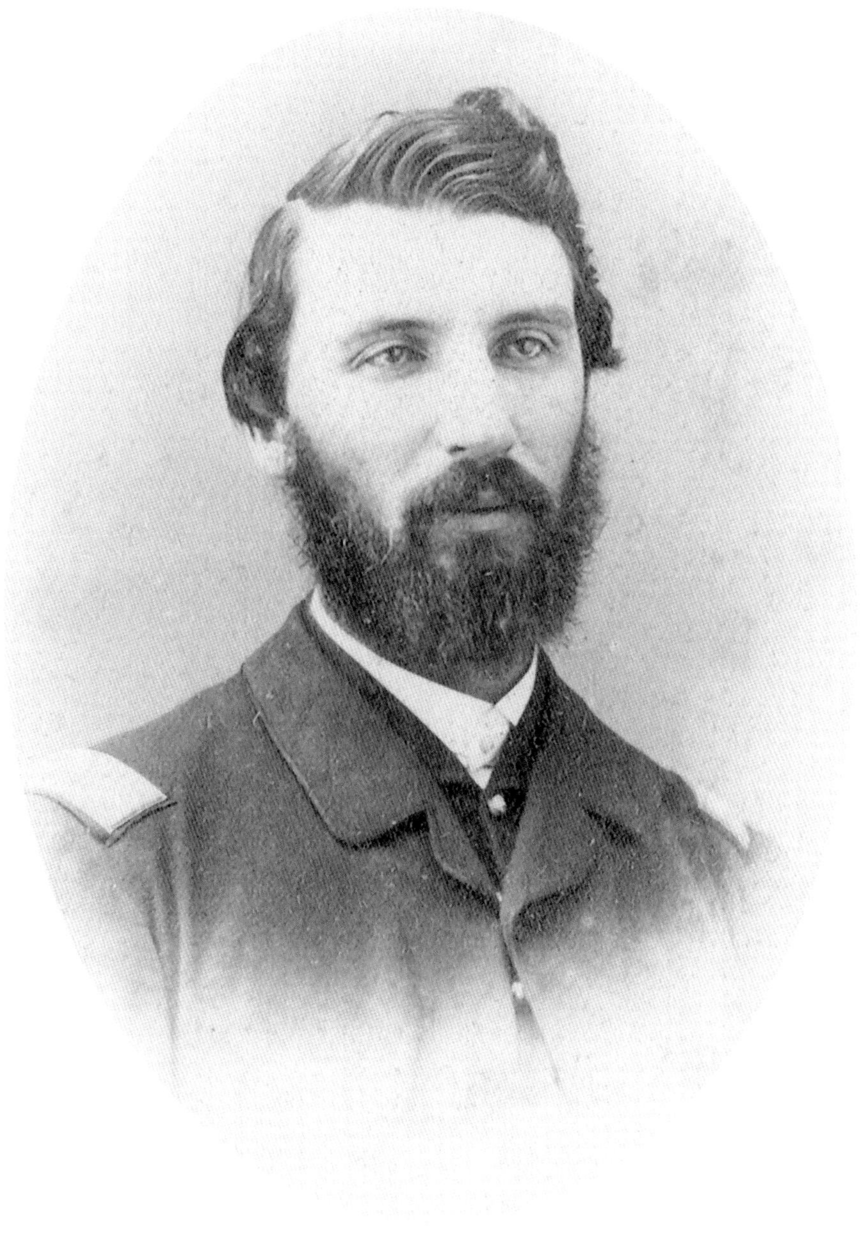

George H. Hildt

Like many men of his era, George Hildt felt a call to duty and an obligation to preserve the Union. Shortly after the war broke out in 1861, Hildt enlisted in Company F of the 16th Ohio Volunteer Infantry.

After the initial three months of the war ended, Hildt continued in his commitment and enlisted in Company I of the 30th Ohio Volunteer Infantry. By doing so, he was named a major in his company. He was later promoted to lieutenant colonel. Hildt was mustered in at Camp Chase in Columbus on August 18, 1862. During his service with the 30th OVI, George Hildt commanded his company at the Battle of Antietam, the siege of Atlanta, and another siege of Atlanta. It was during the later siege that Hildt's health failed. Once Atlanta was taken, George Hildt was forced to resign his post due to ill health.

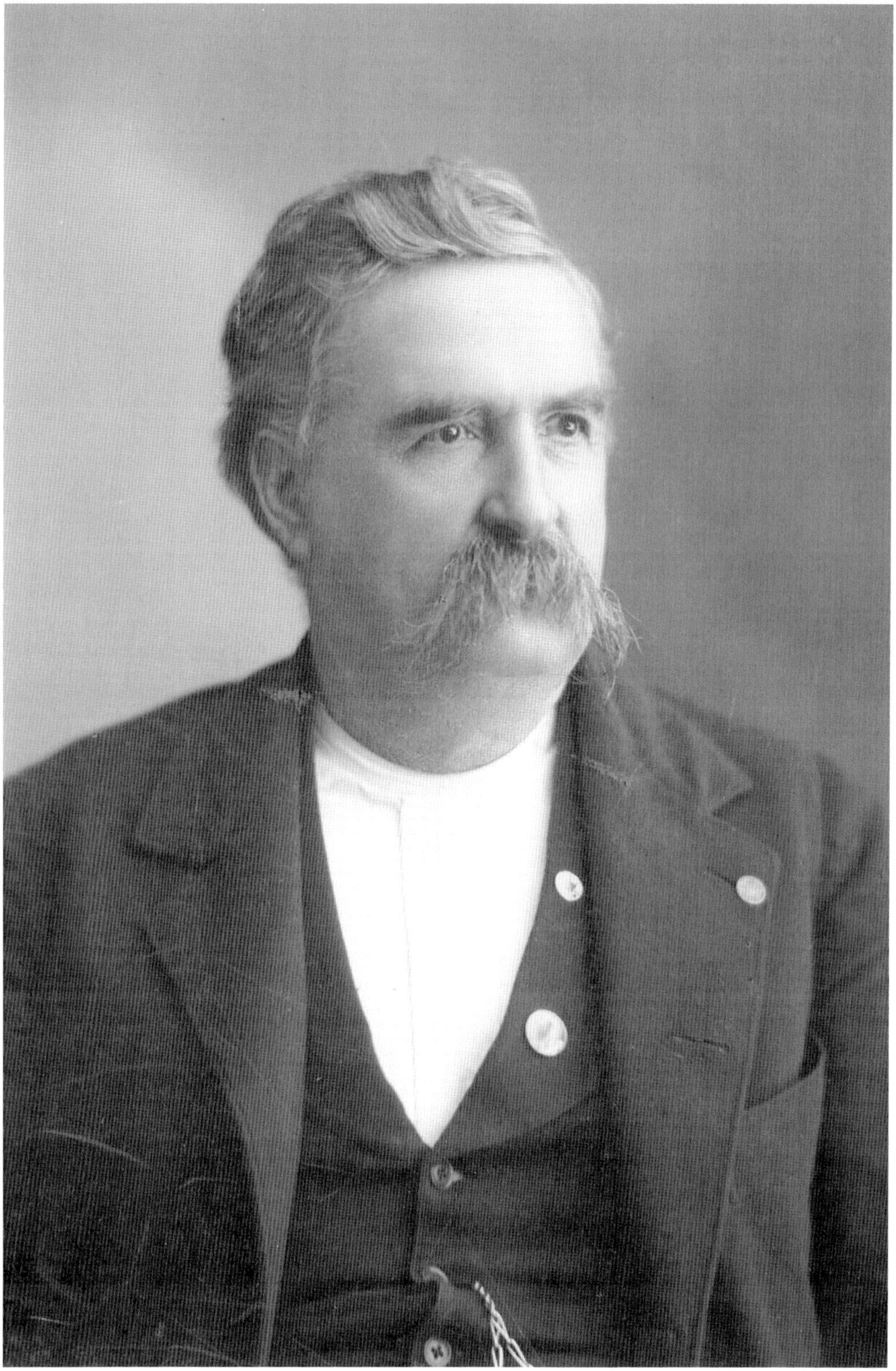

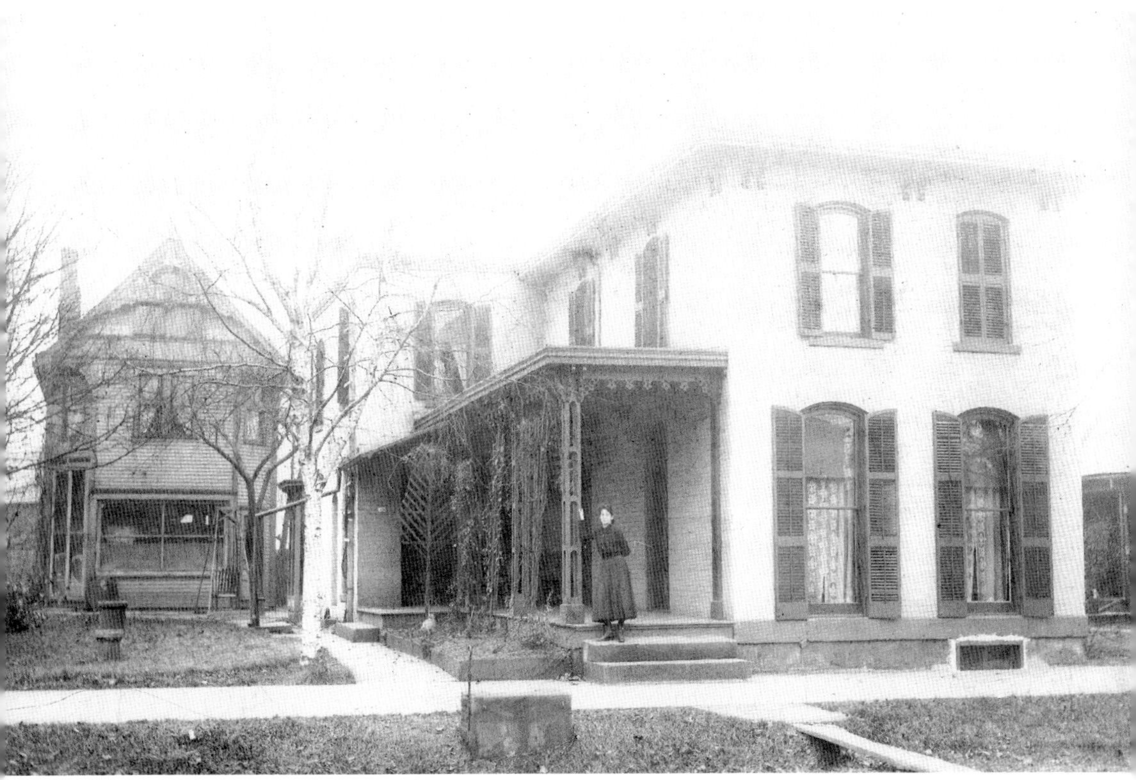

W.W. Scott (ABOVE AND OPPOSITE PAGE)
Born in 1838 in Dover, William W. Scott, or W.W. as he was better known, was a childhood friend of the notorious Confederate raider William Clarke Quantrill. At the age of 23, Scott enlisted as a private in Company G of the 16th Ohio Volunteer Infantry. Although, later that same year, he was discharged for a disability, Scott immediately reenlisted and spent the remainder of the Civil War as a hospital steward of the 12th Regiment of Regulars.

Following his service in the Civil War, Scott returned to Dover where he worked in the drug business, initially with Robert Figley and then with George W. Crites. For many years, Scott and Crites operated successfully in Dover.

Despite his success in the drug industry, Scott's real passion was as a newsman. After returning from the Civil War, he was a constant contributor to the local news, eventually taking over publishing duties of the *Iron Valley Reporter* in 1879. Scott was known for his sensational reporting and cutting edge editorials. Scott's final job was as Dover's postmaster, a position he held until his death in 1902. Pictured above is the Scott residence and the office of the *Iron Valley Reporter.*

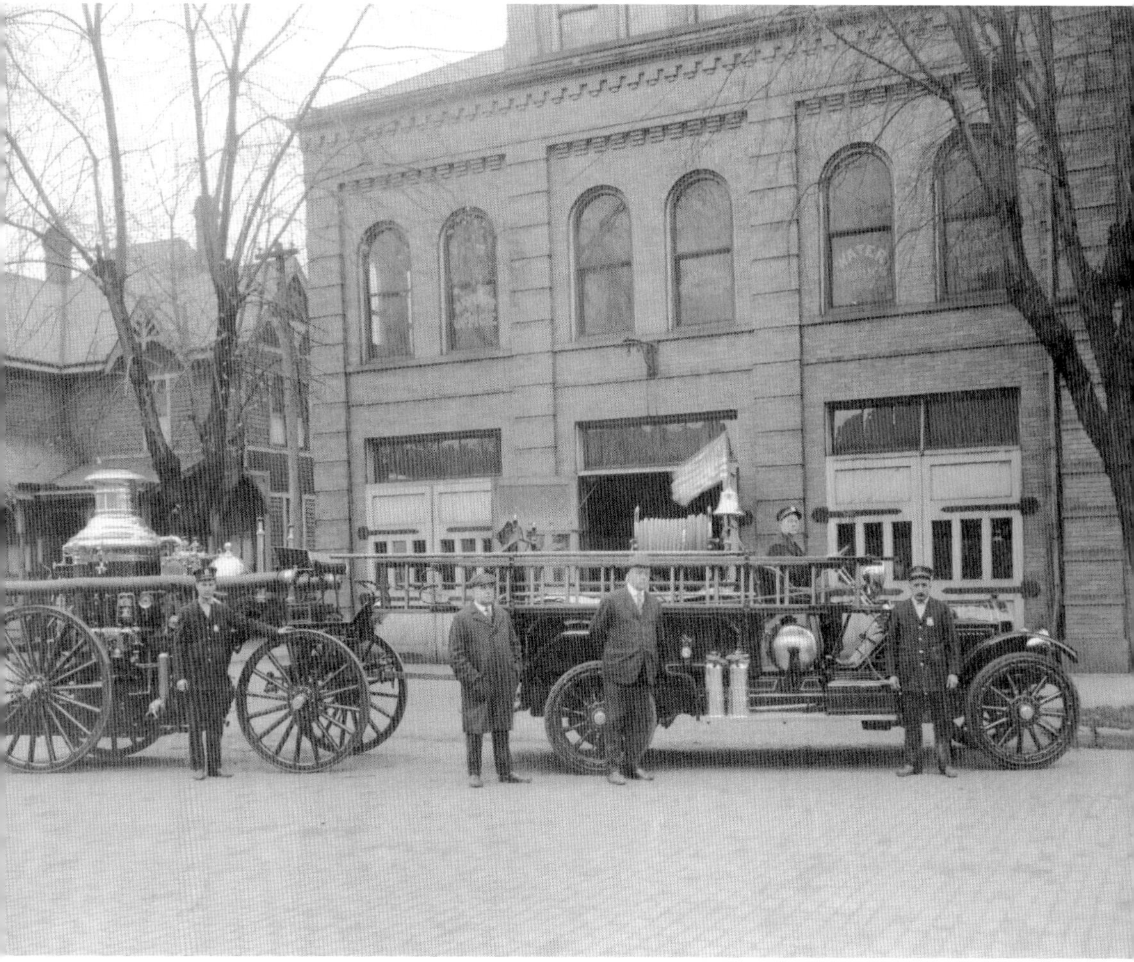

Walter H. Scheu

Born May 27, 1876, Walter H. Scheu (third from the left) rose to prominence in one of the more interesting decades of Dover's history. Among his service to the community, Scheu served as mayor from 1920 to 1923 and as postmaster from 1930 to 1934; he was also a member of the county board of elections. When he was not working on politics, Scheu worked as a paymaster at the American Sheet and Tin Plate Company.

What qualifies Walter H. Scheu for a book like this is the fascinating role he played during the early 1920s and Prohibition. The Prohibition movement in the United States began on January 16, 1919, with the passage of the 18th Amendment to the US Constitution. As time passed, and as the Depression deepened, the law against alcohol consumption became less popular. Prohibition was repealed with the passage of the 21st Amendment in December 1933.

First elected mayor in 1920, Scheu fell into the crosshairs of overzealous county prosecutor Bowers. Bowers successfully called for the resignation of many public officials including Dover and New Philadelphia's police chiefs and succeeded in indicting Uhrichsville's police chief. After Scheu refused to resign due to pressure from Bowers, he, too, was indicted by the county prosecutor on charges of receiving illegal liquor. Scheu would eventually beat the charges and was acquitted.

The climax locally of the Prohibition movement happened in 1921. In June of that year, the homes of both Prosecutor Bowers and Dover safety director Haug were bombed. Luckily, no one was injured. Two men were eventually convicted of masterminding the bombings and were sent to prison.

 106

Lindsay Williams

Prior to his election as mayor of Dover in November 1913, Lindsay Williams lived a fairly unremarkable life. The city directory of 1907–1908 lists him as a plasterer living on Dover's Tuscarawas Avenue.

Like many towns in the early 19th century, Dover had several other political parties in addition to the Republicans and Democrats. During this time, Dover's Socialist party saw an interesting upswing. During the elections in 1913, the Socialists won the mayor's office, council president, the auditor, and city solicitor positions. The city council beginning in 1914 was made up of four Socialists and three Democrats. At the time, Dover was the only Socialist-run town in the county.

In his election, Williams faced incumbent mayor T.P. Peters and former Republican mayor Daniel Defenbacher. When the votes were counted, Williams had 607, Peters 525, and Defenbacher 267. Lindsay Williams was the first and only Socialist mayor in Dover's history. Williams would serve the city in 1914 and 1915. His administration is remembered for very little. He stalled plans for both the construction of a new water works off of Seventeenth Street and put off purchasing steam engines for Dover's light plant. One accomplishment he is noted for is diverting state funds intended for a sewer plant and using the money to pave Dover's streets.

Throughout his administration, rumors abounded that the party, not Williams, was making all the decisions. There must have been some truth in this as Williams eventually became fed up with the Socialists and left the party. In 1914, he ran for reelection as an Independent. His old adversary Democrat T.P. Peters defeated him. Pictured is Dover City Hall around the time Williams was mayor.

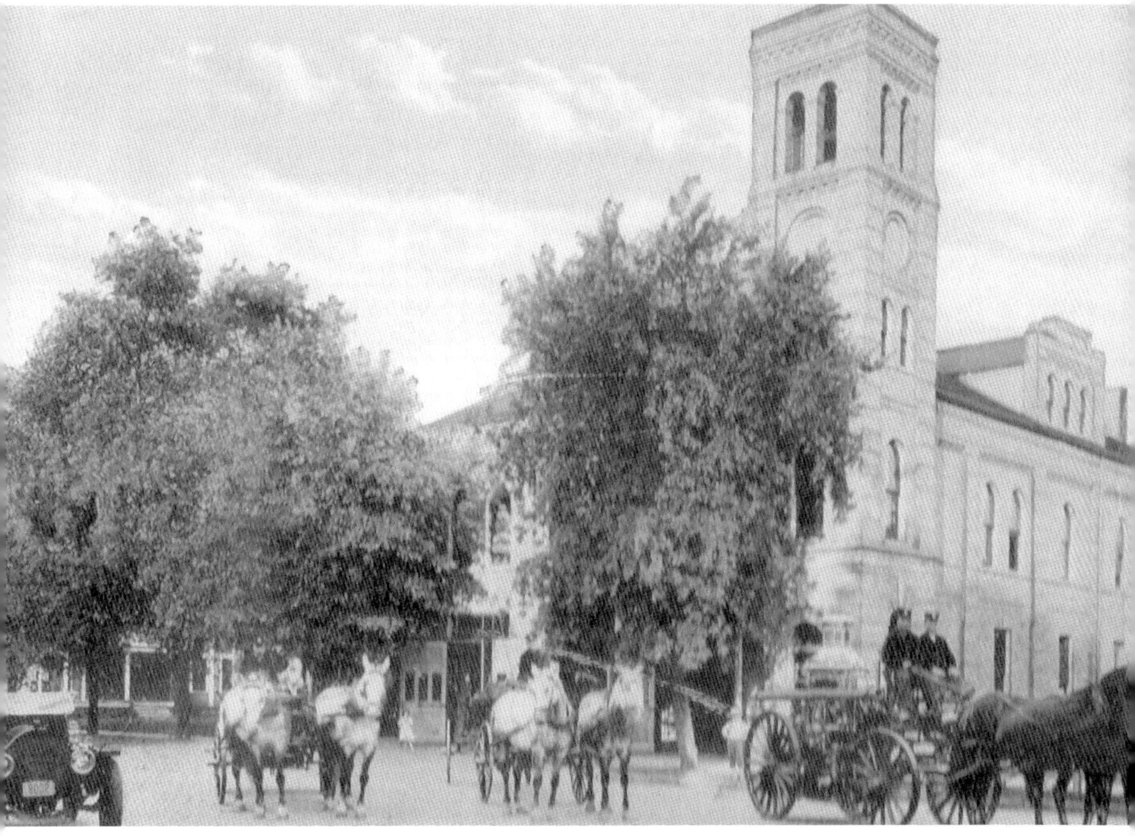

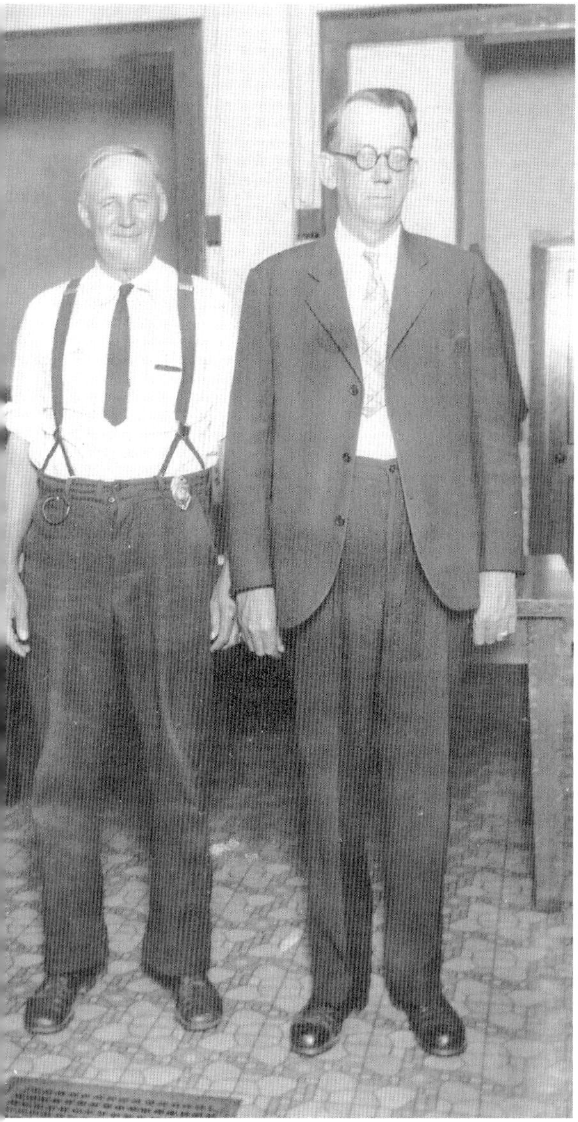

Peter J. Groh

Born in the late 1870s near Ragersville, P.J. Groh (right) moved to Dover just after the turn of the 20th century. His primary business in Dover was the Groh Insurance Agency, which he founded on West Second Street. Outside of his business interests, Groh held several local government posts. These include a stint as mayor from 1926 to 1929 and service as the justice of the peace from 1931 to 1950.

Perhaps what Groh is best known for is his rather controversial run as Dover's mayor. He was elected in 1926 and again in 1928. During his second term in office, on March 21, 1929, Groh was arrested by state Prohibition agents and charged with accepting a $50 bribe. Groh, Dover's mayor, was then forced to spend the night in jail before being released the following day on a $10,000 bond.

Two weeks later, at the recommendation of Dover City Council, Ohio governor Myers Cooper relieved Groh of his duties as mayor. That same month, Groh was indicted by a county grand jury. Stripped of his responsibilities, Groh focused on preparing for his trial. In May 1929, Groh's hearing was held in an electric atmosphere, and he was acquitted of all charges. Despite the court's finding that Groh was not guilty, he was never reinstated as Dover's mayor. Groh then chose not to run for the position in the November election.

Groh remained in Dover, operating his insurance business until 1949 and was elected Dover's justice of the peace in 1931. (Courtesy of Todd Groh.)

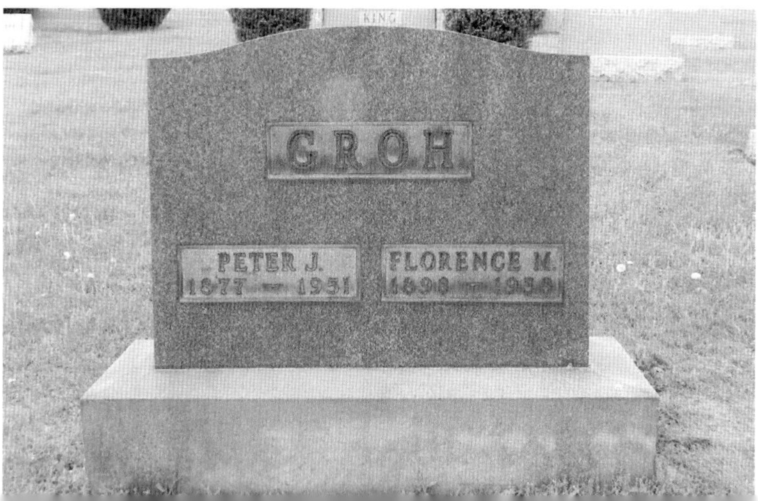

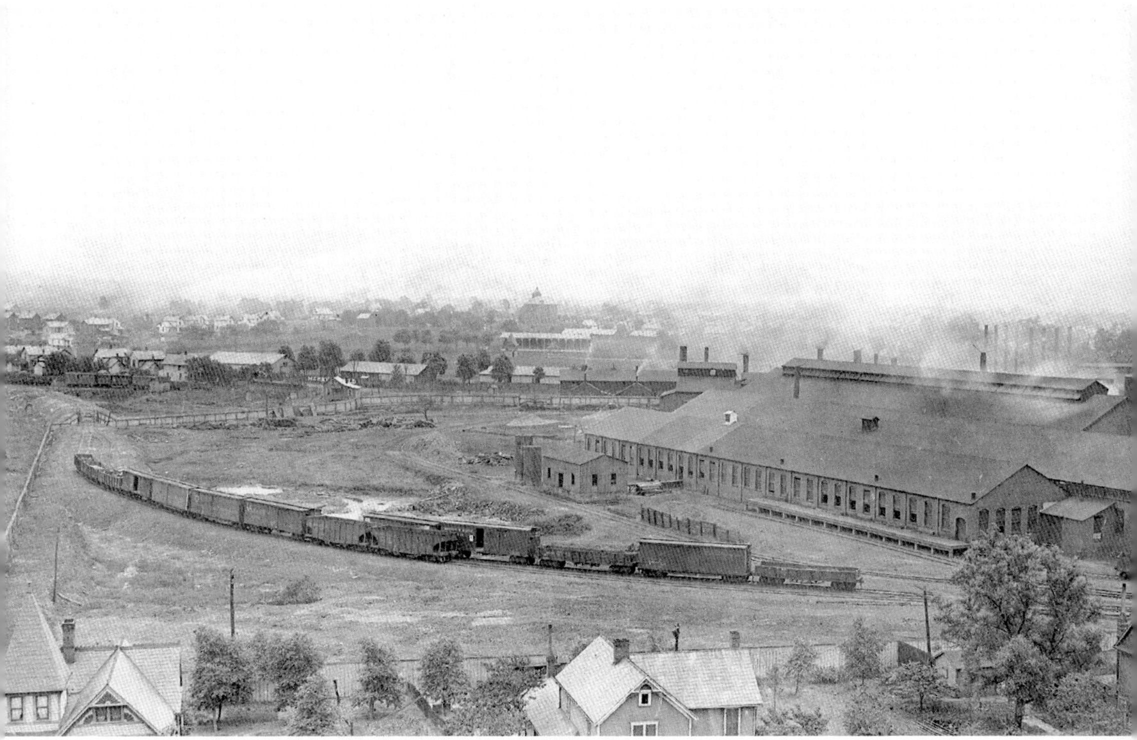

D. Alfred "Jack" O'Neil

Like many small industrial towns at the dawn of the 20th century, Dover dealt with violence associated with union versus nonunion employment. Union strikes were commonplace, and unfortunately, so was violence. Perhaps no single event left a more lasting impression than the shooting of striking union worker Jack O'Neil.

O'Neil was with a group crossing the Wooster Avenue Bridge when they encountered a group of nonunion strikebreakers. According to one source, the union workers had already had one row that evening with mill marshal Hiram Dotts, not long before meeting the nonunion men. The group that the union men met consisted of six out-of-towners from Pennsylvania. Because the men were nonunion, they were imported to cover the jobs left open by the strike. For obvious reasons, the men did not care for each other. A fight soon broke out, culminating in gunshots.

When the sheriff arrived on the scene, he found a mob gathered outside the home of Andrew Godfrey at 77 Front Street. The police also found two of the local union men shot. Jack O'Neil and "Rubber" McDowell were both injured in the melee. The police took the six Pennsylvania men into custody and dispersed the mob. The arrests were made as much to protect the outsiders as to actually charge them with the crime. While McDowell was able to recover after being shot in the arm, O'Neil died from his wounds two days later.

The funeral for O'Neil was one of the largest in Dover's history. It featured a parade of 600 mourners, the Reeves Military Band, and 25 young girls dressed in white with black sashes. O'Neil was interred at Maple Grove Cemetery. The six men initially arrested would never be charged with a crime; charges were eventually dropped because the investigators were unable to determine who fired the fatal shot.

Pictured above is the American Sheet and Tin Plate Company, where the striking men worked.

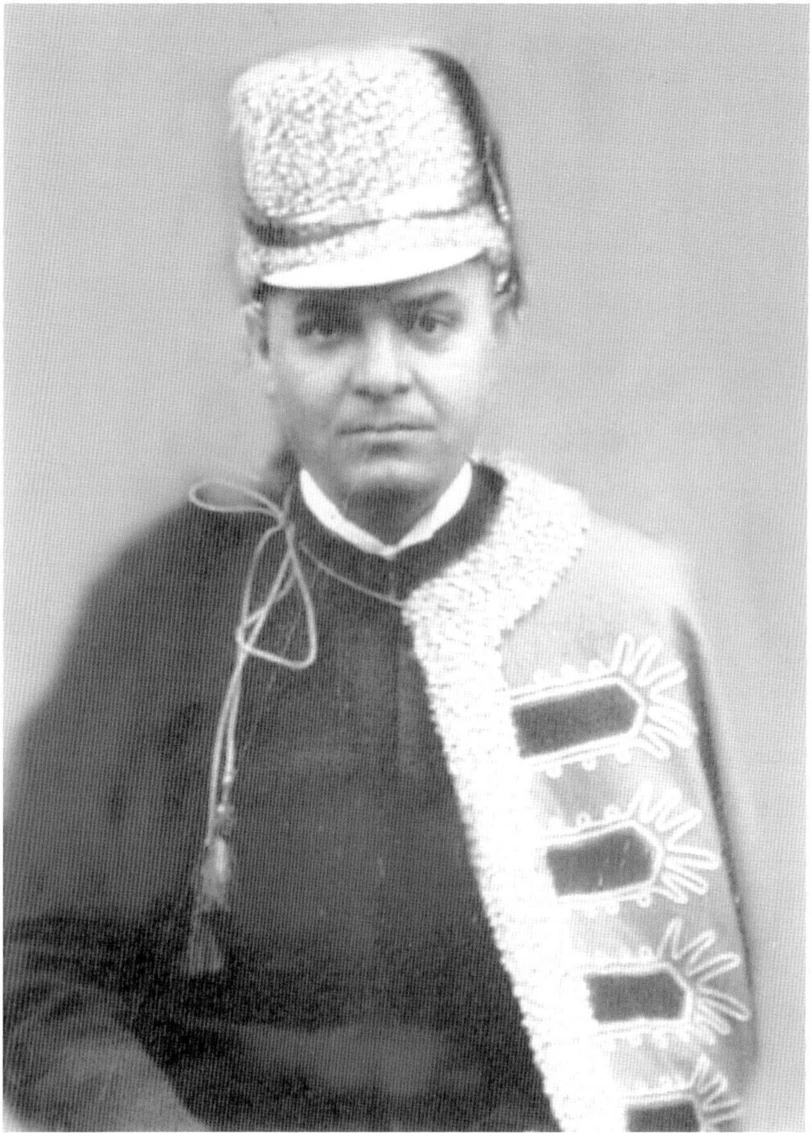

Dominic Greco

Dominic Greco was a true music lover. He carried this love with him when he moved to Dover in 1917. Almost immediately after settling here, he engaged the Italian community to form an Italian band that would play locally. After World War I, the band continued to grow and officially adopted the name the Dover Concert Band. By 1926, the band had begun to develop a reputation for quality in its performances. Feeling they needed uniforms that lived up to their performances, the Dover Concert Band members purchased dual-colored capes and plumed hats.

In the 1930s, their reputation continued to grow, and they performed six times at the state fair. Also during the 1930s, the band was photographed with then-governor and Tuscarawas County native Vic Donahey. In one of those memorable state fair performances, Dominic Greco's band performed on the same stage as the legendary John Philip Sousa Band. Dominic Greco conducted the Dover Concert Band for more than 40 years. In 1973, the members of the band voted to change the name from the Dover Concert Band to the Dominic Greco Band.

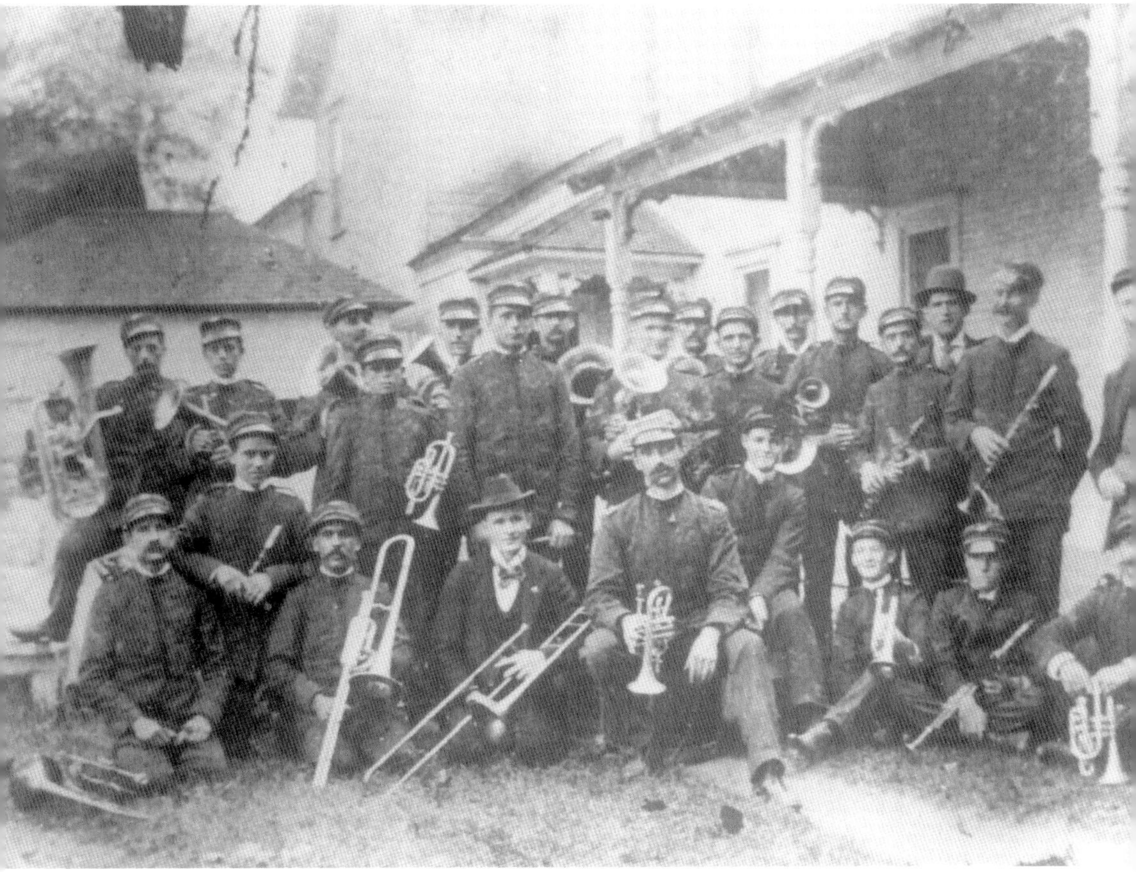

The Reeves Military Band

Formed in the 1890s and active into the first decade of the 20th century, the Reeves Military Band was an entertainment staple locally. The band's primary patron was Dover industrialist Jeremiah E. Reeves. The band also took subscriptions for its concerts that were given weekly during the summer. The repertoire of the band featured both group arrangements and excellent soloists. A typical program involved the band marching to several points and performing several numbers at each. Many times, this march included a stop in front of the Reeves home on East Iron Avenue, where they serenaded their benefactor. Among the more popular numbers the band played were patriotic songs and a rendition of "Old Kentucky Home" by baritone Joe Goodwin. The Reeves Military Band was easily recognized thanks to its unique uniforms. The uniforms were military blue, braided in black. The collars of their jackets were close fitting, and they wore caps with a "strop" visor and the letters R.M.R. monogrammed in gold.

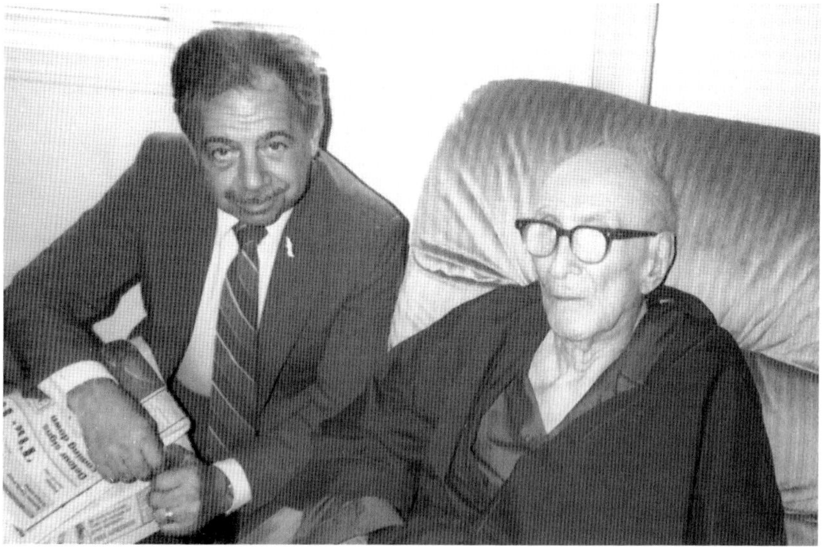

L.H. Alexander

Lawrence H. Alexander was born on April 10, 1890, in Jackson, Ohio. In high school, he played football, but his main activity was the piano. Beginning at the age of 10, he began lessons and quickly showed an aptitude for music. After high school, he attended the Oberlin Conservatory of Music. He graduated from Oberlin in 1913 and would later go on to do graduate work at Cornell University in Ithaca, New York.

After graduation, Alexander's first job was in Sullivan, Indiana. He remained in Indiana for three years before accepting a position at Dover's Roosevelt High School. At the time he began work at Dover in the fall of 1916 he was the school system's only music teacher. L.H. did not waste time once he was settled in. In his very first year at Dover, Alexander started the school's first orchestra, and in his second year, he created the marching band. Under Alexander's guidance, the band grew quickly, and in 1933, it competed in the National Band Contest at Evanston, Illinois. After its performance, the marching band was crowned Class B National Champion. Upon his return to Dover, the band was honored with a parade, and L.H. was given the key to the city.

Among his many other accomplishments, L.H. Alexander composed both Dover's Alma Mater and the school's fight song. After a 42-year career in education, L.H. Alexander retired in 1958. He would remain in the community throughout his long retirement. (Courtesy of Fred Delphia.)

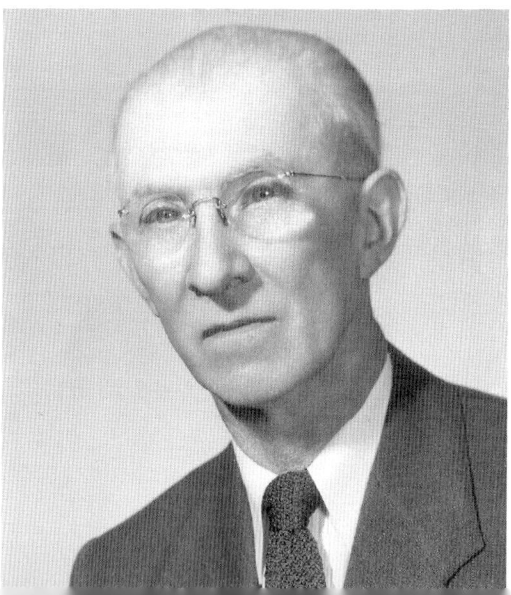

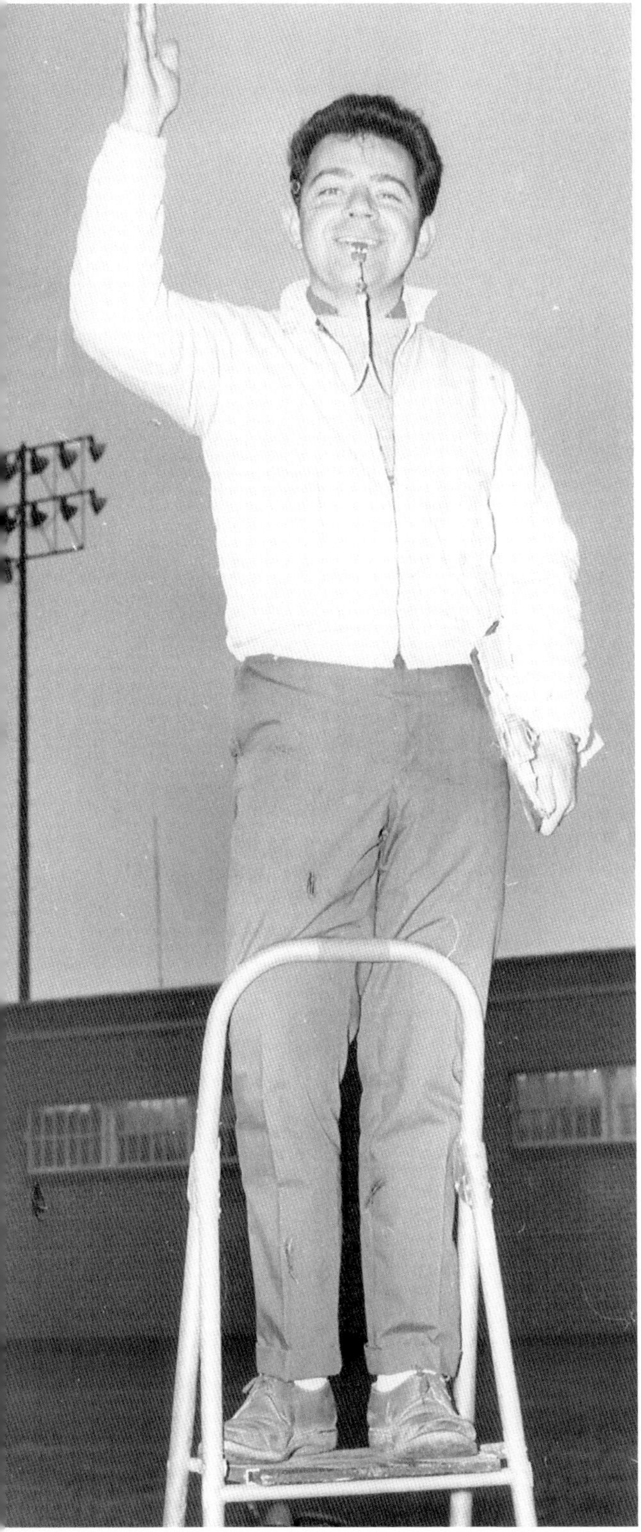

Frederick Delphia
Born in East Liverpool in 1938, Fred Delphia's life has nearly always involved music, and his passion for it has led him down many paths and opened many doors. After finishing high school at Steubenville in 1956, Delphia joined the US Navy as a musician. He trained at the Navy School of Music in Washington, DC, and, later, served aboard two heavy cruisers in the Mediterranean. His final year of service was spent in the Navy shipyard in Philadelphia.

Following his service to his country, Fred attended Ohio University. He graduated in 1964 with a degree in music. Later, he would attend the University of Akron, where he was awarded a master's degree in music supervision. Delphia's first teaching job was at Milan, Ohio, where he remained until 1966.

In the fall of 1966, Delphia was hired at Dover. He took over both the orchestra and band duties. He would remain in both positions until he moved into an administrative position in 1981. That year, he became Dover's assistant principal. Eight years later, he would rise to become the high school principal, holding this position until his retirement in 2000. Even with his rise in the ranks of Dover's administration, Delphia always remained active in music. Since the 1970s, Delphia has led the outstanding Dominic Greco Band. The Greco Band performs many shows throughout the summer months. It never fails to draw a crowd.

One of Delphia's favorite memories of his band years is when the Dover band marched in the 1975 Indy 500. With record-setting temperatures hovering near 90, many of the bands looked lethargic. That was not the case with Delphia's marching Tornadoes. As *Car and Driver* magazine later noted, "Most of the bands were struggling hard against the heat," but "the red-uniformed, white-feathered gang from Dover (Ohio) High School came high-stepping like they were on amphetamines." (Courtesy of Fred Delphia.)

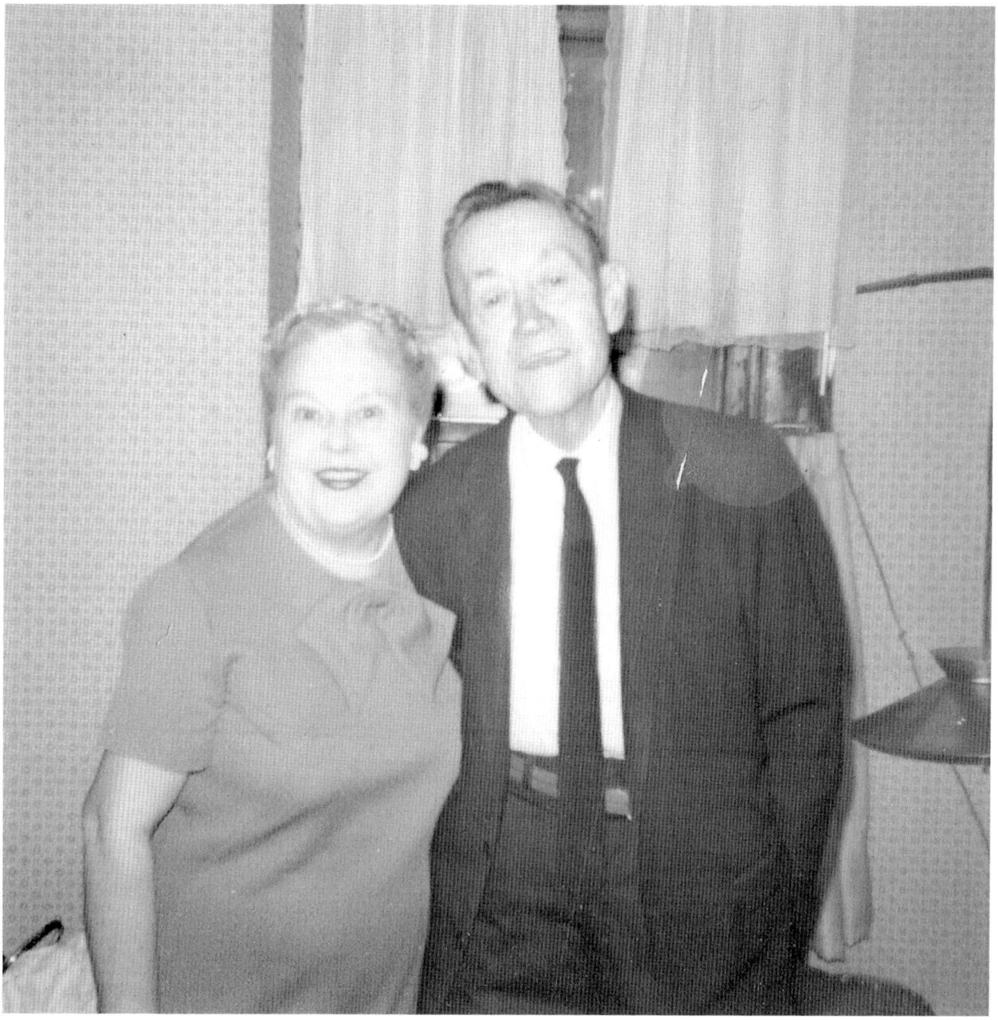

Henry Hagloch

Henry Hagloch was born on July 15, 1887, in the town of Maryville, Missouri. At the time of his birth, his parents, Isaiah and Margaret Hagloch, were working on farms in Missouri. When he was just a year old, his parents returned to Dover. Hagloch found his true calling in 1910, when he went to work in the newspaper industry. By 1913, he was a member of the staff of the *Reporter.* The majority of his 50-year career in the newspaper business would be spent there. By the time he retired in 1960, he was the *Reporter*'s editor, despite having no formal training in journalism. Henry Hagloch learned his trade by doing it.

Outside of the newspaper, Hagloch was an enthusiastic local historian. He helped organize the Dover Historical Society, and in 1956, he collected all of his historical articles to form his *History of Tuscarawas County*, which was published by the Dover Historical Society. (Courtesy of Les Williams.)

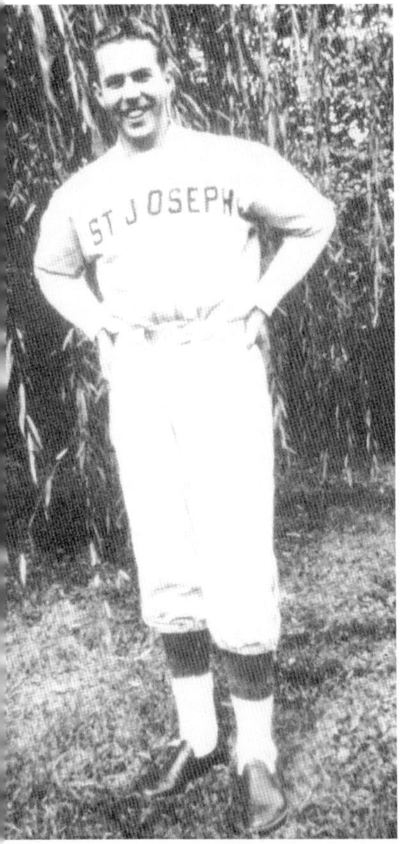

Max Krantz

Max Krantz was born on April 12, 1917. He attended St. Joseph's High School in Dover, graduating in 1933. After high school, Krantz attended Fenn College in Cleveland. After college, he took a job with the Weigand Companies in 1935. He spent the next 30 years with the company, eventually rising to the position of director.

In 1965, Krantz decided to try something different. After resigning from Weigand, he founded several of his own companies. Included in these business ventures was the Dover Transportation Company. He eventually retired in the 1980s, selling off many of his businesses and working as a consultant locally with companies like Baker Highway Express. Despite his retirement, Krantz still had the drive to work and would later founded two additional companies. One of these, EMKO Leasing, he ran well into his eighties.

Outside of business, Krantz was a civic leader within the community. He served on the commission that located Interstate 77 and was active with Union Hospital and Tuscarawas Valley Comprehensive Mental Health, CIC, and the local Kiwanis club. Krantz also worked with St. Joseph's to found the school's first football team, served for a time as a coach, and was one of the founders of Dover's Little League. Despite all of Krantz's accomplishments professionally and with his community service, many know him for the gardens he kept at his home on Fourteenth Street in Dover. For many summers, Krantz's award-winning gardens were open to the public. His green thumb would eventually earn him an award for Ohio's Most Beautiful Garden given out by *Ohio* magazine.

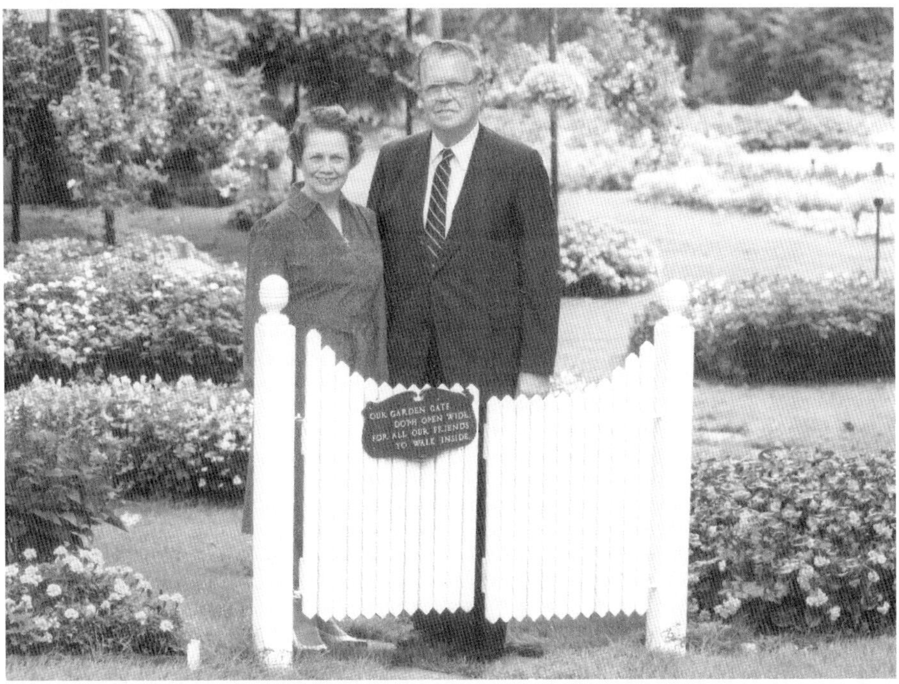

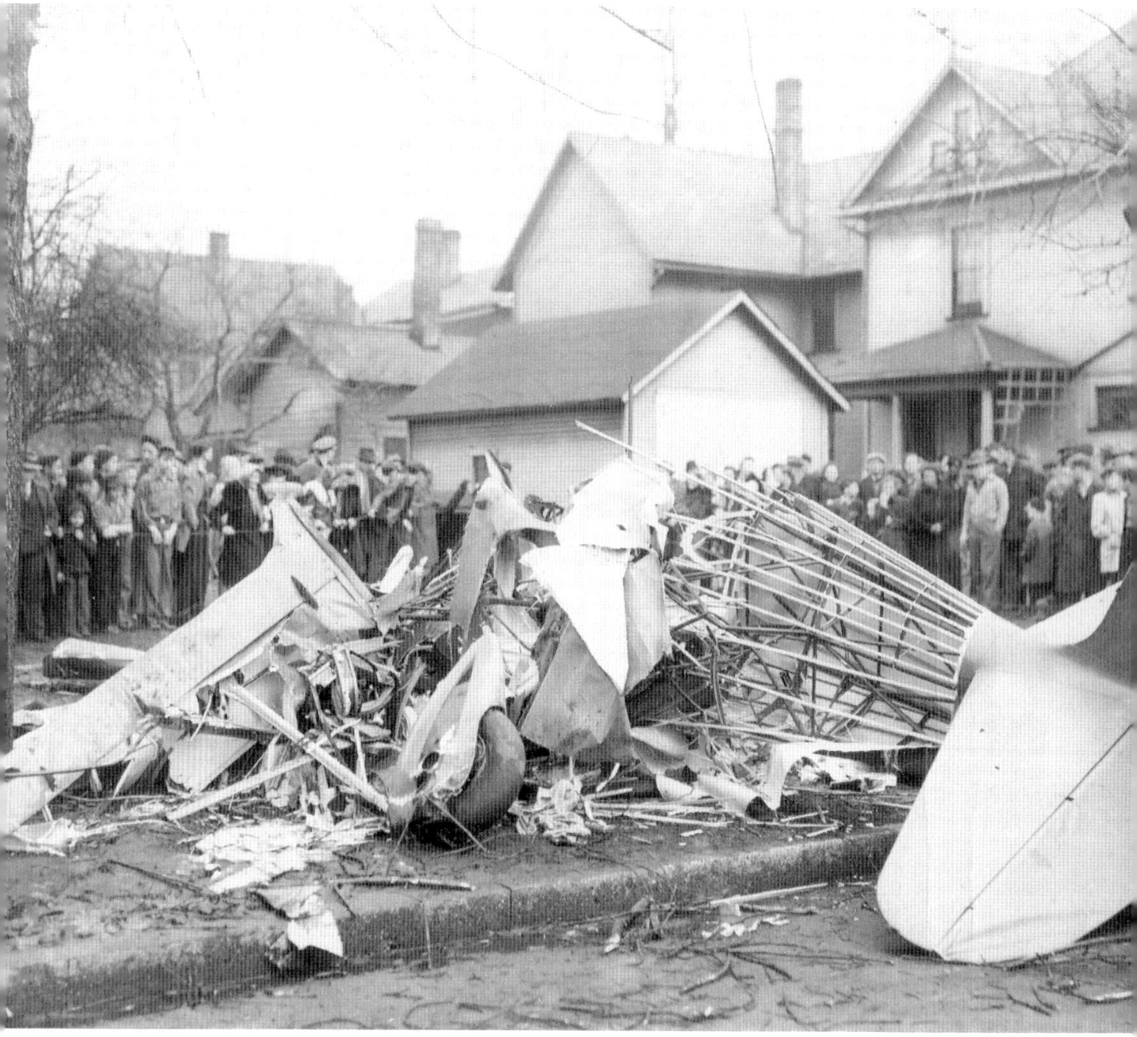

Adam "Addie" Wendling

One of the most tragic events in Dover's history during the 20th century is the plane crash that killed Addie Wendling, Edward Early, and Early's son Ed Jr. Addie Wendling was serving as the commander of the Tuscarawas County Air Patrol during World War II. One of the responsibilities of the air patrol was to spread information over the area. Many times, this was done by dropping leaflets over the city. On one such mission, on January 23, 1943, Wendling and his passengers took off from New Philadelphia with the plan of dropping flyers to promote a new film that was being shown at Dover's Bexley Theater. The film was about the War Bond program. Tragically, for Wendling and his passengers, the plane had mechanical difficulties just after crossing the Tuscarawas River. The engine stopped, and the plane crashed on Walnut Street near Second Street. All three were killed instantly.

With Wendling's death, the community lost not only an active supporter of the war effort, but they also lost an important local businessman. Wendling was the proprietor of the Wendling Brothers Construction Company. His company was responsible for the construction of Dover High School, the old Wooster Avenue Bridge, New Philadelphia Airport, the Bexley and Quaker Theaters, and the Dover Elks Lodge.

116

Josephine "Grandma" Zifer

Josephine Zifer was born in the Village of Oriolo, Cosenza, Italy, on January 5, 1898. Even today, Oriolo is a small village of less than 3,000 people. It is located in the southern end of Italy in the Calabria Region. Calabria is a typical Mediterranean area with rich agricultural blessings including abundant olive and orange groves.

Josephine Zifer came to the United States in 1916, passing through Ellis Island. Once arriving in Dover, in 1923, she and her husband, Antonio, or Anthony as he would later be known, operated a grocery on the Boulevard in Dover. Together, they operated the grocery and a restaurant until 1966, when Anthony died. A year later, with the help of two of her grandsons, Josephine opened Grandma Zifer's Pizza Shop. The pizza quickly became a favorite, as did the business's matriarch. Grandma Zifer's Pizza operated for many years on the Boulevard in Dover, with Josephine contributing and working in the kitchen well into her nineties. At the time of her death in 2002, Josephine had reached the age of 104. (Courtesy of Ray Hisrich.)

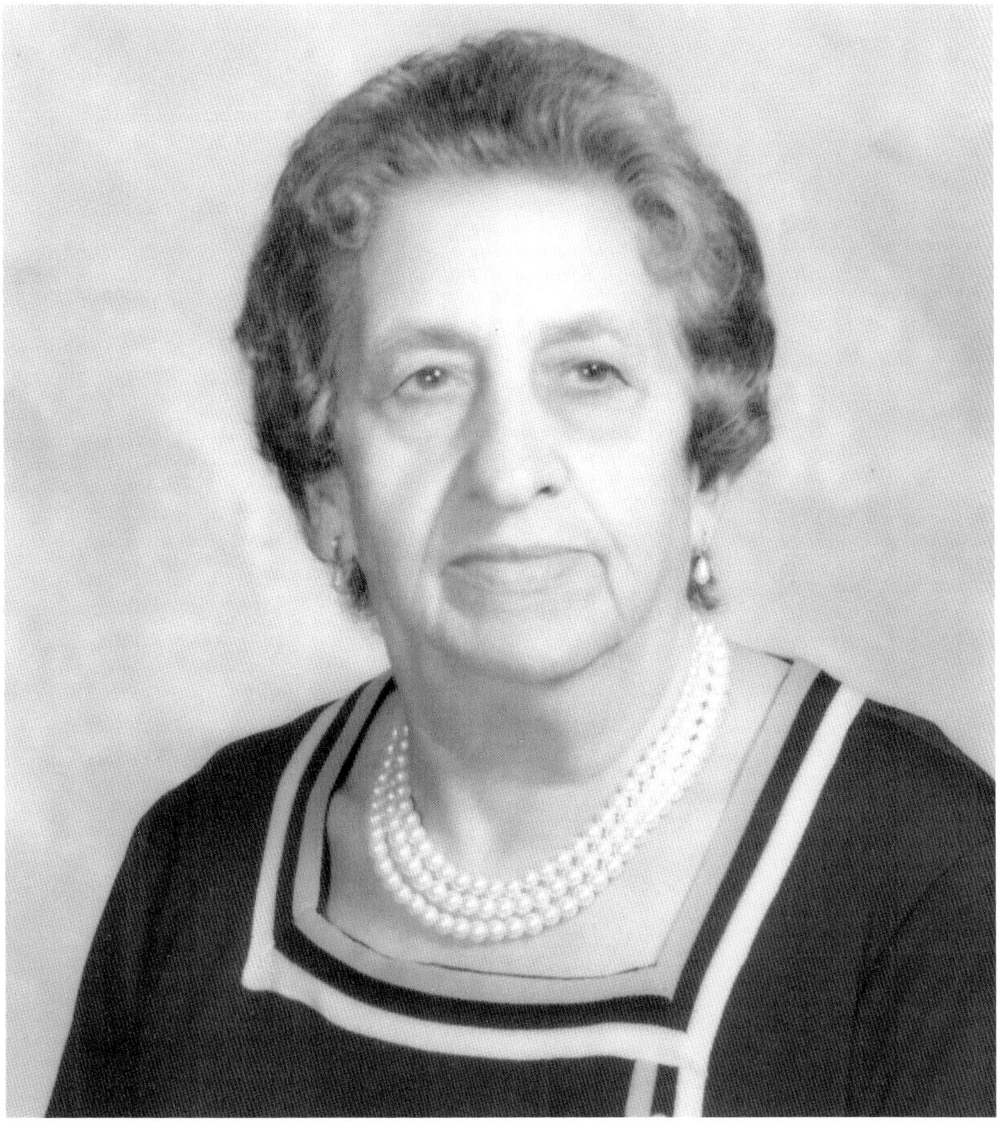

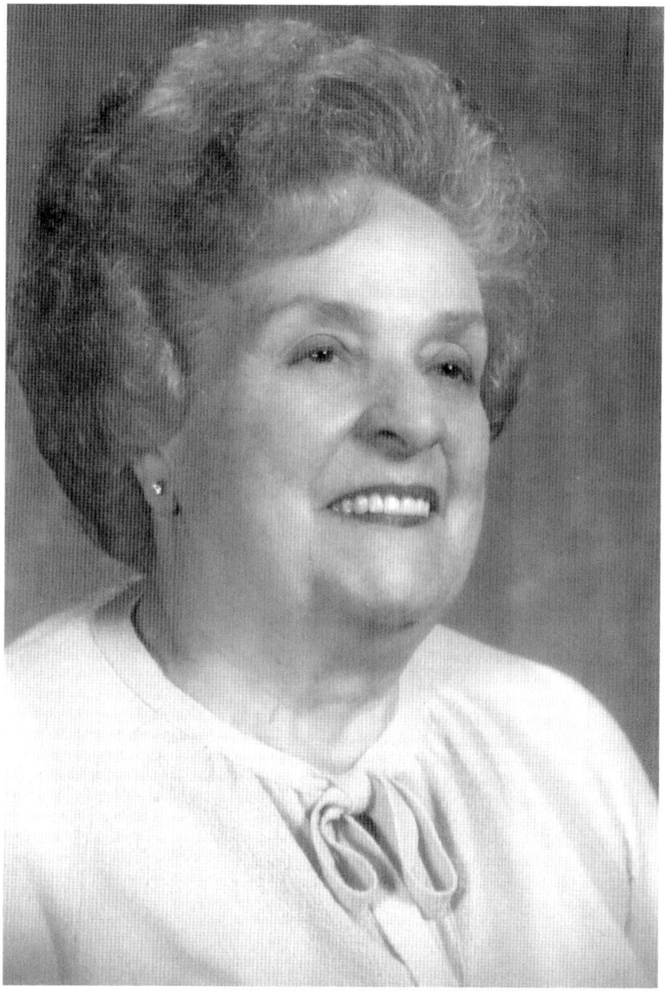

Mary (Tornabene) Zifer

Born on August 5, 1910, Mary Tornabene attended New Philadelphia's Central Elementary School through the sixth grade. Her father, Natale Tornabene, operated Tornabene's Italian Import Store in New Philadelphia. When she was 12, Mary moved to Elyria, Ohio, to live with an aunt and uncle. She would return to the area a few years later and meet her future husband, Joe Zifer. Mary and Joe were married on November 27, 1926, at Dover's St. Joseph's Church. Mary Spent a period of years working for US Quarry and Tile. During this time, she periodically made homemade dishes to the delight of her coworkers. In those days, pizza shops were a new phenomenon; however, that changed after World War II as the pizza industry began to grow.

In 1953, after a layoff at the ceramics plant, Mary decided to go into business for herself. In the early years, she made pizzas out of her home kitchen and distributed them through her father's store, Navarre IGA, and Stallard's and Riggle's markets. The business quickly grew, and soon, Mary had enclosed the porch of her North Tuscarawas Avenue home, where she opened her first pizza shop. Mary Zifer's Pizza was also the area's first pizza delivery service. Mary's husband, Joe, would take pizzas to workers at the Reeves Manufacturing Company, Greer Steel, Shenango, and General Electric.

The pizza shop proved a family business, and soon Mary's children had opened several additional locations. Mary retired in 1976 and died in 1994, but her legacy lives on as well as her pizza. Mary's original Peerless oven is still in use at Mary Zifer's Dover location and continues to turn out great pies.

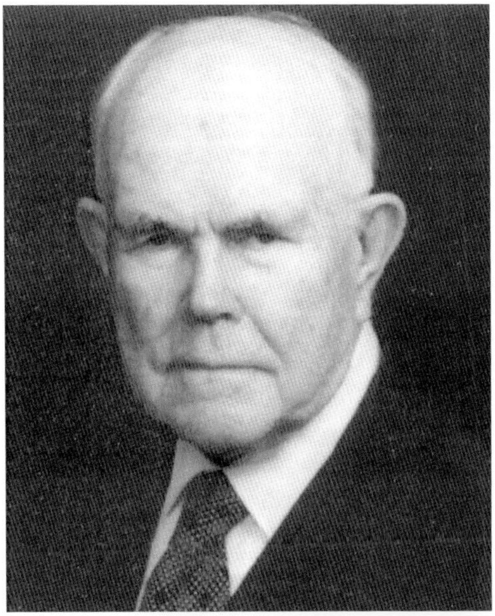

Johann J. Zabka

At once, the budding artist, poet, and historian Zabka loved his adopted home. Born in Sohrau, Germany, on March 11, 1911, Zabka lived through extraordinary times. After the conclusion of the World War II, Zabka worked as a machinist for several years while dreaming of immigrating to the United States. His dream became reality in 1952, with the assistance of Dover's Grace Lutheran Church. The church also helped Zabka find work. He was hired at Gradall, where he remained for the next 19 years. After his retirement from Gradall, Zabka became passionate about Tuscarawas County's history. He was active with the Tuscarawas County Historical Society, where he founded the Zeisberger-Heckewelder Medal. In addition to his work with the historical society, he penned his own autobiography, titled *My Determination*, and an epic poem of Tuscarawas County. (Both, courtesy of John Nelson.)

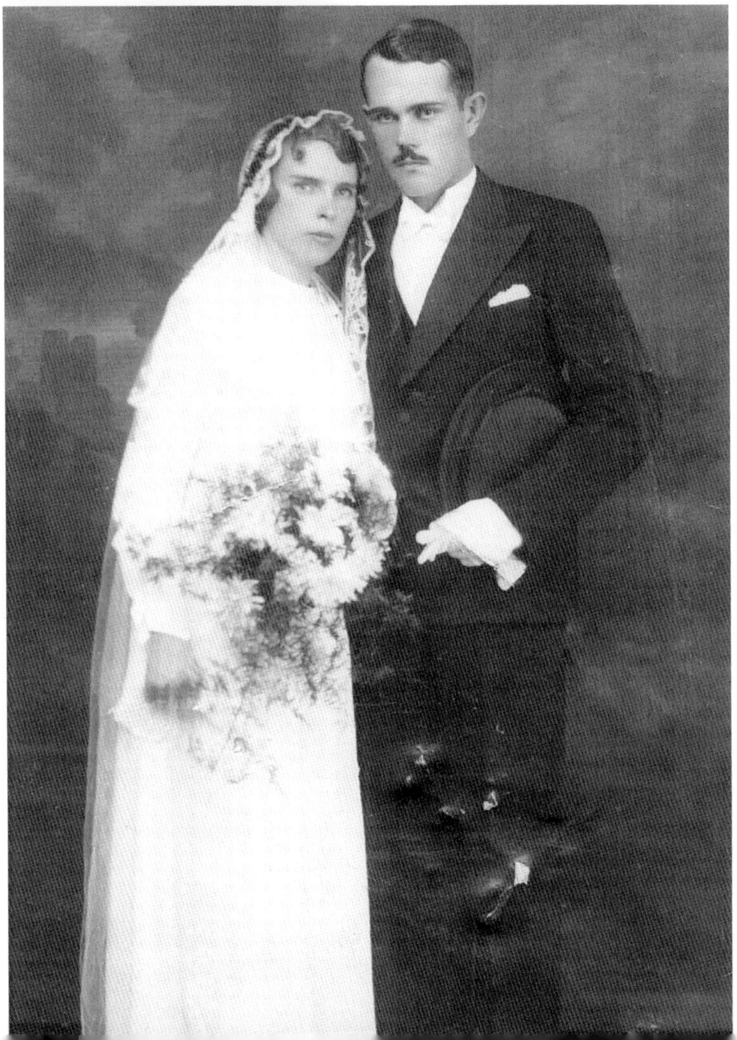

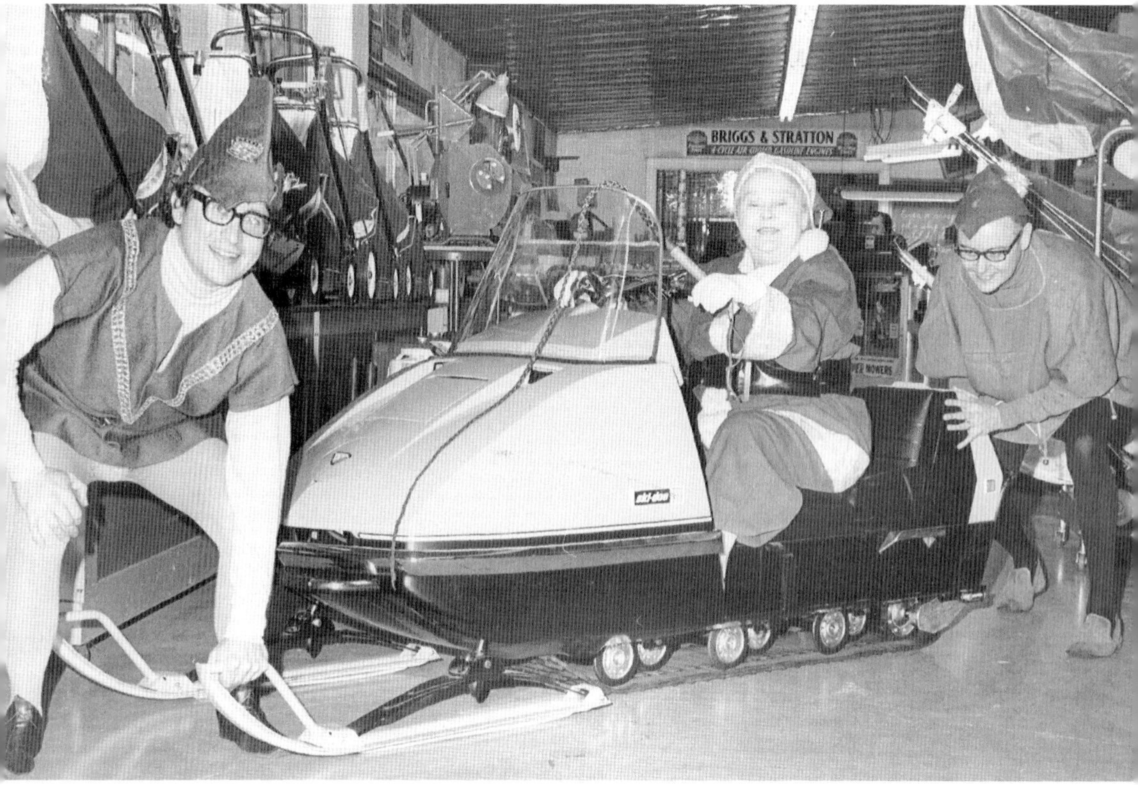

Fannie Marlowe

Born in 1899 in Sherrodsville, Ohio, Fannie Marlowe became one of Dover's most beloved citizens. Recognized for her kindness, in 1974, the residents of Dover turned out to honor her as part of "Fannie Marlowe Day." Held to celebrate her 75th birthday, the day sought to repay the kindness of a woman who was long a fixture of Dover's downtown landscape.

A graduate of New Philadelphia High School, Fannie Stratton married William "Mac" Marlowe on February 25, 1920. After their marriage, the couple moved to Cleveland, where they lived for several years. In Cleveland, Mac attended Western Reserve University to study pharmacy. Fannie, too, worked in those early years and developed a sense of caring customer service. The William Taylor and Sons Clothing Store employed her.

Later, the couple decided to return to Tuscarawas County and open a pharmacy in downtown Dover. When they first opened in 1931, many did not expect the young couple and their business to last. The hours were long, and with few staff, the couple spent all of their time at the store. Their big break came when they decided to install a soda fountain at Marlowe's and begin selling ice cream and other snacks. Although it meant having the store open from 7:00 a.m. to midnight, it allowed the store to thrive. Now, they could supplement their prescription business with income from hungry moviegoers just out of the Bexley Theater.

After her husband's death in 1952, Fannie carried on with the help of her sons Dave and Jerry, eventually growing the business to three additional stores. Fannie remained active in the business until her retirement in 1986. Away from the business, Fannie was an active part of the community. This involvement earned her the Exchange Club's Golden Deeds Award.

Probably the greatest story of Fannie's kindness comes with her famous baked great northern or lima beans. For many years, Fannie would make her famous dish for families who had lost a loved one. At one point, she was circulating more than 20 pans of her famous dish at a time and would receive daily calls from two local funeral homes. (Courtesy of Jerry Marlowe.)

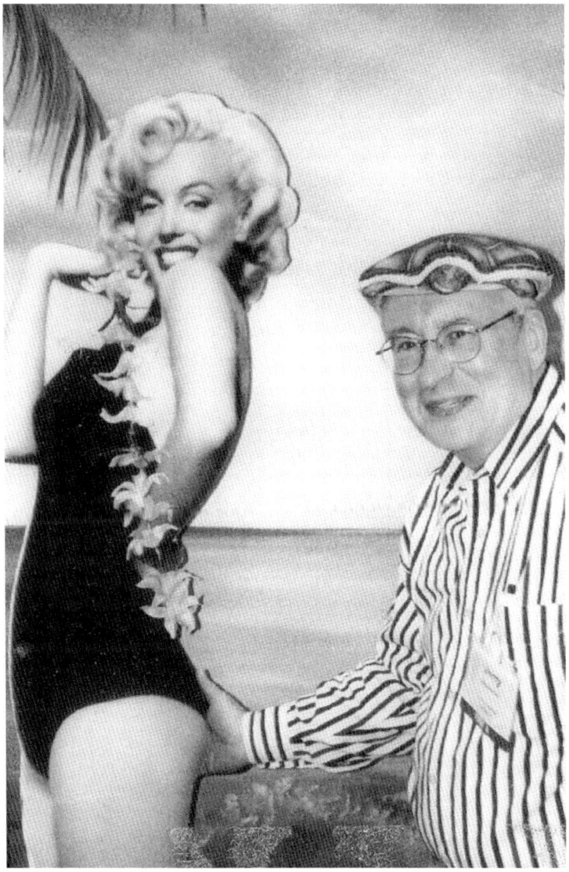

Jerry Marlowe

It is quite possible that Jerry Marlowe is one of the most interesting men to have ever called Dover home. Born in Dover February 12, 1936, to Fannie and Mac Marlowe, Jerry grew up in the family business. Jerry attended Dover High School before taking what many would describe as the scenic route through college. Although he started his work toward a degree in pharmacy in 1954, he did not finish until seven years later. He received his pharmacy degree in 1961.

On the surface, Jerry is a mild-mannered pharmacist; however, he never lost his childish enthusiasm for life. Among his interests are a love for cooking and his title as Ohio State's No. 1 gate-crasher. Jerry studied at both the Culinary Institute of America in New York and Le Cordon Bleu in London, England. Recognized as a trained chef, Jerry even had a cooking show on WOAC, a local cable channel in Canton, Ohio. Beginning in 1987, *Wild in the Kitchen* ran for two years.

Marlowe's real attention came from repeatedly crashing the gate at the Ohio State-Michigan football game. The tradition began when Jerry was still a graduate student at OSU. Over the years, he has succeeded in a variety of costumes, including a pizza delivery boy, a Boy Scout leader, and OSU band director; he even managed to sneak in one year in a nun's habit. Although Marlowe manages to sneak into the game without a ticket, it does not mean he is looking to cheat the university out of its ticket price. Every year, Jerry gives generously to his alma mater's pharmacy department.

Although he is best known for his zany stunts and more than 200 hats, there is a serious and caring side to Jerry. Along with his mother and brother, Jerry expanded the family business to three locations and successfully converted the pharmacy into a compounding pharmacy when the traditional store was no longer viable. He is also active civically. Jerry was instrumental in the establishment of hospice in Tuscarawas County. (Courtesy of Jerry Marlowe.)

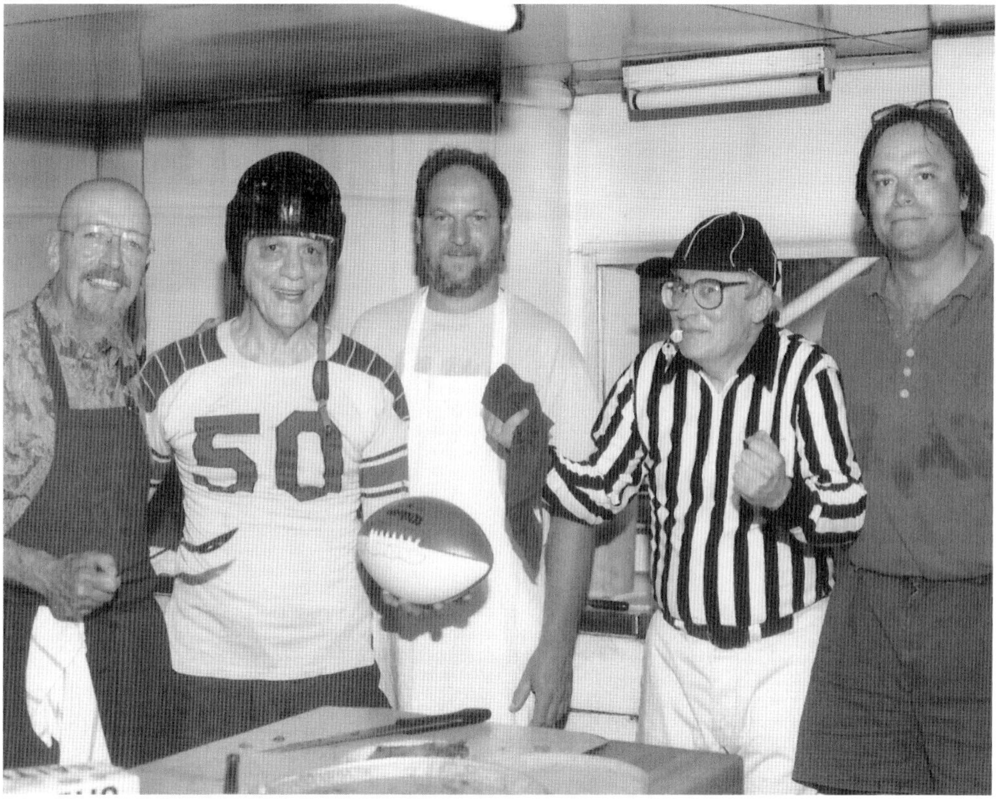

Larry Dinolfo

The story of Larry Dinolfo (second from left) and of the Dinolfo family in Dover is a long and colorful one. Born in Dover in 1923, Dinolfo was enterprising from a young age. As a boy, he performed for millworkers outside the Reeves Mill for spare change. Later, he refined his talents as a musician performing for a much more select audience. This included any attractive lady who happened into his restaurant. He was known to perform quite a serenade on the kazoo.

As a teenager, Dinolfo was an outstanding athlete for the Dover Tornadoes. He starred on the football team, scoring his first touchdown as a sophomore against Uhrichsville. During his senior season in 1942, the varsity team sported a 10-0 record. Dinolfo scored eight touchdowns that year, despite breaking his leg during the fourth game of the season. Larry Dinolfo graduated from Dover in 1943.

What most remember Larry Dinolfo for today is not his football prowess but his cooking skills. Getting into the family business, Larry operated Dinolfo's Restaurant in Dover for many years. Legend holds that his family opened its first restaurant prior to 1900. In the old days, the restaurant was known as Curly Ross's, but later, folks simply called it Dinolfo's. Known throughout the county, the pizzas at Larry Dinolfo's pizza shop were famous for their signature deep-fried crusts. Surrounded by an interesting cast of characters, the restaurant and its food never disappointed. Larry Dinolfo died October 28, 2001. (Courtesy of Jerry Marlowe.)

Rear Adm. Herald Stout

Herald Stout was born on June 15, 1903, in Dover. As a boy, he attended Dover schools while working part-time at a local print shop. The promising young man was forced to grow up quickly after his father was killed in an industrial accident when he was only four. By the time he graduated Roosevelt High School as valedictorian in 1923, Stout was also a foreman at the shop.

After high school, Stout attended the US Naval Academy at Annapolis, Maryland, graduating in 1926. His first commission was on the USS *Cincinnati*. During his time on the USS *Cincinnati*, Stout attended the Naval Torpedo School in Newport, Rhode Island. It would be the first of many times that Stout pursued additional education. Incredibly intelligent, Stout constantly worked at improving his knowledge and skills. Just a month before World War II broke out, he was named the lieutenant commander of the USS *Breese*. On December 7, 1941, the USS *Breese* was docked at Pearl Harbor when the Japanese attacked. The ship not only managed to survive but also managed to down a Japanese bomber. Later, during the war, Stout commanded the destroyer USS *Claxton*. For his service in World War II, Stout was awarded three Navy Crosses.

Stout further distinguished himself during the Korean War as commander of Mine Squadron Three. The squadron's responsibility was to sweep ocean channels prior to landings or gun strikes for mines. For his effectiveness in this post, Stout was given a Distinguished Service Medal. He retired from active service on June 30, 1956, and was immediately given the rank of rear admiral. Perhaps his greatest honor, though, came after his passing in 1987. In 1994, the Destroyer, USS *Stout* was commissioned in his honor.

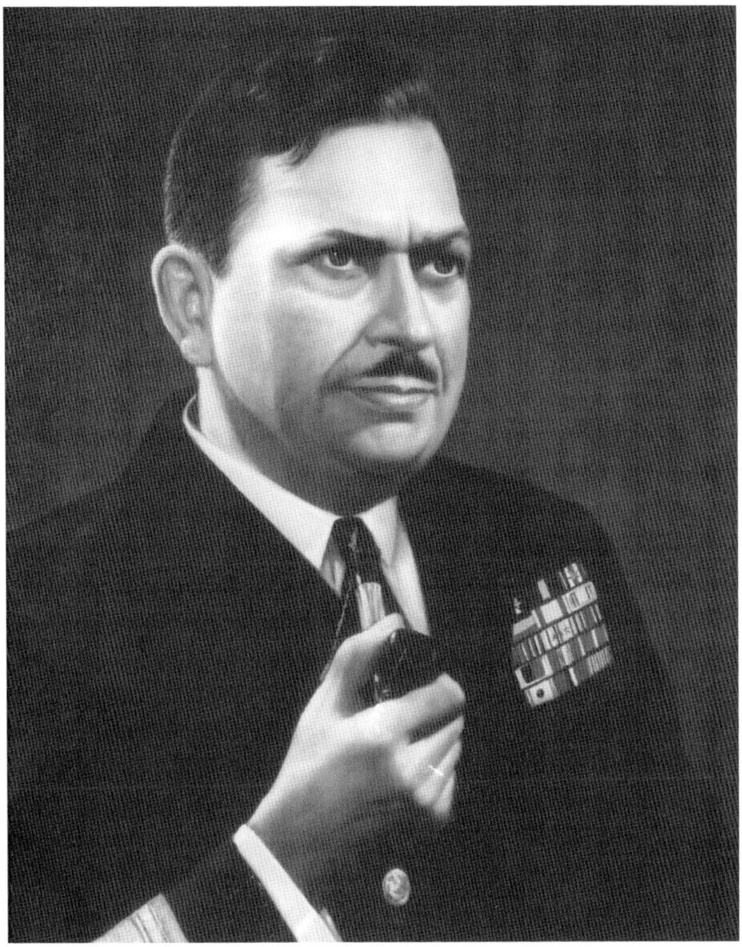

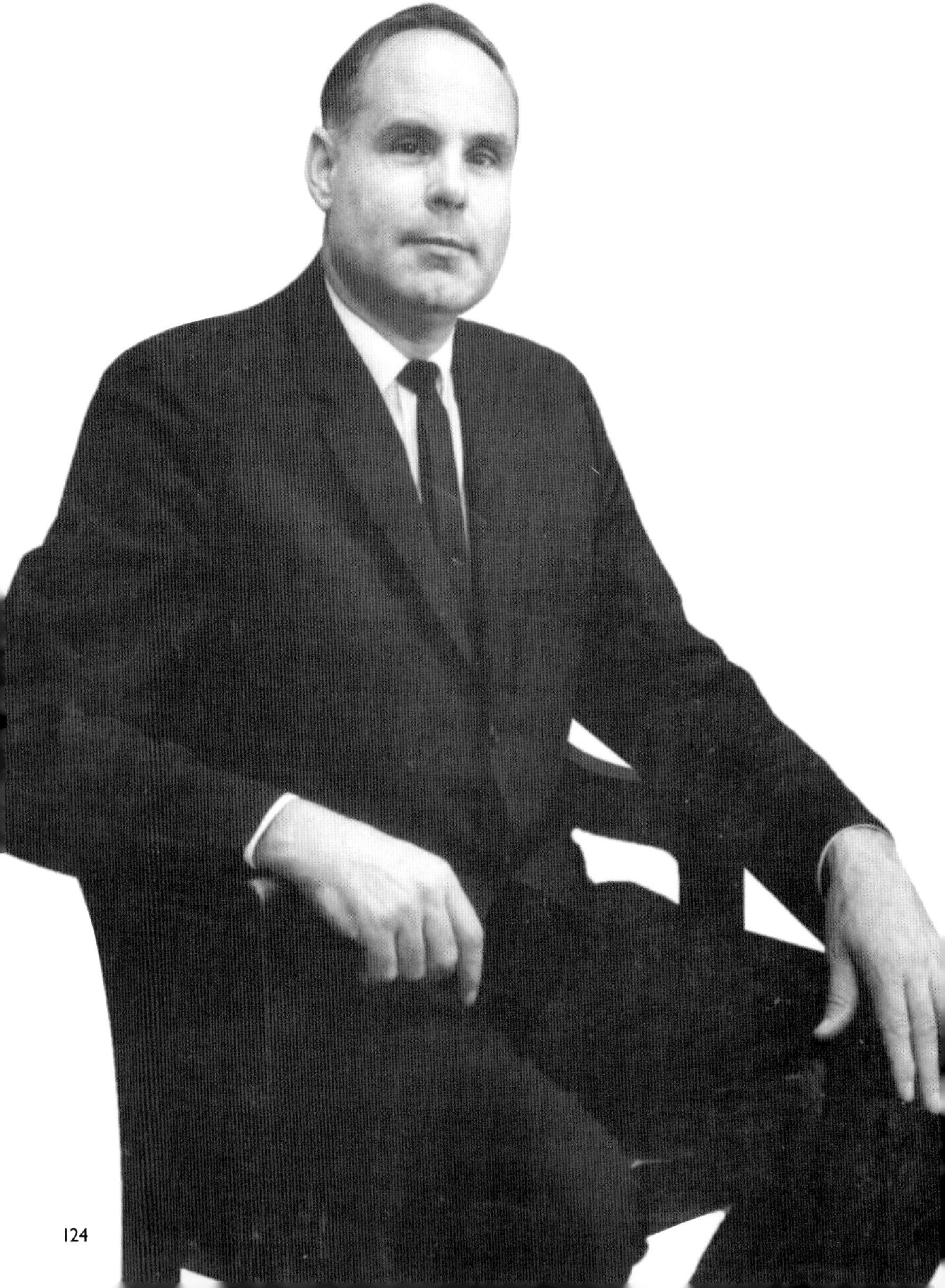

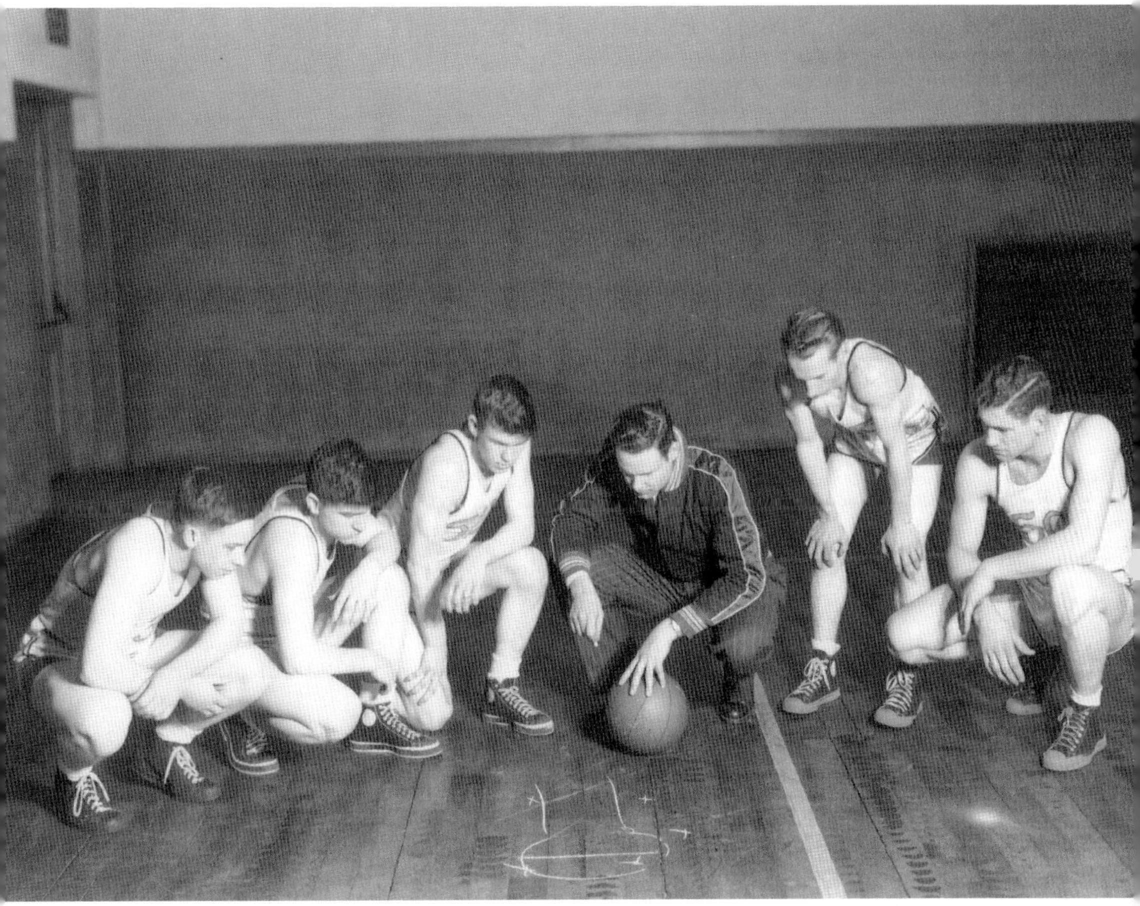

Emmet L. Riley (ABOVE AND OPPOSITE PAGE)
Born in New Philadelphia on August 17, 1917, Emmet Riley grew up in the Dundee-Winfield area just outside of Dover. After graduating from Dover in 1934, Riley attended Kent State University. While he was studying at Kent State, he had his first teaching job at Wooster. He was 17 when he broke into the field. Riley would later teach at Mineral City and Strasburg. While at Strasburg, he coached both basketball and football. As a coach he led Strasburg to the 1946 regional finals.

He entered school administration when he accepted a position in Montclair, New Jersey. He would later return to the area, where he served as superintendent at Dover from 1961 to 1970. After his retirement, he continued to substitute teach until he reached the age of 83. Away from the classroom, Riley married Ester Mizer in 1941. In 2011, they celebrated 70 years of marriage.

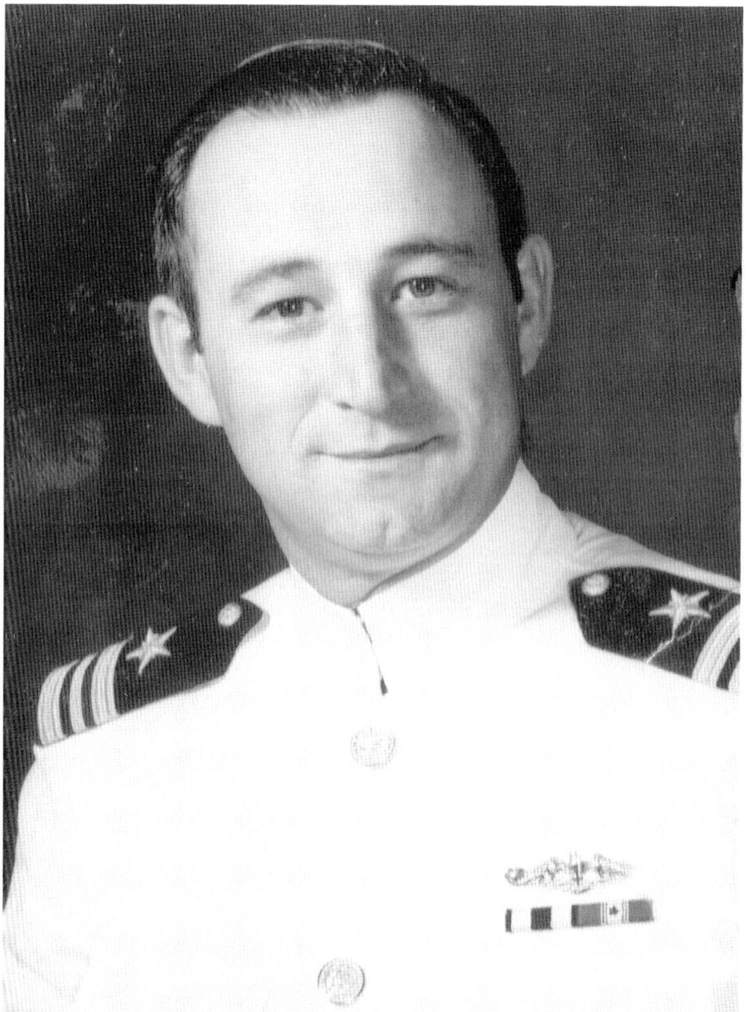

Harry M. Yockey

Harry M. Yockey was born in Canton, Ohio, in 1933. During his formidable years, Yockey's father, Harry, moved to the Dover area to become editor of the Dover–New Philadelphia *Times Reporter.* Young Harry came of age here in the community and attended Dover High School, where he excelled in everything he attempted. He is noted as a scholastic achiever, member of numerous clubs, a member of the football team, and even prom king.

After his high school graduation in 1951, Yockey attended Case Western Reserve University before enlisting in the US Navy. He was appointed to the Naval Academy at Annapolis earning his degree in 1957. Yockey would eventually go on to earn a master's degree in electrical engineering from the Naval Post Graduate School in Monterey, California.

While Yockey's early successes are important, his greatest gift and most important achievement was his work on the US Tomahawk Cruise Missile Program. After serving as commander of the USS *Salmon* from 1970 to 1972 and on several other assignments, Yockey began work in 1976 on the Tomahawk Missile Program. He continued with the Tomahawk project through his retirement in 1983. Many believe Yockey played a crucial role in the overall success of the Tomahawk Missile System, and in 1979, he was inducted into *Aviation Week & Space Technology* magazine's Laureates Hall of Fame for Achievement. He was also honored with a Meritorious Service Medal.

INDEX